Minority Women Entrepreneurs

Minority **Women** **ENTREPRENEURS**

How Outsider Status Can Lead to **Better Business Practices**

Mary Godwyn and **Donna Stoddard**

Stanford Business Books
an Imprint of Stanford University Press
Stanford, California

© 2011 Greenleaf Publishing Limited

Published in the USA by
Stanford University Press
Stanford, California

Library of Congress Cataloging-in-Publication Data

Godwyn, Mary, author.
    Minority women entrepreneurs : how outsider status can lead to better business practices / Mary Godwyn and Donna Stoddard.
         pages cm
    Published simultaneously in the United Kingdom by Greenleaf Publishing.
    Includes bibliographical references and index.
    ISBN 978-0-8047-7477-2 (cloth : alk. paper) -- ISBN 978-0-8047-7478-9 (pbk. : alk. paper)
    1. Minority businesswomen--United States I. Stoddard, Donna, author. II. Title.
    HD2358.5.U6G63 2011
    658.4'21082--dc22

                         2010048498

Published simultaneously in the UK by
Greenleaf Publishing Limited
Aizlewood's Mill
Nursery Street
Sheffield S3 8GG
www.greenleaf-publishing.com

British Library Cataloguing in Publication Data:
    A catalogue record for this book is available from the British Library.
    ISBN-13: 978-1-906093-48-8 (paperback)
    ISBN-13: 978-1-906093-49-5 (hardback)

Cover by LaliAbril.com

FSC
www.fsc.org
MIX
Paper from
responsible sources
FSC® C013604

Printed in Great Britain on acid-free paper by
CPI Antony Rowe, Chippenham and Eastbourne

Contents

All people are born entrepreneurs. There are no exceptions.

Muhammad Yunus

Acknowledgments

The authors thank the editorial staff at Greenleaf Publishing, especially John Stuart for his tireless devotion to this project and expert guidance through the publishing process, and also to Dean Bargh for his kindness and patience; the editorial staff at Stanford University Press, especially Margo Beth Crouppen; the anonymous reviewers who provided us with such valuable comments; the Babson Faculty Research Fund, especially Susan Chern for her enthusiasm and encouragement; Mary Driscoll, Sheila Dinsmoor and Karen McDonald for keeping this study running smoothly; Fritz Fleischmann, Steve Collins, Jim Hoopes, Ann Marie McCauley and Graham Godwyn for generously reading and providing suggestions on the manuscript; the student coders who patiently went through the data, especially Divya Subramanyam Paratala; the Center for Women's Leadership at Babson College, especially Nan Langowitz and Janelle Shubert; the Women's Business Center of Northern Virginia, especially Barbara Wrigley; Gwen Martin for introducing us to some of the entrepreneurs through Accelerating the Growth of Minority Women Entrepreneurs Project; and, above all, the entrepreneurs who gave their time, energy, and shared so much of themselves with us.

Mary Godwyn would also like to thank her family and dedicate this book to them: Phil, Sam, Graham, Emily, and Henry – you give me so much happiness.

Donna Stoddard would also like to thank her family and dedicate this book to them: Al, Alicia, Alvie, and Alex.

The 12 entrepreneurs

The 12 entrepreneurs in this study are:

- **Margaret Henningsen and Legacy Bank.** This bank specializes in mortgages and business loans, with a mission to serve the underserved minority population of Milwaukee. Henningsen identifies as African American.

- **Judi Henderson-Townsend and Mannequin Madness.** Located in Oakland, California, this Mannequin liquidator offers, sells, rents, and recycles mannequins featuring diverse gender, race, and age representations. Henderson-Townsend identifies as African American.

- **Pauline Lewis and oovoo design.** An international company designing and manufacturing hand-embroidered bags, purses, and wallets located in Virginia and Vietnam. Lewis identifies as Asian American.

- **Barbara Manzi and Manzi Metals.** Located in Tampa, Florida, Manzi Metals is a multi-metal distribution company. Manzi identifies as Black Portuguese.

- **Angela Patterson, Gretchen Cook-Anderson, and Saphia Water.** Located in Silver Spring, Maryland, Patterson and Cook-Anderson manufacture vitamin-fortified water for pregnant and nursing mothers. Patterson and Cook-Anderson both identify as African American.

- **Najma Jamaludeen, Maryam Jamaludeen, and Basketmate and Temsah Shea Butter.** Najma Jamaludeen invented an expandable laundry basket, and both Najma and Maryam created, manufacture, and distribute Temsah Shea Butter. They are located in Detroit, Michigan. Najma and Maryam identify as African American Muslims.

- **Nancy Stevens and NancySpeaks.com.** Nancy is an inspirational speaker and life coach, as well as a Paralympian. She has also run camps for disabled women who seek to expand their physical abilities. Located in Bend, Oregon, Stevens has been blind since birth.

- **Kathy Deserly, Child Advocate for Native American Children.** A consultant based in Great Falls, Montana, Deserly travels around the U.S. working as a liaison between tribes and government offices. She identifies as Hispanic, with Guatemalan and Choctaw Indian roots.

- **Kim Edwards and Pampered Paws.** Located in Havre, Montana, Edwards runs a dog-grooming business. She identifies as Eskimo/ Native Alaskan.

- **Rita Chang and Classroom Encounters.** A teacher and inventor of innovative pedagogy, Chang produces and markets educational DVDs for high-school science classes. Located in Wellesley, MA, Chang identifies as Asian American.

Introduction: challenging the elegant theories of economics

Thirty years ago, Muhammad Yunus, a university professor, founded the Grameen Bank. His goal was ambitious, but simple: to eradicate world poverty (Tharoor 2006). Initially, the idea of lending money to desperately poor people was completely out of the question. The very suggestion was outlandish. It went against the fundamental principles of economics; it violated well-established assumptions about human nature, conventions about who should be trusted, who deserved loans, and, most important, who would pay back with interest so that banks would remain competitive and profitable. Convinced that poor people would never repay their loans, conventional bankers said Yunus was hopelessly naive, even crazy, and would not help him. But seeing the deprivation and human suffering in the villages of Bangladesh made Yunus doubt some of the basic assumptions behind "the elegant theories of economics" he was teaching in the university classroom (Yunus 2006).

Yunus would eventually provide a passionate critique encompassing economic theory, free-market capitalism, and conventional banking practices. He would also disrupt the notion, sacred to so many, that classical economic assumptions are necessary for democracy and freedom. Instead of accepting banking policies as rational and responsible, he declared banks discriminatory. By rejecting the idea that credit should only be a "rich man's prerogative" (Yunus 2007b), he exposed conventional banking policies as "anti-poor" and, less obviously, "anti-women." He declared the world "so mesmerized by the success of capitalism it does not dare to doubt that system's underlying theory" (2007a: 18). Not only did Yunus doubt the theory: he challenged it, and by testing some of its basic tenets, he improved capitalism.

The main problem, according to Yunus, was that rather than freeing people, "free-market" capitalism limits freedom and constrains human potential; it creates a "repressive economic milieu" (Yunus 2007b). He writes:

> Capitalism takes a narrow view of human nature, assuming that people are one-dimensional beings concerned only with the pursuit of maximum profit . . . In the conventional theory of business, we've created a one-dimensional human being to play the role of business leader, the so-called entrepreneur. We've insulated him from the rest of life, the religious, emotional, political and social. He is dedicated to one mission only – maximize profit. (Yunus 2007a: 18)

By refusing to accept this narrow view of human nature and the equally narrow goal of profit maximization for entrepreneurial activity, Yunus successfully changed the paradigm of banking. Ignoring the formidable power of economic and cultural prohibitions against lending money to the poor, especially to poor women, he started Grameen Bank, the village bank. In Yunus's words, Grameen bank "reversed conventional banking practice by removing the need for collateral and created a banking system based on mutual trust" (Yunus 2007b).

As it turned out, conventional bankers were wrong about poor people not repaying their loans: the repayment rate for the Grameen Bank has always been about 98%, much higher than for traditional banks. For over three decades, Grameen has served populations of people who had never before had fair access to capital. An entrepreneurial miracle, Grameen has made small loans to almost 100 million of the world's poorest people, and delivered 50 million from poverty (Fraser 2007). Grameen's micro-credit is now available in over 40 countries. At the current rate, Yunus predicts that poverty could be eradicated by the year 2050, and he dreams of creating poverty museums documenting this retired social ill.

Minority women: outsiders demonstrating better entrepreneurship

Early in the development of the lending process, Yunus made another controversial claim: because they use the money primarily to benefit their families and their communities, **women are "better" borrowers**. He explains:

> Money going to the family through the women brought so
> much more benefit than the same amount of money going to
> men. In every case, you cannot fail. In the beginning, we had
> no idea that this kind of thing would emerge. It is so clear, so
> transparent, you don't need to be smart researchers to find it,
> but just by casual observation you see the difference of what
> happens within the family if the mother is a borrower and if
> the father is a borrower. You can almost write a book about it,
> what a difference [it makes]. Children become the immediate
> beneficiary if the mother is the borrower.
>   [So we said] Let's focus on women because you get so much
> social impact. Money-wise, it's the same. Everybody's paying
> back – men [were] paying back and women [were] paying back
> – but the impact is so different. So we changed our minds and
> quickly we moved from 50/50 to 60 and 70 and so on – 90%.
> Today we have seven and a half million borrowers – 97% of
> them are women. (Yunus 2008)

Though Yunus was roundly accused of being unfair to men and of not supporting gender equality, Grameen became one of the first banks to lend almost exclusively to women. (The Mahila SEWA Cooperative Bank, Ltd. was founded in 1974. This bank was started by the members of the Self-Employed Women's Association, a trade union in India started by Ela Bhatt.)

This unorthodox policy changed the world. Many of these women's children, once counted among the ranks of the very poorest, have moved through the educational system. Some are now in graduate school becoming doctors, lawyers, and other professionals. This degree of class mobility in Bangladesh was virtually nonexistent before the Grameen Bank and the invention of micro-credit. Putting money in women's hands has meant the end of generations of unremitting poverty for their families.

In this book, we make our own controversial claim: women, especially minority women, are not just better borrowers: **they provide examples of better entrepreneurship**. That is to say, because of current, prevailing social definitions of gender and minority status, minority women are more likely to be highly innovative and direct their business practices and profits towards social good. We support this claim by examining ten businesses owned and operated by 12 minority women entrepreneurs. We apply a multi-dimensional analysis that not only addresses the difficulties and opportunities experienced by minority women business owners, but also investigates how gender and minority status pertain to their entrepreneurial decisions. Though our findings are based on a small sample size, they are consistent with Yunus's observations, the opinions of major economists including Lawrence Summers, Joseph Stiglitz, and Amartya Sen, and considerable empirical evidence that women, as a group, are more likely than are men to direct money to "their children and their communities" (Kristof and WuDunn 2009: xx).

How do gender and minority status shape entrepreneurial decision-making? This question seems long overdue, not only because women are more likely to spend their earnings on social good, but also since minority women in the U.S. start new businesses at **four times** the rate of nonminority men and women (MBDA 2008). Voluminous quantitative findings from around the world reveal that women contribute a much higher proportion of their earnings and their time to social good than do men (Crittenden 2001: 129). However, theoretical explanations for this behavior are scarce. Quantitative studies are crucial to establishing general patterns of behavior among populations of people, but they do not chronicle the micro-interactions and decision-making processes that provide an understanding of how patterns develop and are enacted on a day-to-day basis. In our study, we employ qualitative methods grounded in social and psychological theories and provide first-hand accounts – narratives – of minority women entrepreneurs, as they talk about and act through their businesses, their communities, and their partnerships. We hope that this qualitative study provides insight into the largely unexplained quantitative data.

By focusing on broad categories such as gender and minority status, our claims reflect patterns and probability. We are, therefore, not claiming that every individual minority woman entrepreneur exhibits the characteristic pattern of being highly innovative and prioritizing her children and community. We readily acknowledge that there are examples of specific minority women who do not, by these standards, provide examples of better entrepreneurship practices. Additionally, we are not claiming that only minority women fit this pattern: Muhammad Yunus and other men fit this pattern as well.

Statistically, women are likely to contribute more of their earnings towards public good than are men. Some explain this behavior as resulting from inherent or essential gender difference. In fact, a key concept in social psychology is the fundamental attribution error: the tendency for people to attribute behavior to an individual's character or group membership rather than to situational factors such as norms and social expectations (Nkomo 1992: 494). However, we found that this type of generosity that is generally associated with women does not emanate from some essential aspect of gender or minority status, but instead is learned, considered socially more appropriate for women, and has historical precedent within minority communities. The same behavior is available to majority men, but they must contend with the diminishment of masculinity and majority class privilege when they act this way, so it is less likely to be the path they follow. We are therefore not claiming that women and men, or minorities and those in the majority, are essentially or inherently different, but that the social expectations for them are. Social expectations and behavioral norms become the context in which all people make decisions and develop self-identity. In the cases of the minority women we interviewed, innovation bends towards social justice and community benefit. As mentioned, many quantitative studies have established that women are more likely to spend their money on social good than are men (Crittenden 2001: 129). Our study suggests that minority women **entrepreneurs**, to the degree they demonstrate typical identification with female gender characteristics and with minority status, **are also more likely to fit a pattern** of directing their innovative practices and their profits to social good. However, since these behaviors are learned and acquired over time, anyone – men and women, minorities and majorities – can consciously adopt these priorities.

We do not compare specific minority women with a control group of specific majority men. In fact, the broad definition we use for minority status eludes quantifiable and precise definitions of race, ethnicity, and other aspects of minority membership making control groups untenable. Moreover, the preponderance of business case studies feature white, male protagonists, so there is no penury of interviews with this population of entrepreneurs. Instead of comparing our interviewees with other specific entrepreneurs, we compare their narratives with the dominant discourse in entrepreneurial research, case studies, and educational literature. Our intention is not to elevate women at the expense of men, or minority members over members of the majority, but to explore how aspects of the entrepreneur's identity influence entrepreneurial activity. We hope this study leads to a reconsideration of conventional definitions of successful entrepreneurship and a revision of the assumptions about human nature found in classical economic theory.

Clearly, the one-dimensional, profit-driven definition of human nature is inadequate to explain the well-documented and widespread non-instrumental behavior evident among some entrepreneurs. We found that the methods and goals of entrepreneurship are culturally embedded and socially defined. That is to say, business practices are not inevitable, universal or culturally neutral, and do not follow from a narrow set of human characteristics and economic motivations. Instead, we found that practices arise organically from within populations of people and vary according to cultural values and group affiliations.

Profit in a social context

Because economic theory has such a monopoly on the subject areas of business and commerce, social and psychological theories are not typically applied to these areas of study. However, the latter disciplines offer more developed and nuanced understandings of the complexity of human behavior and interaction. Like Yunus, we reject some basic assumptions of economic theory, including the idea that entrepreneurs are one-dimensional people who are primarily interested in profit. We reject this idea because it is not borne out in our data or in the abundance of empirical research on women's spending habits. In our study, we found varied and complex human values and behavior expressed through and developed in entrepreneurial business activity. These values provide a social context to profit accumulation.

For instance, it was not unusual for the entrepreneurs in our study to use highly emotional language and terms usually associated with intimate relationships to describe their businesses, their products and their employees. One of the entrepreneurs in our study, Judy Henderson-Townsend, remarks, "A business is an organic process like reaching enlightenment. When you look at it this way, you enjoy it more. My business is my baby. I have a six-year-old child right now." Another entrepreneur, Barbara Manzi, describes her business as "the love of my life," and says it gives her such energy that she wants to "work all day and all night." Manzi explains, "My employees are as close to me as my own children. I start every day with a friendly 'Good morning!' You have to say something tender and kind because they might not be getting that at home."

When Yunus claimed that women were better borrowers, he was not saying women were *economically* better – better because they paid their loans more dependably or because they paid a higher interest rate. He claimed women were better borrowers because they were better managers of resources and directed their money to social goals much more often than did men. Like Yunus, we do not accept the definition of business success as being primarily about measuring economic worth. The entrepreneurs in our study maintain the perspective that profit is situated in the context of personal values and social relationships. Again from Manzi:

> It's not about individual profit. That's where most entrepreneurs fall through the cracks. Profit will come. But the one thing that entrepreneurs should know is: Don't be so material. It's not about buying the latest clothes, the newest cars. It is not about the money or growing the industry. It's about the

> passion, the appreciation. Money doesn't make you happy. My
> employees and me, we are a family. They give back. They know
> I am very passionate about their welfare and the welfare of
> their families. This is their business. When they have a family
> problem, they can go home and take care of it. Someone else
> will step in and run their desk. They'll have their turn. If the
> company makes money, the wealth is shared. They don't come
> here for a job, they come for a career.

Sociologists are interested in the relationship between group affiliations and behavior, and therefore it is not the size of the business or how much money it makes that matters here, but rather how minority and gender status influence entrepreneurial activity. We apply sociological, and to a lesser degree, psychological, theories to explain our qualitative data, to recognize and study the phenomenon of non-instrumental entrepreneurial activity more generally and to suggest new paradigmatic standards that might be applied to business and entrepreneurship research.

Paradigms

People rely on broad theoretical frameworks, also called worldviews or paradigms, to explore, understand and explain the empirical world. There are many ways to interpret data; sometimes these ways are discretely contained within disciplinary lenses, and at other times these lenses overlap. The sociologist William Levin provides a fine description of different disciplinary interpretations of a simple act: arriving in a college classroom. For instance, Levin observes that a physicist would focus on the way gravity and friction work to allow human ambulation; a biologist might focus on the degree of physical health and well-being necessary to enroll and attend classes; an architect might address how the design and structure of the classroom influences attendance; a psychologist might be interested in why some people are motivated to attend college, and how rewards and punishments are associated with various types of performance (Levin 1994: 10). Depending on the theoretical lens, or paradigm, different aspects of empirical data are emphasized. In this way, interpretations, even of common phenomena, are paradigmatically dependent.

In addition, the process of study and examination – that is, the initial questions that direct exploration, experimentation, and data gathering – can also be paradigmatically dependent. Some paradigms are more likely to be applied to certain subjects and questions of inquiry than are others.

For instance, biologists and chemists might be more likely to explore the processes involved in cell structure development and mutation, while theories and paradigms in political science or history would less likely be employed. Even within disciplines or types of disciplines there are competing theories and paradigms that are more or less applicable depending on the subject matter and inquiry. For example, though many consider that psychology, sociology, and economics fall under the general category of social science, these disciplines have wide variability with regard to their assumptions about human nature and the goals of research. Further, there are many competing theoretical areas within each social science. As will be discussed later, sociologists generally recognize at least three basic paradigms, or theoretical perspectives: functionalism, conflict theory, and symbolic interaction.

So far, there is no unifying theory, no one universal way to organize inquiry and data, and different theoretical perspectives have strengths and weaknesses. They also have biases and ramifications; content and interpretation of data are paradigmatically dependent, as are the outcome and findings of any inquiry.

For instance, though management and sociology both have theories of organization, one important difference between these disciplinary lenses is that management theorists study organizations – mainly formal, for-profit organizations such as companies – from an instrumental point of view. The beginning assumption in management and economic theories is that an organization is a means to an end to achieve its goals. The goals for companies are most commonly to increase profits and thereby create economic value for shareholders. If managers do not prioritize economic value above all else, they are doing something wrong, something "irresponsible" (Yunus 2007a: 17) that must, according to the initial assumption, be fixed.

Sociology on the other hand is engaged in the study of both formal, structured organizations – such as corporations, the military, and government bureaucracies – as well as informal, spontaneously formed organizations, such as student activists, online communities, and romantic couplings. Unlike management, or those disciplines that use management and economic theoretical assumptions as their basis, sociological research primarily employs a non-instrumental or non-utilitarian perspective. That is to say, as a social science, sociology is concerned with the study of organizations because such study yields knowledge that is worthwhile in itself, whether any utility is discovered or any instrumental goal is met. Similarly, the study of chemistry is predicated on the assumption that understanding chemical compounds and reactions is valuable in itself, even if there is no other evidence of use or need. That is not to say that some chemists are not motivated by the idea of achieving chemical reactions that would produce low-cost energy or eradicate disease. However, the study of chemistry, like that of sociology, transcends instrumentality by assuming worth based on knowledge alone.

In the investigation of a group of managers who, despite the dominant economic mandate, do not prioritize profit above all else, a sociological study would differ from an economically based one. A sociologist would try to understand what such behavior explains about human social interactions, about patterns of relationships among individuals, and how such behavior is shaped by group membership. Additionally, rather than treating profit as an ahistorical, culturally neutral goal, a sociologist would likely examine profit within the context of the social norms and cultural practices that reward profit-driven behavior.

Sometimes, to the detriment of generating new perspectives and fruitful solutions, areas of knowledge and inquiry become bound by stagnant understandings and theories that are incompatible with empirical evidence. In such cases, rather than useful organizational tools, paradigms can prove to be impediments to interpreting data and evidence.

Early signs of the inadequacy of established paradigms are often dismissed as mistakes in observation, miscalculations in measurement or some other misperception. Ruling paradigms can be so powerful and pervasive that they pass for objective truth, common sense or even sacred understanding. Therefore, there can be overwhelming loyalty to particular paradigms and strong, even violent, resistance to change, especially to changing paradigms that define conventional wisdom (what people have come to take for granted) and advance the interests of those in power. A common example of loyalty to a faulty paradigm was the initial refusal of the Catholic Church to recognize that the earth revolves around the sun. In this case, resistance to the new heliocentric paradigm was manifest in the persecution of Galileo and others who rejected the popular geocentricism of the day.

In Western society, we use a foundational paradigm or worldview that Riane Eisler calls a "domination system." This paradigm always uses a hierarchy to understand empirical data about relationships. In the domination system, there are only two alternatives: dominating someone else or being dominated by someone else (Eisler 2007: 30). Those who accept this paradigm use it to interpret empirical events, sometimes without regard to its accuracy or applicability.

For example, Temple Grandin, the author of several books about animal behavior, notes there is a long-standing but inaccurate belief that alpha males dominate and control packs of wild dogs and wolves. There has long been strong evidence that dogs and wolves live in families, not in packs, and are organized by a single mating pair of adults rather than an alpha male. Dog and wolf families do not use a dominance hierarchy to keep the peace. Yet the alpha dog myth persists. This persistence is an example of misapplying a well-established paradigm by trying to force empirical evidence into a familiar theory. Writing with Catherine Johnson, Grandin remarks:

> The crazy thing about all this is that Dr. Mech wasn't the first person to say that wolves live in families, not packs. His oldest citation of a publication with this observation goes clear back to 1944, to a man named Adolph Murie, who wrote a book called *The Wolves of Mount McKinley*. I think it's a really interesting question why Adolph Murie's observations didn't catch on with the public, and the captive wolf research did, especially since the wolf family idea makes so much more sense. (Grandin and Johnson 2010: 28)

People sometimes use established paradigms to disguise or ignore evidence to the contrary; by emphasizing certain aspects of data and neglecting others, our understanding of the empirical world can be manipulated. Although Dr. Mech did modify the ruling principle of the domination system enough to recognize that wolves live in families, he did not change his personal view, despite the lack of evidence, that males dominate females. Grandin writes, "Dr. Mech thinks the mom probably is subordinate to the dad, although the mom's subordination wasn't obvious in the pack he observed" (Grandin 2010: 27). Though it can be a long and conflict-ridden process, when theories are repeatedly found inadequate to explain evidence and predict trends, paradigms are modified – they shift.

Yunus noticed that devotion to the assumptions of capitalism and conventional economics, like the lingering misperception of the alpha dog, resulted in forcing "reality to imitate theory" (Yunus 2007a: 18). He not only claimed that economic and management paradigms were inadequate to explain human nature and the characteristics of entrepreneurial activities, but that despite their inadequacies, these theories went unchallenged and unchanged largely because they protected the interests of the powerful few at the cost of the many. In other words, widespread acceptance of economic and management theories does not necessarily come from their descriptive or predictive accuracy, but because these theories privilege members of the economic and social elite. Yunus saw clear evidence that the routine acceptance and application of these theories caused enormous human misery. He therefore came to reject the assumption that human nature and the nature of entrepreneurial activity are primarily instrumental and profit-driven. Moreover, Yunus began to hold business activity accountable to social standards, not just economic goals.

Purpose and research

Our research investigates how gender and minority status influence the way that the women we interviewed develop their personal identities and maintain ties to their communities through entrepreneurial activity. We attempt to explain how and why the minority women entrepreneurs in our study often demonstrate non-instrumental behavior and act counter to the assumptions that rule economic theory and free-market capitalism. Moreover, we interrogate economic theory with sociological concepts to bring fresh solutions to economic inequality and humanistic alternatives to exploitative business policies. This book is both a sociological study of a group of minority women entrepreneurs and also a critical analysis of the ruling economic paradigm.

Our data collection methods are surveys, observation, and in-depth interviews. In this research, we adopt Louis Wirth's definition of minority:

> a group of people who because of physical or cultural characteristics, are singled out from others in the society in which they live for differential and unequal treatment, and who therefore regard themselves as objects of collective discrimination. (Wirth 1945: 347)

Further, the women in this study are what sociologist Erving Goffman refers to as deviant and stigmatized; that is to say, they are outside the normative expectations for entrepreneurs. Goffman (1963) theorized that people were subject to stigma for three reasons: physical deformities such as being blind or missing a limb; so-called character flaws such as being a drug addict or mentally ill; or because of group membership, such as being a minority in race, gender, class, age, or sexual orientation. According to Goffman, those who are stigmatized are "discredited" people.

Group membership certainly includes demographic referents such as race and gender, but it can also include *what* people do – their occupations – and *the way they do it*: that is, how closely they conform to societal standards and expectations. The minority women in this study do business differently; they are deviant not only because of minority status in gender, race, age, religion, or physical disability, but because they reject conventional business assumptions regarding the primacy of profit and the separation of business goals from social good and personal identity. Their behavior as business owners, therefore, is not well explained or predicted by the economic paradigm. In fact, due to the prioritization of economic goals that dominates management and entrepreneurship studies, business owners who do not put profit over all else are commonly dismissed, ignored, or even disparaged. Despite their impressive numbers, minority women are virtually absent from media images, workplace research, business case studies, and sociological and women's studies literature. Kathy Deserly, an entrepreneur in our study, explains, "Sometimes I feel that I'm doing 'woman's work' which doesn't command the same level of respect that other forms of entrepreneurship do." Ironically, because they provide empirical evidence that counters the assumptions of economic and management paradigms, these entrepreneurs remain invisible to the very theories that dominate entrepreneurship research.

The purpose of this book, then, is threefold. First, this research gives voice and representation to the fastest-growing population of U.S. entrepreneurs – women entrepreneurs, with special attention to women with minority status. Second, we describe how and why their businesses revolve around humanitarian social impact and employ ingenious entrepreneurial strategies that fly in the face of conventional business assumptions. Third, by situating our empirical data in social and psychological perspectives, and by documenting specific business policies, we provide theory and practice for other entrepreneurs, students of entrepreneurship and sociology, and all those who might also want to challenge the notion that entrepreneurs are one-dimensional profit-seekers. The strategies described here can be used by anyone and applied to a wide range of ventures.

Why this book matters

A re-evaluation of business

The global economic calamity that began in 2008 was a wake-up call. It disrupted the authority of conventional wisdom and created the space for a long-overdue re-examination of the distribution of economic and political power. There is widespread agreement that we need radically new configurations of business integrated with social responsibility to avoid financial mismanagement, to protect our environment, and to provide for our children's future. Many people are disoriented and disillusioned; they are looking for new business models, new role models, and new ways of understanding the interface between economic, social, environmental and personal goals. In a 2009 meeting at the United Nations (UN) that has been called the "highest level meeting on climate change ever," Secretary-General Ban Ki-moon stated that warmer temperatures would: "increase pressure on water, food and land; reverse years of development gains; exacerbate poverty; destabilize fragile states and topple governments" (Kolbert 2009: 23). Noting the connection between conventional business practices and the impending environmental disaster, UN delegate President Mohamed Nasheed of the Maldives, an island country south of India, declared, "If things go business as usual, we will not live. We will die. Our country will not exist" (Kolbert 2009: 23).

Even business students are disappointed in conventional business education. In a 2009 survey of over 1800 students from U.S. and international business schools:

- 90% blame a focus in business on short-term results as a contributing factor to the global financial crises

- Only 16% strongly agree MBA programs are helping them learn how to make business decisions that will avert similar financial crises

- 88% believe the for-profit sector should play a role in addressing social/environmental issues

- 77% believe that being responsible leads to corporate profits

- 56% strongly agree business schools should introduce financial models that consider long-term social impact

- 78% agree MBA curriculum should include more sustainability/corporate social responsibility (CSR) content

- Students see costs of healthcare (75%), sources of energy (74%) and quality of public education (47%) as very important factors for CEOs of U.S. corporations, yet report that business schools place moderate/little emphasis on these challenges. (Net Impact 2009)

Economic hard times, disappointment in business conventions and in business people have affected undergraduates as well. The Higher Education Research Institute (HERI) at the University of California at Los Angeles has conducted a freshman survey annually since 1966. In 2009, the percentage of freshmen who listed their "probable career" as being one in business dropped from 14.1% to 12.1%. This is an all-time low for the survey.

The number of first-year students who plan to major in business has also dropped to the lowest rate since 1974 (Moltz 2010).

As a response to increased criticism and scrutiny, business schools are looking for ways to dissociate themselves and their students from a culture of "personal greed" (Fox 2009). *The New York Times* reports that changes are under way in business courses and curricula. Some schools are refocusing on long-term relationships and leadership, and many are adding seminars to address the economic crisis. Rakesh Khurana, a professor at Harvard Business School and author of *From Higher Aims to Hired Hands* (2007), says that the problem began when

> a company's stock price was the primary barometer of success, which changed the schools' concept of proper management techniques. Instead of being viewed as long-term economic stewards, managers came to be seen mainly as the agents of the owners – the shareholders – and responsible for maximizing shareholder wealth. (Holland 2009)

As an indication of their new commitment to social values, the Thunderbird School of Global Management has instituted an "Oath of Honor" to help establish the professionalism of its graduates. Angel Cabrera, dean of Thunderbird, remarks:

> It is so obvious that something big has failed. We can look the other way, but come on. The CEOs of those companies, those are people we used to brag about. We cannot say, "Well, it wasn't our fault" when there is such a systemic, widespread failure of leadership. (Holland 2009)

The centrality of entrepreneurship: small is the new big

It is important to recognize the ongoing critical necessity of small, entrepreneurial enterprise to the growth of the U.S. economy. Sydney Finkelstein, professor at Dartmouth's Tuck Business School, reminds us that there are only three ways for large, multinational businesses to grow: from the inside (otherwise known as organically), through alliance with other businesses, and through mergers and acquisitions. According to Finkelstein, each way is problematic (Day 2009). Organic growth is difficult for big business because of the hierarchal, quasi-"military" culture: alliances are complicated to oversee and control, and 70% of all mergers fail to provide value for stockholders (Kusstatscher 2006: 92).

On the other hand, small businesses are characteristically more flexible, nimble, and responsive. In the United States, very small companies, those with no additional paid employees, make up 70% of all businesses (U.S. Census 2006). In 2003, U.S. small businesses generated US$830 billion, up from US$586 billion in 1997. According to the National Small Business Association (NSBA), an advocacy group for small business owners, small companies have created 21.9 million jobs in the last 15 years, while large businesses have created only 1.8 million.

It is no wonder that the March 12, 2009 issue of *The Economist* cites the engine of entrepreneurship as the solution to the current international financial crisis. According to *The Economist* (2009), entrepreneurs are "global heroes" whose "time has come," and entrepreneurship has become "cool." After all the recent devastating economic losses, people are hungry to hear stories of American ingenuity again, and the United States is by far the most entrepreneurial nation. But entrepreneurship is not just an American story. As Thomas Friedman argues (2005), the world is flat, and technological advances have given even small businesses access to global markets.

Regardless of articles in the popular press and the demand for an increase in corporate social responsibility (CSR), actual social change does not originate by keeping the current goals and assumptions intact. As long as the goal of businesses remains profit maximization, then CSR efforts will be subordinated to financial priorities, and no real change will be accomplished. Camouflaged by a façade of progress, CSR is often a vehicle that extends the stagnation of the current and untenable business culture, rather than an answer to environmental deterioration and alarming social problems (Reich 2007: 170-72).

Remarking on the origins of change, Malcolm Gladwell notes that current business leaders "can't fight the establishment because they are the establishment" (Gladwell 2009: 48). Even as they experience the failings of underlying economic theories, those who are part of the business establishment are often unwittingly locked into old modes of thought and continue to look for ways to salvage familiar conventions.

As outsiders, these women reject many of the tenets of economic theory because they are inadequate to address the complexities of the relationships involved in material exchange and social value creation.

Men still own far more businesses than do women (Minniti, Arenius *et al.* 2005: 12); however, the minority women in this study are entrepreneurs, not merely business owners. They are visionaries – resourceful outsiders who have had years of practice and generations of examples of actively creating alternatives to the conventional. To survive in hostile environments, they simply have to think of novel solutions. As Audre Lorde famously asserted: "The master's tools will never dismantle the master's house. They may allow us temporarily to beat him at his own game, but they will never allow us to bring about genuine change" (Lorde 2001: 23). The entrepreneurs interviewed here provide practices and insights that we argue are central to developing new and better ways of understanding business and entrepreneurship. The global financial crisis exposed the greed and avarice of top-heavy, homogeneous, corporate bureaucracies and has created the need for different definitions of successful business. We need new narratives of success and new images of social heroes.

Color is the new white, and women are the new men: or why it's in everyone's best interest for today's children to be economically successful adults

The U.S. Census Bureau reports that 47% of children under 5 years are minorities and the average age of non-Hispanic Whites is 41.1 (U.S. Census 2005). That means the aging population of White baby-boomers will depend on young people of color to support them in their twilight years. Additionally, the U.S. Census projects an increase in single mothers and in women-headed households (U.S. Census 2005). The social and economic future of the United States is in the hands of young ethnic and racial minorities, and it is in everyone's best interest to make sure that the mothers of these young people are economically solvent. Moreover, a consensus is building that "women will rule business" because the so-called "female management style" has been linked to greater productivity and increased profits (Shipman and Kay 2009: 47).

"There are extraordinary things taking place in business education, and a lot that is very promising," says Judith F. Samuelson, executive director of the Business and Society Program at the Aspen Institute. "But what's the central theorem of business education? It's wanting" (Holland 2009). In this climate, minority women entrepreneurs are a welcome antidote to the large, corporate business orthodoxy that has produced the current corruption, greed, and poor management. Minority women entrepreneurs provide a new "central theorem" for business: a fusion of social good with profitability where business no longer lives in a separate, autonomous sphere but is situated in and governed by social values.

How to read this book

This book is intended for a variety of overlapping audiences: students of business, sociology, race, and gender studies, as well as practitioners of entrepreneurship, aspiring entrepreneurs, and those looking for new, socially responsible and sustainable business practices.

Part 1 (Chapters 1–4) sets the theoretical and methodological context for the empirical data. Intended for scholars and students of sociology, race, and gender studies, these chapters discuss theory and scholarly research, the intellectual foundations of sociology, and the empirical research literature investigating issues of minority status, gender, and access to the economy.

In Part 1, we examine the following:

- The study of entrepreneurship within the discipline of sociology, as well as sociological theories of selfhood, social reproduction and power

- The relationship between individual confidence and institutional evaluations of competence

- The place of minorities and women within entrepreneurship and entrepreneurship literature

- The sociology and history of entrepreneurship, classical economic theory and business-as-usual.

Part 2 (Chapters 5–7) is thematically organized and devoted to minority women entrepreneurs as business innovators, partners, and community members. Those who want to focus on our empirical research – the stories of the entrepreneurs – can begin reading at Part 2. Our 12 entrepreneurs are listed at the beginning of the book (pages ix-x).

Finally, Part 3 (Chapter 8) explores opportunities and challenges going forward.

PART 1

1

The unique position of minority women entrepreneurs

Correcting the invisibility

In 1915, Aimee Semple McPherson, an American Pentecostal evangelist, drew crowds larger than Teddy Roosevelt, Houdini, and P.T. Barnum. A young widow and entrepreneur, McPherson supported both her mother and her child, created the first Christian radio station in the United States and sowed the seeds of the enormously powerful evangelical movement. Though it is common for today's ministers to refer to their "evangelical forefathers," it was McPherson's innovative delivery of sermons that laid the foundation for popular U.S. televangelists. During her lifetime, McPherson's message affected millions, and she set social and political standards that continue to inform the evangelical movement. After almost a century, Roosevelt, Houdini, and Barnum remain well known, but despite the political clout of evangelical Christianity, few have heard of McPherson.

In 1884, over a decade before *Plessy v. Ferguson,* Ida B. Wells sued the Chesapeake and Ohio railroad company for forcing her to give up her seat to a White man. When the conductor tried to remove her, she refused to be ladylike and deferential. Instead, Wells sank her teeth into his hand and braced her legs against the back of the seat (Baker 1996; Franklin 1995). It took three strong men to drag her from the train. As a founding member of the National Association for the Advancement of Colored People (NAACP), a newspaper owner, publisher, author, and political activist, Wells watched the lynching of several friends and fellow African Americans (Baker 1996;

Franklin 1995). Risking her own life, Wells wrote a scathing indictment of southern law in her book *Southern Horrors: Lynch Law in All Its Phases* (1997). But how many people know her name?

In 1903, prior to Henry Ford's Model A, Mary Anderson invented and patented the windshield wiper; women subsequently invented the carburetor, a clutch mechanism and an electric engine starter. Grace Hopper, a computer scientist and mathematician, invented COBOL, the first computer language. She joins the ranks of forgotten women entrepreneurs: scientists, inventors, mathematicians, athletes, peace activists, Nobel Laureates, authors, political leaders, and business owners. Given this trend, we can expect that contemporary influential women such as Oprah Winfrey, Condoleezza Rice, Shirin Ebadi, Hillary Clinton, Shirley Chishom, Aung San Suu Kyi, Katharine Graham, Margaret Chase Smith, Barbara Jordan, Corazon Aquino, Ann Richards, Rigoberta Menchú, and Benazir Bhutto – and all of their accomplishments – will disappear from our social consciousness as well.

Therefore, our initial goal in writing this book was to right a wrong. Despite the fact that their numbers are growing at an astounding rate, four times that of non-minority men and women (MBDA 2008), minority women are virtually invisible in entrepreneurship literature and woefully under-represented in business case studies. In fact, with few exceptions, representations in the media and in typical business school case studies portray entrepreneurs as White, male business owners (Brush 1997). Complaints about the dearth of scholarly research, media coverage, teaching tools, and business cases that feature women and entrepreneurs of color are not a recent phenomenon (Baker, Aldrich *et al.* 1997; Langowitz and Morgan 2003; Davies, Spencer, and Steele 2005; Greene and Brush 2004; Ogbor 2000). John Ogbor writes that the "concept of entrepreneurship is discriminatory, gender-biased, ethnocentrically determined and ideologically controlled, sustaining not only prevailing societal biases, but serving as a tapestry for unexamined and contradictory assumptions and knowledge about the reality of entrepreneurs" (Ogbor 2000: 605).

In addition, for the sake of simplicity, research definitions of marginalized groups often include only one status characteristic that differs from the norm: see the aptly titled compilation of essays *All the Women are White and All the Blacks are Men, But Some of Us are Brave*, edited by Gloria T. Hull, Patricia Bell Scott, and Barbara Smith (1982). Despite the growing numbers of minority women entrepreneurs, the separation of race and ethnicity on the one hand and gender on the other contributes to their invisibility. If, as Helen Hacker argues (1951), women have the status of a minority, then women of color have a double minority status that puts them even further outside of what African American feminist Audre Lorde calls "the mythical norm":

> Somewhere, on the edge of consciousness, there is what I call a *mythical norm*, which each one of us within our hearts knows "that is not me." In America, this norm is usually defined as White, thin, male, young, heterosexual, Christian and financially secure. It is within this mythical norm that the trappings of power reside in this society. (Lorde 1984: 116)

Furthermore, there is evidence that under-representation of women and minorities in entrepreneurial narratives and workplace images anchors low social and psychological expectations for these groups. Regardless of the increase of women in the paid labor force, feminine characteristics are not as likely to be associated with workplace leadership as are masculine qualities (Valian 1998), and the pay gap between women and men persists. Women are therefore more likely to turn to entrepreneurship as a way to circumvent discrimination (Minniti, Arenius *et al.* 2005: 12). However, business ownership does not neutralize gender and racial prejudice. Research over the last 30 years has established that women are less likely to be identified as business leaders even though women-owned businesses in the U.S. succeed at a rate equal to male-owned enterprises (Eagly and Johannesen-Schmidt 2001; Heilman, Block *et al.* 1989). Gender and racial stereotypes negatively affect self-esteem (Clark and Clark 1939) and measurably diminish performance (Steele 1997: 620). According to Minniti, Arenius *et al.*:

> a woman's perceptions of environmental opportunities as well as her confidence in her own capabilities, are powerful predictors of entrepreneurial activity ... and a strong negative and significant correlation exists between fear of failure and a woman's likelihood of starting a new business. (Minniti, Arenius *et al.* 2005: 12)

Simply put, this is a human-rights issue: under-representation in scholarly research, teaching tools, and media coverage effectively impedes minority women's access to the economy through entrepreneurship. Since entrepreneurship has been a lifeline for populations facing employment discrimination, impediments to business ownership threaten the life chances, and the very survival, of minority women and their families.

This general lack of confidence has been documented in numerous studies, and ours was no exception. Barbara Manzi recounts her former boss telling her she would not succeed as an entrepreneur. "He said I wasn't business-savvy enough to pay attention to the accounting. He said, 'You're still a salesperson'." But after working for ten years and bringing in millions for the company, Manzi was denied a raise. She resigned, bought a desk for US$89 and started Manzi Metals. She is often asked why she waited so long to start her own business. Manzi explains:

> Well, I had no business background and no experience. I didn't think I had the right stuff. When you come from a family where you don't see much that's good . . . when you turn over at night and roll over your sisters, you don't think, I'm going to grow up and be an *entrepreneur*. As a Black women, you start to think you can't do some things, but over time I learned that others were no smarter than me.

Judy Henderson-Townsend concurs:

> Many times, women undervalue our skills. We are more desperate to get the money. I had to watch my language and stop describing my business as "wacky." At first I thought, "Who am I to think I am a business owner?" But then I got the award from the Renaissance Center. And then I got the EPA [Environmental Protection Agency] award, and I thought: "I am the *Queen* of mannequins!"

There is a growing body of evidence confirming that frames of reference can be changed and performance can be positively affected. The inclusion of women and minorities in normative representations can work to lift debilitating stereotypes (Steele 1997; Davies, Spencer, and Steele 2005; Godwyn 2009c). Claude Steele found that the standardized test scores of African American students were higher if tests were introduced as "academically insignificant," thereby removing the expectation that Black students would perform less well than their White counterparts (Steele 1997: 619-20). Further, when women acquire entrepreneurial training and role models in a female-oriented culture, such as Women's Business Centers, they develop a frame of reference, different than that of the larger society, which positions women as normative business leaders. Unlike those in control groups, these women are much more likely to perceive women, rather than men, as business leaders (Godwyn 2009c). And women trained at Women's Business Centers start businesses at a rate of almost **four times** the national average for women (Langowitz, Sharpe *et al.* 2006). Pauline Lewis, who took entrepreneurship classes at a Women's Business Center, puts it this way:

> This is a fantastic time for women to start the enterprise they've always dreamed of, and I think the reason for that is we have examples out there now. And that is making all the difference in the world to have other women that you can look at and say, "If she can do it, I can do it," and I know it goes as far as being able to pick up the phone and saying "I want to call her because she's been in business now for seven years. I'm going to call her and ask her for her help."

By disseminating their accomplishments, their stories and their faces, the first purpose of this book is to right the wrong done each time women's entrepreneurial contributions are diminished, marginalized, and forgotten.

Why minority women are uniquely positioned to provide better business

The importance of minority views for entrepreneurial innovation

Inherent to entrepreneurial enterprise is the valuation of change, novelty, and difference; therefore, **entrepreneurial vision is by definition a minority perspective residing outside of the norm**. Charlan Nemeth argues that majority and minority views contribute differently to processes. The views of majorities "foster convergence of attention, thought and the number of alternatives considered" (Nemeth 1986: 23). While minority views

> are important . . . because they stimulate divergent attention and thought. As a result, even when [minority views] are wrong, they contribute to the detection of novel solutions and decisions that, on balance, are qualitatively better . . . for creativity, problem-solving and decision-making, both at the individual and group levels. (Nemeth 1986: 23)

Entrepreneurs, therefore, must be willing to entertain the notion that ignorance might be disguised as expert knowledge and conventional wisdom. In other words, a minority viewpoint influences entrepreneurial decision-making.

Jane Margolis agrees. She describes why it is important for a wide range of people and perspectives to be involved in computer science and product development:

> In terms of design teams and designing products, there's evidence from other industries that if you have just a male team, you could have a flawed product. Let's look at air bags, for example. Only 8% of mechanical engineers are female, and most of the teams working on air bags were predominantly male . . . Air bags were invented based on the male body as the

norm, [and] they ended up being potentially deadly to women and children. That's also happened with heart valves and voice-recognition systems; they were geared toward the male. Add more design experts of different viewpoints, different genders and different races, and you're going to get products that are much better in terms of meeting the needs of a broader number of people. The other thing is, it's almost a question of democracy and equity. If technology jobs can really lead to economic opportunities and educational opportunities, they shouldn't just fall into the laps of a very narrow band of males. (Gilbert 2002)

The significance of providing narratives and images of minority women business owners is to gather data on this group of heretofore neglected entrepreneurs, to begin to redefine the established framework about who will succeed in entrepreneurial activities, and to challenge the narrow model of business goals and assumptions informed by classical economic theory. Our intention is to disseminate the views, experiences, and images of minority women entrepreneurs, to give them voice and visibility, and to integrate their perspectives into the discourse of entrepreneurship literature. As Nemeth notes, minority views sharpen and deepen the analytical edge of critique and problem-solving by providing divergent, nonconforming perspectives. Hannah Arendt puts it this way:

> The more people's standpoints I have present in my mind while I am pondering a given issue, and the better I can imagine how I would feel or think in their place, the more valid my final conclusion, my opinion. (Bottomly 2007: 29)

As our interviews progressed, we had a dawning realization. We were not merely providing the minority women in our study with the visibility and recognition they had been denied – they were demonstrating new and better ways of doing business. It became clear that these entrepreneurs were using strategies and goals not typically associated with business ownership and not typically taught, or even mentioned, at business schools. Though our research began as a simple demographic study on an underrepresented population, identity is not only about *being*, about who people are; identity is inseparable from behavior, what people do and how they do it. In this case, identity is constructed through entrepreneurial activity that includes what products or services are delivered, who delivers and receives them, how workers are treated, and how profits are distributed.

We had two primary criteria for the entrepreneurs included in the study: they had to be female, and they had to identify themselves as minorities. In addition to gender, the entrepreneurs could have minority status in race, class, ethnicity, religion, sexual orientation, age, disability, or any other aspect of their identity that positions them outside of the majority of business owners. Second, we chose to interview entrepreneurs who represent a range of industries and geographic locations across the United States. Since our focus is on how minority status affects variation in the quantity and quality of opportunities that are available to and perceived by individuals, we use a modified version of Scott Shane and Sankaran Venkataraman's broad definition of the scholarly examination of the field of entrepreneurship to organize our research:

> The scholarly examination of how, by whom and with what effects opportunities to create [*values and understandings as well as*] goods and services are discovered, evaluated and exploited. (Shane and Venkataraman 2000: 218 [our addition in italics])

The addition of "values and understandings" to Shane and Venkataraman's definition was necessary to accommodate the political, social, and personal impact that was so central to these women's descriptions of their businesses and their experiences as entrepreneurs. In the following narratives, each entrepreneur offers a sensitive and highly self-reflexive understanding of how her business is integrated into her personal and social identities, how her values are manifest in her venture and how she envisions giving back to the community – as Pauline Lewis puts it, sharing with "people like me."

True to Shane and Venkataraman's definition of entrepreneurship, these women focus on economic opportunities produced by the creation of goods and services, but they also conduct their businesses within the context of their social and personal values. Most significantly, they uniformly reject the narrow model of business owner as self-interested actor making decisions that prioritize individual wealth and shareholder power at the cost of public good, environmental health, family, and emotional attachments. That is yesterday's model that has proven unsustainable, even disastrous, today.

In the tradition of entrepreneurial innovation, these women reconfigure the world to reflect their vision. This vision represents a new paradigm of equal commitment both to social and environmental, and to personal and economic good. They simply do not recognize divisions among these priorities, nor do they assume one must be traded for the other. Pauline Lewis describes how helping women in South-East Asia is central to her business: "When you build something like that into your core mission, your core value, you live and breathe it every day." Margaret Henningsen explains the reason she started Legacy Bank: "When you look at our mission state-ment, it is about serving the underserved. They have the right to walk into a bank and be treated with respect." The social mission and entrepreneur's values are not applied *after* profit is made or *instead of* profit, but *together with* profit.

Because they have never been in the majority, the entrepreneurs in this study have developed techniques and strategies for challenging and chang-ing the regular, accepted ways of doing things – ways that have often felt like Procrustean beds to them. Because they are *minority women business owners* – a population devalued on multiple levels – their entrepreneurial devices are idiosyncratic, biographical, and individual, but also genera-tional, familial, and historical. Margaret Henningsen explains:

> If I walk into a room and no one knows I am Margaret Henning-sen, I get treated just like someone on welfare. There are some historical carry-overs and some recent experiences that keep showing me we are not quite on the same level as that White male.

These women consistently mention their marginalized, outsider status; their identification with disadvantaged populations directs their social mission and informs their personal values.

The significance of gender

In addition to minority status, there is an important gender component at work as well. In *The Second Shift,* Arlie Hochschild pioneered the concept of gender strategy. She writes:

> A gender strategy is a plan of action through which a person tries to solve problems at hand, given the cultural notions of gender at play. To pursue a gender strategy, a man draws on beliefs about manhood and womanhood, beliefs that are forged in early childhood and thus anchored to deep emo-tions. He makes a connection between how he thinks about his manhood, what he feels about it and what he does. It works the same way for a woman. (Hochschild 1989: 15)

Here is an illustration of gender strategy: Debra and Matt are middle-aged Americans on vacation in Ecuador. Hot and tired after a hike, they sit down in an open-air cafe and order drinks. Matt removes the expensive pair of sunglasses he bought expressly for the trip and lays them on the cafe table.

An enchanting aspect of Ecuadorian life is the diversity of monkeys. Taking the couple by surprise, a capuchin monkey swoops down, grabs Matt's sunglasses and races to the top of a tall tree. Matt's immediate response is to look for rocks or stones to throw at the monkey hoping to knock it, and his sunglasses, to the ground. Meanwhile, Debra runs over to the cafe owner and asks for some food so she can lure the monkey down with a more attractive treat than the sunglasses.

According to the social psychology concept of the fundamental attribution error, people tend to attribute behavior to the characteristics of an individual rather than to social norms and behavioral expectations (Nkomo 1992: 494). It therefore might seem tempting to say that Matt is "naturally" aggressive, even cruel and self-centered, while Debra, a typical woman, is compassionate, nice. But Hochschild explains that the difference in their behavior is **learned** rather than biologically dictated or reflected of essential gender differences. In other words, men and women have been taught to be different kinds of people. They learn to see the world with gendered eyes, interpret problems and generate solutions based on a gendered view. Men are rewarded for masculine behavior that includes aggressiveness, force, and self-centeredness. To be kind and gentle calls their masculinity into question, and they can expect ridicule and loss of respect for their trouble. So for Matt, the monkey was a thief to be caught and punished. On the other hand, women are expected to be self-sacrificing and conciliatory; they learn to attend to the emotional needs of others. If they fail in this, they are criticized for being cold and unfeeling. Debra saw the monkey as innocent and playful, an inquisitive animal that would cooperate.

Consistent with gender strategies, most men approach business one way and women another. For instance, women have been socialized to do the vast amount of unpaid caring work. Ann Crittenden writes, "in industrialized countries, according to United Nation's statistics, women spend about one-third of their time in paid labor and two-thirds of their time on work that is unpaid and unrecognized. For men the numbers are reversed" (Crittenden 2001: 77). It is no wonder that Muhammad Yunus observed women using their earnings to care for their children and community. Women's gendered view creates cooperative, socially oriented goals for their efforts and resources. Historian David Landes states unequivocally: "the best clue to a nation's growth and development potential is the status and role of women" (Crittenden 2001: 129). Women have been taught to work for social and familial good – with or without monetary reward for themselves. Money is important, but to work primarily for money is apt to diminish a woman's gendered social identity, her sense of self and well-being. Self-alienation, unhappiness, and a sense of meaninglessness commonly result. Moreover, given the deep emotions attached to gender identity, and the relational self that is developed in conjunction with a feminine identity, women often experience gratification and satisfaction in taking care of others (Chodorow 1978; Gilligan 1982). Their business goals are therefore likely to promote social justice and ensure the welfare of their family, their community, and the environment.

It is the opposite with men. The prevalent social valuation of men emphasizes economic independence and financial competence, calculated decision-making, and the ability to eschew emotional attachment. Therefore, not only can monetary profit feel like its own reward, the cut-throat competitive game that business has become provides a way to establish masculine credentials. The discipline of economics assumes this masculine orientation by actively ignoring the economic value of caring work and its connection to the production of human capital. This caring work includes childcare and domestic tasks most often contributed by women. The tendency to neglect the economic significance of caring work so dominates economic theory that Shirley Burggraf was moved to remark, "Economists don't know where babies come from" (Crittenden 2001: 74).

As Hochschild notes, these social lessons are embedded in a constellation of feelings, thoughts, and actions – and they carry tremendous emotional weight. Therefore, gendered decisions resonate with personal and social identities and come to feel familiar, almost sacred, in the same way that family and cultural traditions do. Gender strategies are not always conscious: they often feel like second nature – like the right thing to do. **However, since gender strategies are learned, they can also be examined, applied selectively, or changed altogether.** This is evident when individual women act like "one of the guys" (Levy 2005: 4) to succeed in male-dominated environments, or when men demonstrate their "feminine side."

Despite the claim of biological determinists that gendered behavior is mandated by essential, physiological attributes, there is overwhelming anthropological, sociological, and historical evidence that gendered characteristics are adopted in response to environmental rewards and constraints (Chodorow 1978; Fausto-Sterling 2000; Lorber 1995; Kimmel 2004; Risler 2007; Bardo 1999; Caprioli, Hudson *et al.* 2007). Behavior traits such as giving a high percentage of earnings to social good or donating much of one's earnings to children are theoretically available to both women and men, but **these traits have themselves been gendered** and are therefore more likely to be adopted by women than by men. When the Grameen Bank decided to lend primarily to women, it was because it was endorsing these behavior traits, not because it was supporting women over men. Because of an established system of social rewards and punishments, women are more likely to develop and manifest the entrepreneurial practices that combat poverty.

For instance, over the course of thousands of loans, Yunus not only noticed that women tended to spend their money on children and public good much more often than did men, he also noticed the social pressure and gendered expectations for each. Wives had to be exceptionally resourceful to find ways to cover the family's expenses with the meager amount of capital their husbands provided. Otherwise, they would be blamed for their husband's low earnings:

> If you are in a poor family, if you are a woman, your husband earns a little bit and brings it to you, and expects you to take care of every single need of the family with whatever he gives you. And if you don't do it, then you are a bad wife. You don't know how to handle things. You get abused. You get beaten up because you are wasting money. So, in the process, [a woman becomes] an excellent manager of scarce resources, by necessity . . . Men never went through that process, so [they were] not as careful about tending the money as women [were]. So you see the difference in the use of the money and the skill of the management. In case after case you see that, and you get impressed by what happens when the woman is the borrower . . . (Yunus 2008)

Rather than being static, essential, or determined, gendered behaviors differ across cultures, over time in the same culture, within a given culture depending on the context and throughout an individual's development over the course of a lifetime (Kimmel 2004). Additionally, gender identity and gendered behaviors are influenced by other characteristics such as race, ethnicity, age, religion, class, and sexual orientation.

Given their minority and gender status, it is not surprising that the women in this study are all conscientious and diligent in applying their labor to social reconstruction. We adopt the perspective that "self is activity" (Collins and Hoopes 1995: 639), and we focus on the ways these individual minority women negotiate larger historical and structural constraints and find opportunities to challenge and change social, economic, and political assumptions. Their entrepreneurial process is part of a meaningful association with other people as well as a central element of their personal identities and access to the economy. Therefore, business activity becomes a significant aspect of the historical and political process: it is a passport to the world and a way to engage their individual values in a social and economic mission. The cultivation of conscience and civic duty obviate political and personal passivity. Their values are community-focused rather than self-interested, and do not prioritize profit over social impact, but instead illustrate how both can be, and perhaps must be, held in equal balance. This flies in the face of conventional explanations of entrepreneurship, which generally prioritize profit maximization and assume entrepreneurs are primarily motivated by rapid accumulation of material wealth (Banks 2006; Timmons and Spinelli 2007).

The entrepreneurs here tell stories of resisting an artificially imposed separation between their businesses and their values, their emotional attachments and the bottom line. Their stories illustrate a myriad of possible ways to integrate business goals, practices, and policies into the ongoing development of selfhood, social justice, and ethical positions. The narratives here demonstrate how these entrepreneurs manage to maintain various elements working in concert, rather than accept the orthodox business practice of a vertical hierarchy that sacrifices one goal for another. These women do not deploy the philanthro-capitalist model where goals are sequenced such that profit comes first and then, once a surplus of wealth is amassed, philanthropic ends might be developed later; nor do they conceive of their businesses as a zero-sum game where one interest wins because another loses. Their method is so unfamiliar to conventional business models that there is no English word for it. Instead, the Arabic concept of *taraadin* is more applicable. Christopher Moore explains: "Arabic has no word for 'compromise' in the sense of reaching an arrangement via struggle and disagreement. But a much happier concept, *taraadin*, exists in Arabic. It implies a happy solution for everyone, an 'I win, you win'" (Moore: 2004: 69). Perhaps most important, these women do not imagine that business has its own separate rules, discreetly removed from the social sphere where morality, ethics, and human relationships reside. Instead, for them, business is always situated within and guided by social and moral objectives.

The second purpose of this book is to share the conclusion of our research. Though it may sound surprising – even biased – for many of the same reasons that Muhammad Yunus insists women are better borrowers, we conclude that **minority women are uniquely positioned to solve social problems through better business**. They provide examples of better entrepreneurship. By documenting their efforts, we hope to fortify and extend the economic and cultural influence of minority women, while also providing new business models that show how these entrepreneurs use social impact and self-expression to create and sustain healthy, lucrative entrepreneurial enterprises.

Business, but not business-as-usual: theory and practice for entrepreneurs

Our third purpose is to situate the stories of these entrepreneurs in theory and practice. There is a growing enthusiasm among business owners to do right by their employees, the environment, and their communities. Yet business practices corresponding to these desires remain largely uncharted territory lacking the familiar, systemized practices of profit-driven enterprises. This research gives practical tools to students, business owners, aspiring entrepreneurs, and those looking for models of sustainable, socially conscious businesses. The narratives here explain new and creative ways of thinking about the interconnectivity of environmental welfare, division of labor within families, gender, race, and class diversity, and private contributions to the public good. These stories inject the often neglected and undervalued quality-of-life concerns into business considerations and challenge the simple, quantitative calculations associated with classical economic theory and conventional business policies. The minority women featured here discuss specific strategies they employ so that other entrepreneurs can make use of these innovative solutions.

Harry Blackmun admonished that "in order to get beyond racism, we must first take account of race. There is no other way. And in order to treat some persons equally, we must treat them differently" (Breyer 1999: 1394). Following Blackmun, we do not represent minority women as abstract, generic business owners, but as individuals with social status characteristics which, under the prevailing frame of reference, render them nontraditional, atypical and invisible – in other words, as deviant rather than normative business owners (Berger, Cohen et al. 1966; Berger, Fisek et al. 1966; Berger, Fisek et al. 1977).

Since business activity is associated with a dominant gender and race, the women in this study, like all minority women, are what Malcolm Gladwell refers to as "outliers" (2008). To understand why and how they differ so significantly from their majority counterparts – White, educated businessmen – we examine how their minority status in gender, race, age, class, and/or physical disability is situated in social relationships, access to the economy, and constructions of selfhood. As entrepreneurs, all of these women form self-definitions and relationships within minority-based subcultures, but they are also competent social actors who successfully navigate the larger majority cultural and economic landscape. The act of bridging these realms creates conscious recognition of social rules and

assumptions that non-minorities seldom possess. This recognition provides a direction for social change.

Though the techniques described in this study can be adopted by anyone, they are truly revolutionary – and initially might seem implausible,
even hopelessly naive. But to repeat Muhammad Yunus's contention that
women are better borrowers: "it is so clear, so transparent . . . You don't
need to be smart researchers to find it, but just by casual observation,
you see the difference" (Yunus 2008). In-depth interviews help reveal the
relationships and day-to-day decision-making that create the patterns
measured in the many quantitative studies documenting the tendency for
women to contribute their earnings to social good. The methods routinely
used by these and other minority women might provide the next best step
in the evolution of business – one that leads not only to resources for their
own families, but to embedded social responsibility, personal growth,
self-expression, and the ongoing development of moral integrity. This is
nothing short of unifying the seemingly separate spheres of business and
family, public and private, rational and emotional, quality and quantity, self
and society.

Methods and results

Our methodology is qualitative, and our data collection methods are surveys, observation, and in-depth interviews. We employ a sociological perspective on the self as being developed in and maintained through social
relationships, and therefore endeavor to "convey the subjective realities of
those studied" (Emerson 1983: 105) as those realities are described to us.
Qualitative sociological research holds that human behavior can only be
understood from the viewpoint of the actor as she is interpreting and constructing meaning in each social situation (Levin 1994: 50). Therefore, stories that people tell about their experiences are not separate from those
experiences; instead, experiences are continually negotiated through and
constituted by the narratives told about them (Ely and Padavic 2007; Scott
1992).

The narrative approach reveals how individual minority women make
sense out of their experience of business ownership while also illuminat-
ing the larger social, cultural, economic, and emancipatory underpinnings
of entrepreneurship (Miller 2005: 6). By focusing on minority women's narratives of entrepreneurship, by allowing them to tell their stories, we can
see the way entrepreneurship is manifest differently in various contexts.

Kwame Anthony Appiah writes, "Evaluating stories together is one of the central human ways of learning to align our responses to the world. And that alignment of responses is, in turn, one of the ways we maintain the social fabric, the texture of our relationships" (2006: 29). Narratives provide access to the subjective reality of minority women entrepreneurs as they experience, respond to, and influence social structure. Tina Miller writes:

> The study of the narrative is one attempt at coming to terms with how social identity and, in turn, social action, are constituted and guided. This linking of identity and action, the ontological condition of social life, has challenged earlier thinking around narrative as merely textual, non-theoretical representation. It has also contributed to the considerable debate on how selves are constituted and maintained in late modernity . . . Narrative then can help us to understand social life and social practices. (Miller 2005: 8-9)

Narratives create a record. They end the silence. It is also important to acknowledge that individuals make sense out of the chaos and disruptions they encounter by situating their experiences in the telling and retelling of stories. Coherent, culturally consistent, recognizable narratives can arise from a concatenation of events initially experienced as dissonant, confusing and unpredictable. We do not claim that stories are not used strategically at times, and we recognize that narratives are constructed within interpersonal and interactive contexts, that they are affected by past experiences and future expectations, and that they are anchored in cultural significance.

Narratives, and the experiences and selves constructed through them, are not static, nor are they necessarily consistent over time and place. Instead, they are emergent and dynamic. Alvesson and Billing note that identity requires "constant renegotiation as people exert their will and respond to social experiences that change over time and even in the course of a work day" (1997, quoted in Ely and Padavic 2007: 1130). Therefore, the qualitative data gathered here is not valued insofar as it is replicable, but meaningful insofar as it represents "rich detailed data" (Becker 1970: 52, quoted in Emerson 1983: 101) volunteered by the subjects themselves. Regarding the validity and reliability of qualitative field research, Emerson writes:

> On the one hand, the standard logico-deductive approaches to theory do not apply to the analysis of the field data. Such deductive approaches view theorizing as a procedure in which

> formal hypotheses are derived from existing theoretical propo-
> sitions and then checked against data collected specifically to
> test their validity. In contrast, in fieldwork, theorizing depends
> on concepts derived from the data rather than on deduction
> from received theory. The goal is to arrive at theoretical prop-
> ositions after having looked at the social world, not before.
> Hence, prevalent procedures for verifying theoretical proposi-
> tions are by and large of little use in field research. (Emerson
> 1983: 93)

Our data gathering includes observation, written surveys, and in-depth interviews with 12 minority women entrepreneurs. All the interviewees live in the United States. After preliminary interview questions were answered remotely (usually by email), subsequent interview data was collected in face-to-face, semi-structured interviews. Questions were tailored to elicit narratives: the interviewer listens and responds by asking for clarification of the respondent's descriptions of her experiences. In this way, the interactional and relational approach creates another opportunity for the respondent to develop interpretations and build on existing narratives. Tolman writes:

> Both speaker and listener are recognized as individuals who
> bring thoughts and feelings to the text, acknowledging the
> necessary subjectivity of both participants . . . This method
> leaves a trail of evidence for the listener's interpretation, and
> thus leaves room for other interpretations by other listeners
> consistent with the epistemological stance that there is mul-
> tiple meaning in such stories. (Tolman 2007: 303)

The hallmark of field research is flexibility (Emerson 1983: 93); therefore, when practical, we conducted interviews on-site at the entrepreneur's business office; for those entrepreneurs who did not work from an office (e.g. consultants such as Kathy Deserly) interviews were done in conference rooms, cars, restaurants, and residences. Interviews lasted from several hours to several days, and some entrepreneurs were contacted after the initial interview to provide clarifications or elaborations. Each interview was videotaped.

Our sample represents a diversity of minority women business owners. Diversity is maintained across race, ethnicity, physical disability, religion, age, class, type of industry, location in the U.S., and size and longevity of business. Women in this study are single, married, divorced, and divorced and remarried. Some are mothers with partners and some are single parents. Though we invited a range of sexual orientations, we did not have any woman self-identify as other than heterosexual. We chose entrepreneurs who welcomed in-depth interviews and would allow visual representations. We built contacts with minority women entrepreneurs through a variety of venues: Women's Business Centers, the Center for Women's Business Research, the National Bankers Association, and the Center for Women's Leadership at Babson College. Additionally, we reviewed general business periodicals such as *Business Week*, *Entrepreneur Magazine*, *Forbes*, and *Fortune*; publications targeted toward ethnic minorities including *Black Enterprise*, *Latina Style*, and *Essence*; and periodicals that target women, such as *Working Women*. The popular press was a fruitful source of interviewees: Kathy Deserly was featured in a magazine advertisement for BlackBerry phones; Rita Chang was profiled in her local newspaper; and Nancy Stevens was interviewed for *Self* magazine. We then used snowballing methodology to access a broader array of minority women entrepreneurs. We had no requirement or expectation that entrepreneurs would have a social, political, moral, or personal agenda for their businesses – as it turned out, each spontaneously articulated these aspects in the unstructured, face-to-face interviews.

We recognize that typical expectations for business owners have embedded, albeit often invisible and unarticulated, assumptions about social status characteristics. We focus on how those business owners who are outside the current normative expectations negotiate these assumptions. Emergent themes are compared to extant entrepreneurship literature, and analysis is primarily qualitative field research using observation, in-depth interviews, and an iterative process to search for key words and themes (Charmaz 2001).

In addition, we include inter-judge agreement to yield quantifiable results. Each interview was filmed, and approximately ten independent coders viewed the first hour of the interview. Coders watched the interview once and were instructed to pay close attention and take notes on any points of interest, focusing on the ways the interviewee communicated and noting any themes that emerged during the interview. They were instructed to pay attention to such things as the interviewee's comfort level, confidence, facial expressions, gestures, and emotions, and how these might fluctuate over the course of the interview. For instance, coders were asked to note whether there were contradictions in what the interviewee said, and whether there was a reason to accept or reject the interviewee's response on face value. If coders were unsure of something, they were instructed to rewind the DVD and view that section again. At the end of the first viewing, coders wrote down their general impression of the interviewee, the general themes they noticed in the interview and any points of interest or ways they were surprised, confused, and so on.

Twenty-eight coding themes were taken from previous literature in entrepreneurship (Appendix A). Coders were then asked to review the list of 28 themes and determine whether they were relevant to these minority women entrepreneurs. They were instructed to read the themes over several times so that they were familiar with them, and to watch the DVD again, this time looking for the specific themes on the list. In each instance, coders noted whether the theme was mentioned, how often it was mentioned (quantification), and with what intensity (qualification). Coders then wrote down evidence including specific phrases (quotations) used by the interviewee, and descriptions of her facial expressions, comfort level, emphasis, intonation, and gestures, to support their impressions of the interview.

Of the 28 themes, the following six were applied by every coder to every interviewee:

- Theme 6: Personal vision of what workplace should be like (also extends to product service, customer relations) (Johnson 2004: 155)

- Theme 10: Trouble with financing? (Johnson 2004: 156)

- Theme 11: Trouble being taken seriously as business owner/entrepreneur? (Brush 1997: 9)

- Theme 15: Lack of confidence? (Langowitz, Sharpe *et al.* 2006)

- Theme 25: Ability to express personal vision in business enterprise and contribute to wider change (such as workplace policies, new products, and/or social change generally)? (Johnson 2004; Fleischmann 2006)

- Theme 27: Ability to help others like themselves? (Butler 2005)

The minority women interviewed for this study neither seek to extirpate capitalism, nor do they eschew profit, findings that agree with the research on entrepreneurs by Banks (2006). Only one of the entrepreneurs, Rita Chang, identifies herself as a social entrepreneur, and hers is the only nonprofit business. However, the other entrepreneurs in the study have not adopted the model of waiting until they are wealthy to develop a social mission. Instead, the entrepreneurs featured here found ways to develop a moral, social, and political voice, and business ownership was part of this process (2006: 462-63).

Though our sample size here is small, what became clear during this study was that the orthodox view of business ownership is entirely inadequate to describe the experiences, identities, and objectives of these entrepreneurs. Instead, we found, as Banks describes:

> The collapsing of distinctions between public and private realms may well lead to the engulfment of the self by work, but can, potentially, have the converse effect of increasing the range and heterogeneity of (previously externalized) moral actions and judgments that can be brought to bear in the labor process . . . perhaps we should consider equally how non-instrumental, political and social values may be feeding back into the work process. (Banks 2006: 462-63)

In addition to discussing the economic solvency of her business, each interviewee initiated a narrative about imbuing her work with social, cultural, and political values. As John Silbey Butler notes with regard to his own interviews with entrepreneurs, these case studies are also "a mixture of ethnic history and business activity together" (Butler 1991: 4). In a medley of autobiography and cultural, geographic, class, race, and gender history, these entrepreneurs do not merely describe their business activities, but the social, moral, and personal contexts in which they created their businesses. At times their narratives function in harmony with larger historical and structural contexts, and at other times in opposition to them – always negotiating the established social, economic, and political order. In these interviews, each entrepreneur self-consciously and deliberately identifies herself as a minority woman. This identity is not peripheral or incidental: in fact, each woman describes her gender and minority status such that her reasons for starting a business, for choosing the specific business to start, and for constructing the policies that govern her business, all connect to, and resonate with, personal identity and group affiliations.

The women we interviewed uniformly express the importance of reifying their personal values and visions in their businesses and contributing to wider social change, and this agrees with themes coded from previous literature on entrepreneurs (Johnson 2004: 155; Fleischmann 2006). Each woman also reports that part of the motivation for starting her business was to help other people "like herself." This is sometimes a reference to other women, and sometimes to people with a range of shared characteristics that include race, ethnicity, class, religion, family relationships, and physical challenges. In the case of Angela Patterson and Gretchen Cook-Anderson of Saphia Water, this includes those with African heritage, pregnant women, and women nursing children; and in the case of Nancy Stevens, the physically disabled. All of the entrepreneurs also report times when they had trouble being taken seriously as business owners, and all report having trouble securing financing.

Every woman recounts experiences in the course of running her business where she has been subject to prejudice and discrimination based on her gender and/or minority status. Each entrepreneur articulates a conscious attempt to problematize these experiences and then makes deliberate efforts to affect the larger social order through business decisions. Their personal, social, and political values, developed through experiences of being treated like and identifying as outsiders or "strangers" (Butler 2005) help shape their economic choices and market relations. Like the ethnic and racial middle-group minorities Butler writes about, these women develop "a philosophy of life in a hostile society" (Butler 1991: 258). The common experience of encountering and surviving hostile environments encourages solidarity among minority women entrepreneurs and often provides the basis for their determination to effect social change targeted to minority populations.

The entrepreneurs interviewed for this study use various strategies to construct a sense of self that feels authentic and to infuse their values and perspectives into the wider social discourse. They seek to remedy their outsider status through innovations that combine the seemingly contradictory desires both to adopt and to modify prevalent social goals. They negotiate this paradox by finding ways of loosening structural constraints enough to accommodate their personal and social identities, and in this process they offer new interpretations of social order, and create social change. For example, the businesses run by Pauline Lewis, Margaret Henningsen, and Kathy Deserly all attempt to redress specific historical and structural elements of gender, ethnic, and racial discrimination. Lewis focuses on humanizing manufacturing work and forming egalitarian relationships that celebrate ethnic, racial, and gender solidarity. Henningsen rectifies long-standing policies that denied mortgage loans to African Americans yet she enthusiastically supports traditional home ownership as a worthy objective. By acting as a mediator between U.S. government agencies and tribal organizations, Deserly modifies adoption and foster care for Native populations through the prioritization of both the physical well-being and the cultural identity of children. Each entrepreneur articulates her desire and drive to "give something back."

We recognize that our sample is small and therefore, as mentioned, we do not claim that this research is representative of minority women entrepreneurs generally. Instead, the data here suggest a different orientation to entrepreneurship that is not addressed by conventional business texts, but is consistent with the massive amount of quantitative data regarding the high degree of positive social impact routinely achieved by women entrepreneurs. The centrality of social values is evident in the identification of opportunities, business policies and practices, management of resources, and use of profits. These narratives demonstrate that ethical and moral concerns can be accommodated by, reconciled with, and influential on economic objectives. This perspective disrupts the assertion that the economy is an autonomous sphere governed by instrumental logic and suggests instead that the boundaries between self and work, social benefit and personal economic gain have always been artificial – in fact, economic development is highly attuned to, though not always respectful of, the cultural surroundings from which it arises.

Summary and notes on next chapters

This chapter discusses the three purposes of the book: to give minority women visibility, to explain how and why they are more likely to construct better, more socially conscious businesses, and to provide specific theory and practice for other entrepreneurs. Additionally, this chapter details the importance of minority views, the significance of gender and the methodology of the study. Chapters 2–4 provide the theoretical basis of the empirical research. Chapters 5–7 discuss minority women as business innovators, as partners and as community members. The final chapter examines opportunities and challenges faced by minority women entrepreneurs as well as suggestions for recontextualizing business in the social sphere.

2
Sociological explanations for inequality

The Sociological Imagination: 'You're not a wave; you're part of the ocean!'

Sociologists see people in ways similar to how physicists describe beams of light: they simultaneously have the characteristics of particles and of waves. People as individuals are particles – we have isolated individual qualities, concerns, and motivations. We experience separate sensations. As much as we might wince when we see a child fall, we do not experience exactly the same painful impact. Our thoughts are private, and if uncommunicated, remain in our own minds, and our bodies are physically distinct from all others. We have separate histories that are a unique combination of discrete experiences.

On the other hand, people as waves are in social groups and patterns of interaction over time. Our contemporary lives are colored by our connection with the behavior and treatment of our ancestors and their social networks. To understand the significance of thoughts and experiences – even to develop the language to formulate and articulate thoughts – individuals must communicate with words and gestures that have a shared meaning. Social meaning and shared definitions exist beyond any single individual.

Both ways of being, the particle and the wave, are fundamental: one cannot be disentangled from the other. It is a question of emphasis. Morrie Schwartz, the sociologist made famous by Mitch Alboms's book *Tuesdays with Morrie,* had this to say:

> The story is about a little wave, bobbing along in the ocean, having a grand old time enjoying the wind and fresh air – until [it] notices the other waves in front . . . crashing against the shore. "My God, this is terrible," the wave says. "Look what's going to happen to me!" Then along comes another wave. It sees the first wave, looking grim, and it says . . . "Why do you look so sad?" The first wave says: "You don't understand! We're all going to crash! All of us waves are going to be nothing! Isn't it terrible?" The second wave say: "No, you don't understand. You're not a wave; you're part of the ocean." (Winter and Birnberg 2003: 629)

In addition to our unique, individual selves, we also are members of groups. Tim Wise describes group membership this way:

> when we first draw breath outside the womb, we inhale tiny particles of all that came before, both literally and figuratively. We are never merely individuals; we are never alone; we are always in the company, as uncomfortable as it sometimes can be, of others, the past, of history. We become part of that history just as surely as it becomes part of us. (Wise 2005: 2)

We are women, men, or some combination; we have racial, ethnic, and class identities, and these identities might change over time depending on social definitions. We often have religious, national, and political loyalties. We are chocolate lovers and teetotallers, cat or dog people, Baby Boomers, GenXers, or members of some other age cohort, mothers, fathers, sisters, brothers, daughters, and sons, soccer players, ice skaters, and rock climbers. In fact, there are no qualities that we possess as individuals that are not shared with, related to, and defined by others. We understand our individual selves only as we are situated in larger social values and meanings. Society then, is *sui generis* – a thing in itself. In the same way that the ocean is independent of any single wave, society is independent of any single person. It exists before, will continue to exist after, and yet is inseparable from, any individual.

Sociology, like all disciplines, developed over time and originated from many different sources, both ancient and modern. As an early sociologist, the French theoretician Emile Durkheim sought to establish how sociological analysis was substantially different from the analysis in the other nascent social sciences of psychology, political science, and economics. To accomplish this, he chose a highly controversial subject for one of his most well-known works: *Suicide: A Study in Sociology* (1897).

At the time of Durkheim's study, suicide was proscribed in Christian and Islamic doctrines, and both Catholics and Protestants perceived suicide as a sin worthy of eternal damnation. Not only was suicide a sensationalistic and arresting subject of study, conventional wisdom defined suicide as a private, personal act, often performed in isolation. Suicide was associated with some characteristic of the individual ranging from mental distress, psychological trauma, lack of strong moral character, or incurable insanity (Levin 1994: 367). Many believed that individuals took their own lives when they could no longer cope with some catastrophic personal event. This view of suicide reflects the central role of the individual in the societies of Western Europe and the United States, where personal responsibility, agency, and free will were emphasized. Because of the emphasis on the concepts of individual selfhood, independent action, and unconstrained choice, the concept and study of suicide had been very narrowly focused on personality flaws in suicidal individuals and on traumatic events in their private lives. Therefore, suicides were routinely studied as unrelated episodes of madness.

By examining group affiliation, Durkheim sought to establish that the disciplinary lens of sociology could uncover a different dimension of reality, provide new analytical insights, and find patterns in the probability of suicide. He had to demonstrate that sociological analysis could enlist detachment from and reflection on the very social conventions, traditions, and habits that guide thoughts, perceptions, and explanations within a given society.

Commonsense explanations resonate in a context of conventional thinking: given the centrality of the individual, it was logical to attribute suicide to individual sickness and private experiences. Explanations concerning suicide were therefore limited in Western cultures by a focus on the individual as the unit of analysis.

A main objective of sociological analysis is to study and test traditional social assumptions. By examining underlying patterns of events over time and general principles of causation, sociological analysis reveals nonobvious realities. The work of a sociologist, then, is to see conventional social explanations as emblematic of the society in which they flourish, and not necessarily as comprehensive descriptions of empirical phenomena. Therefore, instead of focusing on suicides as isolated occurrences of individual choice, Durkheim studied suicide within patterns of group affiliation. By challenging what counted as relevant data, Durkheim's analysis supplanted the individual as the frame of reference. The patterns of suicide that emerged included:

- More Protestants than Catholics committed suicide

- More people in urban populations committed suicide than those living in small towns

- In populations where divorce was hard to obtain, women were more likely to commit suicide

- Male suicide was higher where divorce was less difficult. (Lehmann 1994: 65)

Durkheim compared statistical patterns of suicide that had been attributed to individual psychological causes, and found that "individual characteristics could not explain the differing suicide rates" (Levin 1994: 397). Therefore, he postulated that suicide rates were linked to group membership.

Individual members of groups with highly functioning networks – high levels of group solidarity, cohesion, and support – are less likely to commit suicide. In most instances, lower social bonding and lower social integration are associated with higher rates of suicide. Durkheim revealed that the lower rate of suicide among Catholics as compared to Protestants reflected the high degree of social interdependency and solidarity within Catholic communities as opposed to the relative degree of independence and separation in Protestant groups, a result of the doctrine of individualism embraced by Protestants. In our contemporary society, there are higher suicide rates among gay, bisexual, and transgendered people, indicating their outsider status, absence of tight-knit, cohesive communities, and general lack of social support.

However, more rarely, social solidarity can be too strong and overwhelm considerations of individual life, as in the case of suicide bombers and religious martyrs. Using a sociological analysis, Durkheim found that suicide is often either an indicator of the lack of social support, or the inability to balance individual survival and the demands of group membership. Durkheim's study of suicide demonstrates the importance of explaining and predicting human behavior in terms of group membership rather than only in terms of individual characteristics.

Like Durkheim, C. Wright Mills did not explain human behavior in terms of individual choices or personality flaws; he, too, situated the most personal and private decisions in a social context. When analyzing reasons for divorce, Mills encouraged divorced people to look beyond conventional individual explanations and fears such as: they had not chosen the right partner, did not have enough money, or were no longer attractive. Instead, Mills saw marriage as a social institution and divorce as part of the broader social trend reflecting changes in the definition of marriage and in the social demands and expectations of couples. According to Mills, divorces were not disconnected events representing unique dysfunction within a particular couple, but the consequence of larger social forces transcending and acting on individual marriages.

Mills adopted what he called "the sociological imagination" (Levin 1994: 17) which emphasizes the interplay between shared social structures and individual subjective experiences. In relation to divorce, Mills believed that: "In so far as the family as an institution turns women into darling little slaves and men into their chief providers and unweaned dependents, the problem of a satisfactory marriage remains incapable of purely private solutions" (Levin 1994: 18). In this view, each couple operates within a historical, social, and economic milieu that overwhelms the differences among individual couples. As Arlie Hochschild reminds us:

> Each marriage bears the footprints of economic and cultural trends which originate far outside the marriage. A rise in inflation which erodes the earning power of the male wage, an expanding service sector which opens up jobs for women, new culture images . . . that make the working mother seem exciting, all these changes do not simply go on around marriage. They occur *within* marriage, and transform it. Problems between husbands and wives, problems which seem "individual" and "marital," are often individual experiences of powerful economic and cultural shock waves that are not caused by one person or two. (Hochschild 1989: 11)

The sociology of entrepreneurship: 'At least we're getting into the game'

The sociology of entrepreneurship is the study of the relationship between group characteristics and the development of business activity (Butler 2005: 1). Historically, sociological scholarship has emphasized the status characteristics of race and ethnicity (Butler 2005: 1-4; Bonacich and Modell 1980), with gender being a recently added category. John Silbey Butler stresses the self-help, or emancipatory (Fleischmann 2006) aspect of entrepreneurship as it is the process in which "groups develop, maintain and expand business enterprises within the economic structure" (Butler 2005: 1).

Edna Bonacich's theory of "middleman" minorities (1980) and Butler's related concept of "strangers" (2005) attempt to explain how groups of outsiders – those who are socially, politically, and economically marginalized – use entrepreneurial business enterprises as strategies to counteract discrimination. These businesses tend to be family-owned and to concentrate on trade, commerce, and the circulation of goods and services (Butler 2005: 14). Because the number of women in the paid labor force has increased dramatically in the last 40 years, and because women have been discriminated against both by employers and by lending institutions, Butler (2005) and Greene and Johnson (1995) include women under the rubric of "strangers." Women are "strangers," too, in that they often move between domestic and workplace obligations, and because feminine characteristics are not as likely to be associated with the workplace as are masculine qualities (Valian 1998: 125). In addition, until recently women have been largely subsumed into the same class category as their husbands or families of origin, while also having less ability than their male counterparts to generate independent capital (Davis and Robinson 1988; Baxter 1994).

In Bonacich's theory (1980), "middleman" minority entrepreneurs, hereafter referred to as middle-group minority entrepreneurs, exhibit three characteristics:

- They are victims of discrimination
- They are concentrated in service industry business
- They have strong intra-group solidarity.

Like "strangers," middle-group minorities are groups of people who have been subject to discrimination and kept from freely participating in the economy. This population tends to cluster in niche areas of commerce between the elites and the subordinates, such as in small businesses that focus on petty finance, craftwork, and marginalized service industries (Bonacich 1980). Women are minorities not only because they have had to endure societal discrimination, but also because they make up a minority of business owners compared to their male counterparts across all races (Butler 2005; Minniti, Arenius *et al.* 2005: 12). Further, like middle-group minorities, women tend to own small, service-oriented businesses: according to the Center for Women's Business Research (CWBR), women-owned businesses in the U.S. are primarily concentrated in the service sector, and women-owned U.S. businesses tend to be small (CWBR 2009: 7).

Members of middle-group minorities are also characterized by their tendency to "take care of their own" and to maintain a high level of group solidarity (Butler 2005: 16; Bonacich 1980; Greene and Johnson 1995). This intra-group solidarity is most often kept in place by mechanisms of private language; religious affiliation and attendant rituals; urban concentration; social organization; and other specific memberships and practices that serve to reinforce racial, ethnic, class, and religious "relative solidarity within the group and [social separation] from the surrounding society" (Butler 2005).

However, women are neither minorities nor "strangers" insofar as they sometimes have majority status in race, ethnicity, class, and religion. Therefore, unlike the case of middle-group minority entrepreneurs, intra-group solidarity for women business owners has not easily been established, nor have the mechanisms of solidarity been clarified. Greene and Johnson theorize that women entrepreneurs, unlike other minority groups, draw support from their family and friends: in other words, "people who are not [necessarily] exclusively members of the minority group defined as females" (Greene and Johnson 1995: 67). However, subsequent research with female entrepreneurs revealed instances where women's families actively discourage them from starting businesses because the role of entrepreneur can conflict with the role of caretaker (Langowitz, Sharpe *et al.* 2006). Women in more traditional cultures were especially affected: Iranian, Hispanic, rural Caucasian, and Taiwanese cultures were specifically mentioned.

In this study of minority women entrepreneurs, none of the women was in partnerships with her husband, and support was variable. Pauline Lewis says, "He's my number one fan, but he's not allowed to touch anything!" Barbara Manzi says, "My husband doesn't really understand the industry. Women have to support husbands. Husbands don't pay much attention to what women do." Further, disproportionate domestic and family obligations are both a motivation for and an obstacle to women starting businesses (Langowitz, Sharpe *et al.* 2006). Therefore, mechanisms that create intra-group solidarity among minority women entrepreneurs remain unclear and probably case-specific. There is, however, documentation that solidarity can be created in multi-racial groups of women when gender is the emphasized social status characteristic; this is evident in organizations such as Women's Business Centers that offer entrepreneurial training and education to a diverse group of women (Godwyn 2009c).

Sociologists have studied entrepreneurial activity primarily because it produces economic stability and reinforces intra-group solidarity. However, these social consequences of enterprise development are critical not only in generating income to survive day to day, but in promoting self-expression and the representation of group values and perspectives as they are communicated in business practices, products, and services. Johnson writes:

> In short, for female entrepreneurs, small businesses [are] an
> arena where they . . . shape a personal vision of how work
> should be organized. Some women [pursue] entrepreneurship
> as a way to gain control over work processes and advance a
> particular vision. (Johnson 2004: 155)

Evident in the narratives of the minority women entrepreneurs featured here are their personal visions, grounded in their group status identity, and their life experiences. These visions often involve activism imbued throughout their business practices and relevant to a wide range of social issues including lending practices, labor regulations, equal opportunity policies, and environmental impact. Minority women intend to run businesses that are lucrative, but they also talk about using their knowledge and expertise, and their own vision of a just and fair society, to improve the world.

The economist Joseph Schumpeter, one of the earliest theorists of entrepreneurship (1934), recognizes entrepreneurs as innovators and change agents who are necessary for **economic** progress. However, Schumpeter did not identify entrepreneurs as change agents for **social** norms, including aesthetic tastes, knowledge, and conventional wisdom, that come under the rubric of cultural traditions and systems of social valuation. However, in the emancipatory or "self-help" sense (Butler 2005), entrepreneurship is a tangible, practical manifestation of self-expression. It not only offers the entrepreneur access to an economic arena that may have been blocked by social prejudice and discrimination, but also affects her ability to engage with and influence societal discourse – to develop and express personal and group identities by influencing the larger social context. As one Women's Business Center client put it, "There will never be a level playing field, but least we're getting into the game" (Godwyn 2009c). The entrepreneurs in this study reflect the process chronicled by Banks: "they are self-consciously engaged in forms of practice that contain ideas about what is 'good' (and therefore 'bad'), exhibit moral ways of acting towards others, and negotiate the balance between holding instrumental or non-instrumental values" (Banks 2006: 456).

The material aspects of entrepreneurship are granted legitimacy insofar as they reflect shared values. Among these shared values are a commitment to the moral and ethical standards of the community; self-expression; creativity; environmental health; representation of a multiplicity of perspectives; problem-solving; accountability; and the ongoing articulation of the mutuality of social responsibility and personal identity. Fourcade and Healy write:

market exchange is saturated with moral meaning...it
involves more or less conscious efforts to categorize, normal-
ize and naturalize behaviors and rules that are not natural in
any way, whether in the name of economic principles (e.g., effi-
ciency, productivity) or more social ones (e.g., justice, social
responsibility). (Fourcade and Healy 2007: 300)

For the women in this study, entrepreneurship is not only a vehicle for
instrumental economic activity, but also provides ways to influence the
social, cultural, and symbolic realm governed by non-instrumental logic.

The social self: George Herbert Mead

As mentioned, access to the economy through entrepreneurship can give
more people representation in cultural, political, and economic domains.
In this way, entrepreneurial activity influences the way the self is experienced, expressed, and represented in the social. To explore both the
economic and cultural dimensions of entrepreneurship, we first have to
understand how the individual acquires a personal identity (i.e., a sense
of self) over time and within a variety of social contexts. We use the term
"self" in the broadest sense, not to refer to the self-contained, self-interested individual of classical economic theory, "economic man" (Crittenden
2001: 67); but with reference to the multifaceted self that encompasses a
range of social status characteristics including, but not limited to, gender,
race, class, religion, sexual orientation, disability, and marital and family
position. In other words, our *social* self: the cumulative, internalized sense
of who we are that is continuously created and recreated through interaction with others (Collins 1992: 56).

Sociology is distinguished as a discipline with the fundamental postulate
that is there is no pre-social self. Sociologists contend that we construct
our sense of self through our interpretations of the behavior and attitudes
of others towards us. As we attribute meaning to their behavior, we see
the world, and ourselves, through the perspectives of others. Mead calls
this "taking the role of the other" (Mead 1934). Seeing ourselves through
the eyes of others allows us to judge our own actions. This lays the basis
of rationality and morality: "it is necessary for rational conduct that
individual[s] should thus take an objective, impersonal attitude toward
[themselves], that [they] should become [objects] in their own minds"
(Mead 1934: 138).

Sociologists study patterns of interactions among and between people,
and therefore, from a sociological perspective, individuals are all products
of their group affiliations and the various roles they play within groups.

Individuals are then identified and identify with certain groups: "The individual experiences him [or her] self . . . not directly, but only indirectly, from the particular standpoints of other individual members of the same social group, or from the generalized standpoint of the social group as a whole" (Mead 1934: 138). For sociologists, there is no final, definitive core self that is separable from social interaction: "The layers [of self] are added from the outside, which then get reflected on the inside in our consciousness. Each new level of individual is created by a new way of relating to other people. There is no pre-social self" (Collins 1992: 57).

Through a constant interactive process, we evaluate the behavior of others as they are evaluating us. These interactions create the myriad of social networks on which our physical, economic, and psychological survival actively depend:

> The main forms of self-creating interaction rituals are not competitive, but cooperative. People cooperate in building up each other's self-image. People exaggerate, building up incidents in their daily lives to be more than they really are, pretending to be smarter or cooler or richer or more successful than is actually the case . . . Each individual seems to give the other the tacit right to build up a somewhat false view of their own world in return for the right to do likewise when it is their turn to speak. (Collins 1992: 56)

Social interaction, when cooperative, is a mutual, interdependent, circular process wherein "everyone gives another an ideal self and receives back in return their own self from other people" (Collins 1992: 56). The idea that we have no self outside of social interaction, that selfhood is generated in some social context, as a reflection of how we think others see us, is referred to as "the looking glass self" (Cooley 1902). The self is therefore an emergent product of interactions with others.

In tribal and agrarian societies, individuals identify themselves primarily as part of their clan; family names are often stated before individual names. Identity is conceived of as group membership rather than in singular terms. Paula Gunn Allen explains: "An American Indian woman is primarily defined by her tribal identity. In her eyes, her destiny is necessarily that of her people" (Allen 1986: 18). Ayaan Hirsi Ali, a Somali woman, writes, "Somali children must memorize their lineage; this is more important than almost anything. Whenever a Somali meets a stranger, they ask each other, 'Who are you?' They trace back their separate ancestries until they find a common forefather" (Ali 2007: 4).

Rugged individualism, independent thought, and free agency are emblematic of American and, to a slightly lesser extent, Western European, cultural and social values. Therefore, the concept of individual selfhood is so familiar to these cultures that its existence is taken for granted – indeed, psychology and economics typically presume an individual self as the smallest unit of analysis.

For sociologists, the smallest unit of analysis is the group – at least two people. Without a group, there can be no selfhood. A sociological view, then, is consistent with the Scottish proverb: "The greatest gift that God hath given us is to see ourselves as others see us" (Timmons and Spinelli 2007: 26). This proverb is also a reminder that all entrepreneurship, not just social entrepreneurship, is fundamentally a social act. It is the act of creating a product, service, vision, or understanding, not only for oneself, but to be embraced by others.

In the context of sociology, however, God – and all deities and sacred objects – symbolize the abstract good: they are representations, tailored by each society, of social ideals, characteristics, and codes of conduct. Deities transcend the limitations of any individual human and represent the strength of commonly held social beliefs. God, then, is the embodiment of the values of any given society and represents the power of social forces. Therefore, if we read the Scottish proverb from a sociological perspective, then it means that the greatest gift we get from society is the power to see ourselves as others do. Collins writes:

> God (the divine) is society itself: There is one reality that [has] all the characteristics that people attribute to the divine. It is not nature, nor is it metaphysical. It is *society itself.* For society is a force far greater than any individual. It brought us to life, and it can kill us. It has tremendous power over us. Everyone depends upon it in innumerable ways. We use tools and skills we did not invent; we speak a language passed on to us from others. Virtually our whole material and symbolic world is given to us from society . . . Moreover, this something – the feeling of our dependence upon society – exists simultaneously outside and inside ourselves. (Collins 1992: 34 [emphasis in the original])

Power and social interaction

Though sociologists posit cooperation and social cohesion as the foundation of human interactions, they also recognize the obvious: interactions can be highly competitive and conflict-ridden. In these instances, the interactive process of self-creation is wildly skewed depending on the power of those involved. In a hierarchal structure, subordinates must flatter superiors because they are so dependent on their goodwill. In fact, one way to identify the more powerful person or persons in any interaction is to discover who has more knowledge of the other. The person or group with more knowledge is not dominant. Subordinates have more information about the values and perspectives of the powerful. This knowledge is protective; it is necessary to anticipate and meet the needs of those in charge. As Appiah writes, "Thoroughgoing ignorance about the ways of others is largely a privilege of power" (Appiah 2006: xviii).

For instance, in current U.S. society, information about heterosexual relations and rituals of courtship and marriage are widely known, inculcated into the young, embedded and disseminated in families, legal and religious institutions, frequently represented in literature, music and visual arts, including television, film, and advertisements. Heterosexual relationships support and are supported by a huge economic industry that reflects the social and political values of the United States. Regardless of sexual orientation, everyone is familiar with the rituals associated with heterosexual courtship. The same knowledge base does not exist for relationships involving homosexual, bisexual, or transsexual individuals; this ignorance indicates that heterosexuality is the dominant, socially condoned sexual orientation. The difficulties experienced from lack of social support run the gamut from confusion over terminology regarding same-sex partners (are two women who are married both called wives? Partners? Spouses?) to hate speech and physical violence directed toward non-heterosexuals. Social knowledge is a currency that represents social opinion, endorsement, and support, and ignorance reveals societal disapproval, rejection, and sometimes hostility.

Self-creating social interactions, therefore, often contain glaring inequities. This is evident in face-to-face micro-interactions, for instance when one person consistently interrupts the other, as well as in institutional assessments of the competency of groups of people. When Collins writes "society is a force far greater than any individual. It brought us to life, and it can kill us (Collins 1992: 34), he is referencing the authority of social values, values of those in the majority – not necessarily the numerical majority, but those in power who dominate social opinion and dictate social rules – and he is also alluding to what can happen when people violate the ideals and norms of society. Though literal death can be the result, a kind of symbolic death often awaits those who do not or cannot conform to societal demands and expectations. Mead tells us that the self is not created only from seeing ourselves from the particular standpoints of other members in our same social group(s) – our friends – but also from seeing ourselves from the generalized standpoint of the community as a whole. Mead calls this "taking the role of the generalized other" (Mead 1934: 138).

For those who belong to subordinated, marginalized, and stigmatized groups – those people who are granted less social respect than others – the experience of taking the role of the generalized other can be painful and humiliating. Rather than being given an idealized version of selfhood that is mutually exchanged between and among cooperative parties, those individuals in stigmatized groups receive a constant barrage of messages that they lack the characteristics and skills valued in their society. Because of socially defined inferiority, they cannot successfully compete with those in dominant, and therefore superior, groups.

These negative assessments from society at large, the generalized other, are often associated with ascribed social status characteristics – congenital aspects such as race, gender, sexual orientation, weight, height, physical and mental disability, or other attributes that are beyond the control of individuals; this sometimes also includes nationality and religion. Denigrating messages are delivered through micro-interactions with individuals and through larger institutional-level evaluations. These messages can be subtle or dramatic. They are discriminatory: they give rise to unequal treatment based on group membership rather than evaluation based on individual behavior or talent (Levin 1994: 323). Racist, sexist, classist, ageist, homophobic speech and behavior are examples of discriminatory social messages, and, whether intended or not, they result in the stultification of the self-development of those in stigmatized populations: in other words, a symbolic death of self. Levin writes:

> When people make a great deal of money or gain power or prestige, it is common for their success to be attributed to their [individual] talent or hard work. Certainly, that sometimes happens. But it is also clear that *opportunities* to achieve success are not evenly distributed throughout the society . . . I'm not even talking about the person who is handed everything by inheriting the family fortune, for example. I'm just describing the person who has the opportunity to compete without facing special barriers . . . large numbers of people are denied adequate diets, health care, education . . . They suffer reduced life-chances. The result is a system of stratification in which the unequal distribution of money, power, and status is often incorrectly attributed entirely to . . . individual qualities and efforts . . . The system of stratification is stable, because individual differences in the talents and efforts of societal members

> are overwhelmed by the uneven distribution of life-chances.
> (Levin 1994: 302-303 [emphasis in the original])

Symbolic death often takes the form of nullification: societal ignorance of the existence, of the human experience, and the perspectives of devalued groups. In *The Autobiography of an Ex-Colored Man,* James Weldon Johnson explains how African Americans have more accurate and complete knowledge of White people in the United States than Whites have of them, and this inequality of knowledge exposes the social dominance of Whites:

> It is very likely that the Negroes of the United States have a fairly correct idea of what the white people of the country think of them, for that opinion has for a long time been and is still being constantly stated; but they are themselves more or less a sphinx to the whites. (Johnson 1912: vii)

In *The Feminine Mystique*, Betty Friedan speaks of "the problem that has no name" (Friedan 1963). She draws attention to the largely unarticulated dissatisfaction of middle-class, White, college-educated women who, in post-war American society, were often shuttled to the suburbs to become wives and mothers, dependent on their husbands for money and a respectable social identity. Because language to describe the feelings and perspectives of this population had not been supplied by the larger society, Friedan creates a new language. Coining the phrase "the problem that has no name," she demonstrates part of the problem: that these women's voices and their concerns were not being represented in the larger social discourse of the time. As marginalized people, this population of women was silenced, overlooked, forgotten.

Subordinated minorities accumulate knowledge about those in power in part to protect themselves, but a minority perspective on the majority also has another consequence: it can be a source of problem-solving and innovation. Because minorities can more easily identify the weaknesses in the system, they often become resourceful and either circumvent or solve the inadequacies of conventional, accepted methods. As will be discussed at length in the following chapters, all of the women in this study identify themselves as minority women and each had stories to tell about feeling like and being treated as an outsider. For instance, Judi Henderson-Townsend of Mannequin Madness decided not to post her picture on her website because she feared customers would respond negatively to the fact that she is African American. Barbara Manzi, identifying as Black Portuguese and owner of Manzi Metals, now one of the leading metal distributors in the United States, recalls being told "you're just a little Black girl who will never amount to anything. How are you going to start a company? You better learn to cook and sew." Kim Edwards, who identifies as Native Alaskan, is the owner of Pampered Pup. Though her business is a very popular dog-grooming service in Harve, Montana (she estimates that she grooms close to 80% of the dogs in Harve), she has deliberately chosen to stay small in order to maintain high quality. This decision does not reflect the conventional definition of business success, and along with her minority status, her unusual way of doing business elicited distrust at first:

> Being Native made it harder to prove myself. In this area, there are very few successful Native people and when you do come across Natives working in an area, sometimes you still get that attitude that their work might not be that good. I really didn't have people say much, but at first I had to prove myself in their minds.

Kathy Deserly talks about a White man who told her that Indians can't run businesses because "they get welfare money from the government and go out and gamble it away."

On the other hand, outsider status can create opportunities. When Pauline Lewis of oovoo design approached factory owners in Vietnam to discuss making her purses, she did not feel she was taken seriously by male owners – so she decided to work only with women. Lewis now has a very successful partnership with women in Vietnamese sewing circles. Rita Chang reports that from a young age, she was

> always conscious of being different. It wasn't just my ethnicity, but I had a very different background. I grew up in a very international world. I had this multicultural background. At an early age, I became very comfortable with being different.

Chang attributes her innovative outlook to her ability to embrace a minority view, a different way of seeing things.

Conflict theory: Karl Marx

The neglect that some populations face from the larger community is in proportion to the devaluation of their views. The lack of cooperative interactions is indicative of the fact that the interests of these groups are in conflict with the interests of those in power; they are therefore ignored or attacked. In fact, the inability to influence institutional standards of evaluation and cultural values is one way to define minority status. Levin writes, "The distinction between majorities and minorities is one of power, not numbers" (Levin 1994: 329). Conflict theory claims that once dominant and subordinate positions are established, those in dominant positions become convinced that their dominance is deserved, fair, and just. Indeed, the evaluative standards and procedures of the institutional infrastructure (schools, places of worship, legal and economic systems, family and work-place structures) are based on this conclusion. If, as Durkheimian socio-logical theory holds, deities are embodiments of social values, of society itself, then those who dominate society are, by definition, the most divine. The idea that Providence is responsible for the superordinate position of certain groups and the subordination of others (discussed in Chapter 4) is often used to justify power structures.

In addition to ascribed characteristics that define social power, there is also the related characteristic of class. Symbolic death is not only reflected in lack of social knowledge about the perspectives of marginalized groups; symbolic death is also represented in lack of access to the material ben-efits of the community. However, cultural privilege and material goods are not easily separable, as material reflects and defines social status. Michael Moore wrote the forward to Ben's book, *Rivethead*:

> Ben and I both grew up in Flint, Michigan, the sons of factory workers. We were never supposed to get out, and you were never supposed to hear our voices. It all comes down to a mat-ter of class, of knowing our place, and a place like Flint, Michi-gan doesn't really exist in the minds of the media or decision makers. (Hamper 1986: xv)

Material is a crucial dimension involved in social identity and the creation of the self. In part, the way society "brings us to life" is represented in material goods. The exchange and accumulation of material is the tangi-ble evidence of social relationships. For example, Daniel Miller describes the preparations that parents make when they are expecting a child: "The fetus becomes a person as [he or she] become[s] the object of a shop-ping expedition and the gifting of goods" (Miller 2001: 52). We acknowledge the transformations of selves through such social rituals as baby show-ers, weddings, funerals, graduations, and bar/bat mitzvahs, with material exchanges situated in ritualized, highly symbolic practices. These ceremo-nies demarcate the social identity of individuals. Gifts are chosen to reflect the status and roles of those involved. Gifts for female and male babies, for instance, are color-coded and contain expectations for the baby's behav-ior and relationships with others – little girls often receive frilly dresses and baby dolls; boys get overalls and trucks. Similarly, individuals choose material that reflects the social self they would like to have. For instance, types of automobiles are associated with specific genders, racial identities, personalities, and socioeconomic status: different connotations are conveyed for drivers of minivans versus those who drive sporty convertibles. The symbolic significance or social meaning of brands transcends the functionality of the object.

As discussed earlier, conventional discourse regarding economic trends tends to focus on the logic of the free market as distinct from social values and moral considerations; however, Fourcade and Healy contend that "the intertwining of market activity and moral valuation is so pervasive that recent studies have argued the image of a clean division between market and non-market spheres is of limited utility" (Fourcade and Healy 2007: 300).

Viviana Zelizer concurs; she forges an inspired and convincing argument against Georg Simmel's contention that modernity is the "reduction of quality to quantity," and Karl Marx's interpretation that money signifies the process in which "social relationships between individuals were transmuted into material relations between things" (Zelizer 1989: 345). She argues that these material analyses claim money as a neutral object, and therefore, the "link of interdependence is missing" (Zelizer 1989: 347) as if money were not "sociological enough" (Zelizer 1989: 343), noting that in these claims: "The power of money to transform nonpecuniary values is unquestioned, while the reciprocal transformation of money by values is seldom conceptualized or else explicitly rejected" (Zelizer 1989: 347). However, Zelizer contends, "Money is neither culturally neutral nor morally invulnerable. It may well 'corrupt' values into numbers, but values and sentiments reciprocally corrupt money by investing it with moral, social and religious meaning" (Zelizer 1989: 347-48). She also argues that the origin and purposes of money, as well as the amount, payment method, payer, and payee all imbue money with social significance, with quality in addition to quantity. She writes:

> How else, for instance, would we distinguish a bribe from a tribute or a donation? A wage from an honorarium or an allowance from a salary? How do we identify ransom, bonuses, tips, damages or premiums? True, there are quantitative differences among these various payments. But, surely, the special vocabulary conveys much more than diverse amounts. Detached from its qualitative differences, the world of money becomes undecipherable. (Zelizer 1989: 351)

The social meaning of the amount and the method of expenditures is vital to the understanding of money's contribution to self-identity. For example, various methods of paying employees include hourly wages, annual salary, bonuses, stock options, and piecework payments. Fourcade and Healy write that these methods "do not simply reflect specific incentives or bear only a technical relation to the work being paid for. They also incorporate specific status signals, cultural representations (Biernacki 1995) and codes of moral worth" (Fourcade and Healy 2007: 300).

Various payment structures are the product of assumptions about the relationship between employee and employer, and the relationship between people and the work they do. The nature of those relationships is represented by the method of payment. Piecework payment is intended to tie remuneration to each item produced, and therefore motivates workers to produce as much as possible, with the tacit assumption that if they were not so motivated, production would be lower. Collins writes:

> Moreover, the use of a financial incentive system becomes an important influence upon the way workers think of their job. The most important thing for the manager is obviously the monetary controls; this becomes the most important thing for the worker also. In the manager's eyes, all the workers want to do is make as much money as possible for as little effort as possible. The manager's very attitude encourages this. It then becomes a contest between manager and worker over just how much pay can be gotten for how much work. (Collins 1992: 64)

Piecework payment, then, creates relationships that contribute to the sense of selfhood of all parties involved. Adversaries and competitors rather than cooperative collaborators, the manager can easily become stereotyped as the parsimonious boss – while workers can be viewed equally stereotypically as lazy and slow. Fourcade and Healy write, "In a world saturated by economic thinking, actors are thus progressively turned into calculative agencies" (Fourcade and Healy 2007: 302). The work itself becomes valuable only insofar as it relates to money.

There is a very different relationship between white-collar workers – those who have an annual salary, bonuses, and stock options – and their work product. The higher status of white-collar work comes in part from having a social identity of trustworthiness, of mutual loyalty between employees and the company they work for, and, though ironic given that white-collar jobs pay more and are generally more stable, of the inherent worthiness of their work apart from any monetary compensation they receive. For instance, both physicians and attorneys have ethical codes of conduct that separate their professional identity and duties from economic remuneration for their knowledge and skills.

Karl Marx conceptualizes social behavior in largely economic, material terms, and his interpretation of societal conflict is primarily class-based. As he describes the relationship between proletariats (subordinated laborers) and capitalists (those who dominate the economy by owning the means of production) Marx focuses on the significance of each class's access to the economy. He argues that under this class division, workers become separated, or alienated, from their own work product. Marx and Engels used the term "artisan" to refer to those pre-industrial workers, who, as members of craft guilds, maintained creative control over the product of their labor (Marx and Engels 1848: 46). When factories replaced guilds, personal worth was reduced to exchange value, and artisans were exploited by the bourgeoisie, turned into wage-laborers and paid by the pieces they produced. Piecework took the place of creative work, and Marx laments: "[t]he bourgeoisie has stripped of its halo every occupation hitherto honored and looked up to with reverent awe" (Marx and Engels 1848: 11).

After industrialization, workers no longer controlled the transformation of raw materials into usable goods; instead, capitalists dictated the methods workers used to transform raw material, the pace at which they worked, even the jobs they had to perform. Unlike pre-industrial artisans, factory workers were thwarted in their ability to use work as a means of self-expression and creativity. Workers became the commodities of factory owners, interchangeable and reducible to the uniform functions demanded by the assembly line. The class division, therefore, exploits the labor of workers and gives rise to their sense of powerlessness, isolation, meaninglessness, and self-estrangement.

False consciousness

Marx's idea of the conflict between dominant capitalists and subordinate proletariats has been extended to analyze a wide range of relationships: such as those within public institutions, like schools, and those within the domestic realm, like marriage. In each case, the question of how dominant and subordinate positions are either maintained or changed over time has been a central sociological concern. According to Marx, positions of dominance persist in significant part because those in power successfully influence what people "take for granted" (Collins 1992: 75). Therefore, when subordinates adopt a worldview consistent with the norms and values that create and maintain prevailing power dynamics, positions remain unchallenged. Marx calls this adopted worldview "false consciousness," as subordinates are, without conscious realization, internalizing and executing the agenda of those who dominate them. In this way, subordinates unintentionally contribute to their own exploitation.

Accordingly, power is more successfully maintained through controlling ideology rather than by imposing brute force. Cultures are structured such that those in power maintain the most control with the least amount of effort and conflict. John Lye explains:

> [Ideology] is not a matter of groups deliberately planning to oppress people or alter their consciousness (although this can happen), but rather a matter of how the dominant institutions in society work through values, conceptions of the world and symbol systems, in order to legitimize the current order. Briefly, this legitimization is managed through the widespread teaching (the social adoption) of ideas about the way things are, how the world "really" works and should work. These ideas (often embedded in symbols and cultural practices) orient people's thinking in such a way that they accept the current way of doing things, the current sense of what is "natural," and the current understanding of their roles in society. This socialization process, the shaping of our cognitive and affective interpretations of our social world, is called, by Gramsci, "hegemony"; it is carried out, Althusser writes, by the state ideological apparatuses – by the churches, the schools, the family and through cultural forms (such as literature, rock music, advertising, sitcoms, etc.). (Lye 1997)

Marx theorizes that in order for proletariats to successfully challenge capitalists, they have to develop "workers' consciousness." Workers have to begin to identify with their group interests and build solidarity as workers rather than continue to comply with the demands and expectations of capitalists. Collins writes, "For a group to have this solidarity, its members must stop calculating their own self-interest in relation to each other, and emphasize only their common interests as a group" (Collins 1992: 24).

The emancipatory potential of entrepreneurship

Part of the emancipatory potential of entrepreneurship originates in its ability to rejoin workers and their work product. Louis Brandeis wrote, "Real success in business is to be found in achievements comparable . . . with those of the artist or scientist, of the inventor or the statesman. And the joys sought in the profession of business must be like their joys . . ." (Fleischmann 2006: 17). To the degree that entrepreneurs have creative control over their time, products and services produced, alienation does not exist. Entrepreneurship, then, recreates artisan status. William Scott Green writes that entrepreneurship can be seen as

> an antidote to the alienation that both Marx and Weber saw as the ineluctable trait of capitalist modernity. In Marxist terms, entrepreneurship can be seen as the reverse of alienated labor, when workers do not own what they produce. In some basic sense, the entrepreneur is at one with the enterprise of her or his devising. (Green 2005: 4)

Further, an entrepreneur has more direct control over her own compensation. She also has flexibility to dictate various methods of compensation for her employees and suppliers. Entrepreneurship is thereby associated with freedom and self-expression.

Without exception, the women interviewed in this study described that entrepreneurship was a highly satisfying, creative endeavor where they expressed their ideas and values through their work. Rita Chang puts it this way:

> It's much more time consuming – work never ends – and it's much more stressful with more headaches. On the other hand, you're in charge, and you can put your talent and creativity to work for you, and you just have to deal with the risk of not making it financially or otherwise. You make less money, but you have your own vision. For highly independent people, who don't mind taking risks, who have a vision of how they want to do things and believe in themselves, it can be very, very satisfying.

Nancy Stevens explains:

> I love it when a presentation goes well, and people are inspired. I love the flexibility, and the ability to be creative. The best thing and the hardest thing are that you don't have to answer to anyone, but the challenge is that income varies.

And Najma Jamaludeen comments:

> I love it. It is a part of me. I have been doing business with my family since I was seven years old. It is all that I know. It is how I relate to freedom.

In later chapters, we also explore solidarity between minority women entrepreneurs and their communities, as well as the social ideology that can undermine the confidence necessary for women to initiate entrepreneurial enterprises.

Cultural capital and habitus: Pierre Bourdieu

Though Marxism is largely an economic analysis, economic capital, according to Pierre Bourdieu, is inextricably intertwined with other types of capital. The concepts of cultural capital and habitus can help to explain the connection between economic status and social prestige and how power is reproduced generation after generation for the same groups. Bourdieu's concept of cultural capital is the "general cultural background, knowledge, disposition and skills that are passed from one generation to the next" (MacLeod 1995: 13). Cultural capital varies dramatically depending on class. Social values, dictated by those in power, give primacy to the types of knowledge, dispositions, speech patterns, and attitudes of the upper classes and ridicule those of the lower classes. All material trappings, including artwork, automobiles, clothing, vacation homes, even the food associated with the upper classes and the utensils with which it is eaten, are held in esteem by a supportive matrix of cultural knowledge that defines the significance of these material items. The reproduction of class and power is therefore not based only on inheriting material wealth, but on the transmission of cultural knowledge – the training that results in class-based preferences and aesthetic taste.

Bourdieu's concept of habitus describes the meso level on which a sense of belonging and competency, or lack thereof, is developed and cultivated. Habitus is, in Bourdieu's words, "a subjective, but not individual system of internalized structures, schemas of perception, conception and action common to all members of the same group or class" (Bourdieu 1977: 86). In this respect, cultural capital is the currency, and habitus is the social context of interactions among people. When individuals weigh whether to invest time and resources in certain endeavors, they ask themselves if "people like me" (Collier and Morgan 2007) tend to be successful. This concept of "people like me" is, as Bourdieu writes, a subjective experience, but not particular to an individual. Instead, "people like me" includes the status characteristics of group affiliations such as race, gender, class, and sexual orientation, so that individuals within these groups identify others within the same group as "people like me." How people perceive themselves fitting or not fitting into the opportunity structure guides goals and behavior. MacLeod writes:

> Aspirations reflect an individual's view of his or her own chances for getting ahead and are an internalization of objective probabilities . . . A lower-class child growing up in an environment where success is rare is much less likely to develop

strong ambitions than is a middle-class boy or girl growing up in a social world peopled by those who have "made it" and where the connection between effort and reward is taken for granted. (MacLeod 1995: 15)

Children from disadvantaged backgrounds are likely to have developed a sense of self, and a sense of the opportunities open to them, that reflect the messages they receive about the groups with which they are affiliated. Lareau and Weininger (2003) emphasize three key elements in cultural capital and social reproduction:

- Micro-interactional processes

- Institutionalized standards of evaluation

- Differential cultural resources.

Social reproduction depends on the ability of powerful groups to define institutionalized standards of evaluation, and these standards are applied to daily interactions (micro-interactional processes). Powerful groups must also impose differential access to cultural and economic resources. In this way, dominant social members remain in the best position to define and fulfill larger cultural and institutional standards, as these standards, and the values underlying them, reflect their interests.

However, Banks reminds us that

> Bourdieu portrays a social world driven by individualistic instrumentality, albeit within the shared confines of class and habitus, [and therefore] his analysis does tend to overlook the ways in which actors may possess values or follow courses of action that are not automatically geared to enhancing status or reinforcing social position. The emphasis on self-interest in the individualistic pursuit of status, prestige and new kinds of lifestyle tends to underplay the influence of non-instrumental or ethical motives in social and economic reproduction. (Banks 2006: 458)

It is important, therefore, to address the non-instrumental aspects of entrepreneurship. This dimension of non-instrumental decision-making was striking in the stories of minority women entrepreneurs and constitutes one of the strongest counter-examples to "business-as-usual": that is, business that assumes the tenets of self-interested actor and the prioritization of profit. Pauline Lewis describes that when she lost the emotional attachment to her business, despite the fact that she was still making money, she considered shutting down:

> I lost the feel, the emotion, of why I started the business. What it was all about. And so, I was seriously thinking of closing my business and thinking, you know what? Maybe I've had fun and it's time to move on.

Non-instrumental priorities and value-based motives can sometimes make minority women feel that their businesses are not "real." Kathy Deserly explains:

> I find that I often feel that I haven't "arrived" as a business owner/entrepreneur. I am only beginning to realize how few people there are who have my expertise and experience in my particular field. When I talk to others about my work, I sometimes feel that I am not "one of the guys" who are out there blazing trails in technology . . . sometimes I feel that I'm doing "woman's work" which doesn't command the same level of respect that other forms of entrepreneurship do. On the other hand, I really don't care what anyone thinks!

Because Deserly uses standards of assessment for her business decisions that differ from conventional standards, she does not receive the social recognition of the larger community; consequently, her sense is that her business is "woman's work" and as such, does not garner social respect. These minority women routinely make the decision to identify with marginalized groups, and their businesses serve those groups. In other words, in deference to their moral and political positions, they knowingly choose less prestigious platforms of cultural capital on which to construct their notion of self and their presentation in the larger society. As evidenced by Bourdieu's oversight, non-instrumental decisions are not only routinely overlooked in business literature, but also in sociological analysis.

The role of stereotypical images and belief systems in maintaining the status quo: 'Oh, my gosh, this isn't for me'

In the service of social reproduction, stereotypical narratives and images are an underestimated, but enormously effective way to transmit and maintain the cultural capital that connects economic and social power. Self-identified as independent thinkers and committed individualists, members of technologically savvy, modern societies consciously and purposefully resist submitting to the manipulation of narratives, images, and advertisements. Denying our dependence on media representations, and on the opinions of others to shape our self-identity, preserves the fallacies that we direct our fate, that we are in control and that we are "free" from influence. Individualism dictates that we take credit for our successes and not bother with the status characteristics that define our social identity and overwhelm our individual will.

However, if we are individually responsible for our successes, then we are also individually responsible for our failures. Since success (as culturally defined) is statistically much more probable for individuals with certain social status characteristics – those characteristics associated with the mythical norm (White, male, heterosexual, young, able-bodied, middle-class, etc.) – then the cultural focus on the individual is itself a type of ideology. MacLeod calls the myth that success is an individual matter "the achievement ideology" (MacLeod 1995: 1). The achievement ideology is the view held by most people in U.S. society; it states, "success is based on merit, and economic inequality is due to differences in ambition and ability. Individuals do not inherit their social status; they attain it on their own" (MacLeod 1995: 1). When individual merit is accepted as the cause of success, it is understandable that those in privileged social positions might be angry and resentful toward initiatives such as affirmative action programs, which are intended to reduce social advantages.

It is easy to imagine how those with social and economic privilege can be unaware of how this status might affect their life chances. Those who are privileged have directly experienced their own hard work, and they have also experienced their individual setbacks and challenges. Therefore, when they are rewarded for their efforts, especially in a system that gives primacy to individual effort and personal control as causal explanations, those rewards seem justified. Here is a typical scene:

> Ed, a middle-aged white man, raises his hand. "I hear what you are saying – that white people tend to have more money. But I don't like what you are implying – that I should feel guilty about it. I swear, everything I have, I worked hard for." Ed has a point. He says he studied hard in college, worked hard at every job and saved steadily until he could buy a home . . . [When asked] who helped him become prosperous, [he says,] "No one." It turns out that Ed's great-great-grandfather got a farm in Nebraska through the Homestead Act – a program available only to whites. His father, a World War II veteran, got a Veterans Administration mortgage and went to college on the G.I. Bill – programs that Black G.I.s couldn't take full advantage of because of housing and education discrimination . . . It may

> be true that [Ed] studied hard, worked hard and saved – and
> so can claim some credit for his assets. But how much of the
> credit is his? How much is due to public investments in his
> family? A Latina woman . . . asks Ed: "What about me? I studied
> hard, worked hard, and saved just like you. But I didn't get
> the same rewards. Doesn't that mean that your money comes
> partly from your race?" Ed admits that it does. (Lui, Robles *et al.* 2006: 4)

Ed experiences himself as a generic individual, and as such, he does not feel particularly powerful. He does not self-consciously experience his race or his gender every day. As a White man, Ed's race and gender are the social norm, and thus they do not draw attention and suspicion. He remains unaware of how his social status characteristics create patterns of privilege, but he is acutely aware of how hard he has worked. Ed is correct that he is not particularly powerful as an individual. To the extent Ed wields power, it is because his status characteristics are associated with powerful groups. If Ed were to change his status characteristics – become a woman or a person of color – his social power would decline.

Ed's example illuminates discrepancies in treatment that provide economic advantages to Whites, but there are also symbolic and cultural discrepancies that give primacy to White perspectives. Tim Wise describes the cultural milieu in the public school he attended:

> Dances, which began around the seventh grade, almost always
> revolved around "white music," no doubt making a lot of kids
> of color feel like outsiders at their own school. The curriculum
> was almost completely Eurocentric . . . mostly white folks' nar-
> ratives, with a smattering of "other" more as an add-on than as
> a central part of understanding this nation and its collective
> story. (Wise 2005: 16)

Wise also describes his experience of White, male privilege as the luxury of ignorance:

> If you're white, you simply will not, cannot, understand race,
> or even see that race matters . . . There is no reason that you
> should; no experience would have forced the issue, and few
> parents would have sat you down to begin the lesson. That's a
> luxury, a privilege . . . When black mothers have to teach their
> sons to keep both hands on the wheel if stopped by a police
> officer, so as not to get shot – something I have never heard
> a white mother speak of doing with her white son – we know
> we're talking about more than a minor irritant. (Wise 2005: 23)

In her examination of her White, heterosexual privilege, Peggy McIntosh writes:

> I began to understand why we are justly seen as oppressive, even when we don't see ourselves that way. At the very least, obliviousness of one's privileged state can make a person or group irritating to be with . . . Whether through the curriculum or in the newspaper, the television, the economic system, or the general look of people in the streets, I received daily signals and indications that my people counted and that others *either didn't exist or must be trying, not very successfully, to be like [me]*. (McIntosh 2007: 10-13 [emphasis in the original])

Our ideas about ourselves and the world are constantly being shaped by the stories we are told under the authoritative auspices of prestigious individuals and institutions. This conventional wisdom produces pictures in our minds that are so potent, so vivid, and hold such command over our imagination, that they can guide our thoughts and behavior without our conscious awareness.

In her article "Controlling Images and Black Women's Oppression" Patricia Hill Collins writes about negative images associated with Black women that serve to justify their subordinate social position. For instance, the image of the mammy is employed as a way to continue associating Black women with the economic exploitation of house slaves and restrict them to low-paying domestic servant jobs (Collins: 1991: 266). The image of the matriarch serves to discredit Black women as it represents their seizure of the masculine privilege of household head. Social disapproval leveled at Black women for their perceived challenge to male dominance is also a message to White women: assertive, independent women will be abandoned, become impoverished and be rejected as unfeminine (Collins 1991: 269).

The image of subservient mammy opposes the equally disdained image of domineering matriarch, allowing a full range of justification for the rejection of Black women, based on obsequiousness on the one hand and aggression on the other. However, these images are usually passively absorbed, and so remain below conscious scrutiny, reflecting and informing the social status of Black women. Because these images help maintain the current power structure, they are taken for granted and not generally identified as being in need of reform. Over many years, protestations have made these images visible with the intent of creating awareness and a language to reframe these images as pejorative and discriminatory, rather than allowing them to continue being seen merely as benign, natural, and realistic.

Women from various racial, ethnic, class, and religious groups struggle with the persistence of prejudicial social images that facilitate the ease with which discriminatory treatment is exercised and accepted. Yen Le Espiritu writes that the ideological insults that inform "racist and gendered immigration policies . . . keep Asian Americans in an assigned, subordinate place" (Espiritu 1997: 155). Like Patricia Hill Collins, she examines certain images, personas, and symbols associated with Asians including the "yellow peril," and "Suzie Wong." According to Espiritu, "It was fear of the Yellow Peril – fear of the rise of nonwhite people and their contestation of White supremacy – that led to the declaration of martial law in Hawaii . . . and to the internment of over 110,000 Japanese (Espiritu 1997: 156).

Similarly, Paula Gunn Allen writes about the discrepancy between social stereotypes of American Indian women and her personal experience of being an American Indian woman:

> [Through] my formal, white Christian education, I discovered that other people had stories of their own – about women, about Indians, about fact, about reality – and I was amazed by a number of startling suppositions that others made about tribal customs and beliefs. According to the un-Indian, non-Indian view, for instance, Indians barred menstruating women from ceremonies and indeed segregated them from the rest of the people . . . I was surprised and confused to hear this because my mother had taught me . . . that menstruation was a normal occurrence, that I could go swimming or hiking or whatever else I wanted to do during my period . . . No Indian can grow to any age without being informed that her people were "savages" who interfered with the march of progress pursued by respectable, loving, civilized white people. (Gunn 2007: 32)

The images that people hold in their minds often remain unexamined and pre-conscious dictators of social assumptions. In her article "Gender Stereotyping in the English Language" Laurel Richardson writes that "everyone in our society, regardless of class, ethnicity, sex, age, or race, is exposed to the same language, the language of the dominant culture" (Richardson 2007: 99).

She goes on to explain how ideas about gender roles and social power are revealed and propagated in the English language:

> first, in terms of grammatical and semantic structure, women do not have a fully autonomous, independent existence; they are part of man . . . Grammar books specify that the pronoun he can be used generically to mean he or she. Further, man, when used as an indefinite pronoun, grammatically refers to both men and women. (Richardson 2007: 99)

When we hear words, the symbolic representations of objects, we still think in pictures. Therefore, when we hear such conventional occupational titles as fireman, policeman, chairman, spokesman, fisherman, lobsterman, draftsman, mailman, sportsman, or minutemen or phrases such as "man the lifeboats," "man overboard," "man on base," "mankind," research consistently demonstrates that we visualize men, not women (see Richardson 2007: 99). Similarly, the pronoun *he* elicits a male in our mind's eye as well (Richardson 2007: 99); the use of *man* and *he* to refer to both males and females effectively erases mental representations of women:

> One consequence is the exclusion of women in the visualization, imagination and thought of males and females. Most likely this linguistic practice perpetuates in men their feelings of dominance over and responsibility for women, feelings that interfere with the development of equality in relationships. (Richardson 2007: 99)

Similarly, when women hear the word "chairman," they imagine a male, not a person "like them," in that job. Richardson writes:

> Language has tremendous power to shape attitudes and influence behavior. Indeed, MacKay (1983) argues that the prescriptive *he* "has all the characteristics of a highly effective propaganda technique": frequent repetition, early age of acquisition (before age six), covertness (*he* is not thought of as propaganda), use by high-prestige sources (including university texts and professors), and indirectness (presented as though it were a matter of common knowledge). As a result, the prescriptive affects females' sense of life options and feeling of well-being. (Richardson 2007: 100)

Language, then, functions as ideology in that it maximizes control over thoughts and behavior with minimum effort and minimum conflict. Conventional language is usually interpreted as an innocuous, natural, fair consequence of historical progression rather than as a technique of social control. The language of the upper classes, that is to say, the grammar and word use institutionalized in universities and authoritative media, is imbued with a perspective that holds men to be more valuable than and superior to women. However, most women – and women compose the numerical majority of English speakers – have unwittingly internalized and adopted the practices that contribute to their subordinate position. For instance, in addition to the grammatical and semantic examples already discussed, most English-speaking women embrace the convention of assuming their husband's name after marriage and have their children assume the husband's surname as well. In the U.S., a women's birth name, usually referred to as her "maiden name" (her identity before she marries) often becomes the default secret password on the credit card accounts of her children because so few people possess knowledge of it.

Most women who change their last name to their husband's are not consciously contributing to their subordination, the lack of female images in visualization, or the erasure of their personal history and independent identity. Many are complying with social mandates that tacitly pressure women to signal their commitment to marriage by changing their name and relinquishing their identity as single women and/or as career women. Other women embrace their husband's last name as a sign of love and devotion as well as an indication of a change in status. Others adopt their husband's name to signal their dependence on him, and in turn, his obligation to them. Some women do not even imagine keeping their birth name. The very possibility is beyond contemplation because the social convention remains unexamined.

Language is such a vital part of the construction of selfhood that it often falls below the radar of critical evaluation. It becomes, as Collins wrote, part of what we "take for granted" (Collins 1992: 75) and therefore one of the most important ways to ensure the reproduction of current social, political, and economic power dynamics.

This is true not only for the way we talk about women and men, but for the way we talk about race as well. The English language reflects a disparate social valuation of "white" fairer-skinned people and "black" darker-skinned people. The word "fair" has come to mean *just, equitable, dispassionate, unbiased, straightforward, objective, visually beautiful* (fair maiden), *clear and unobstructed* (fair skies), *without irregularity or unevenness* (fair surface), and *stable* (fair condition). Intelligent people are referred to as "bright." White is associated with purity, cleanliness, order, fairness, generosity, and decency, a "white" lie, or the positive comment on character, "That was very white of you" (Morris 1976: 1461). Dark, in contrast, is synonymous with *dim, murky, dusky, obscure, opaque, shady, shadowy, evil* (as in dark-hearted), *ignorant* (as in the Dark Ages), *danger, wickedness, cheerlessness* (dark mood), *secrecy* (deep, dark secrets), *sombre, strange, unfamiliar* (dark horse), *and unwanted* (to "darken" a doorway). Similar findings are associated with black, and additionally, there is the association of dirt, soil, and corruption: "blacken a reputation" and the "black sheep" of the family. It is no accident that villains are dressed in black. Black and darkness have become socially associated with all that is bad; white and brightness are symbolic of all that is good.

Despite what we think we know and what we consciously intend, the assumptions we make and the pictures in our minds inform our understandings of our own competencies and the competencies of others in a surprisingly powerful way; they also inform our aspirations and chances for success. Notwithstanding Grace Hopper's early foundational contribution to the discipline, Jane Margolis and Allan Fisher describe the reasons for the pervasive gender gap in computer science in their book *Unlocking the Clubhouse* (2001):

> Very early in life, computing is claimed as male territory. At each step from early childhood through college, computing is both actively claimed as "guy stuff" by boys and men and passively ceded by girls and women. The claiming is largely the work of a culture and society that links interest and success with computers to boys and men. Curriculum, teachers' expectations and culture reflect boys' pathways into computing, accepting assumptions of male excellence and women's deficiencies in the field . . . The corresponding process of women ceding the field, largely through disinterest and disaffection, is also complex. Careful observation shows that disinterest and disaffection are neither genetic nor accidental. They are not inherent to the field but are the bitter fruit of many external influences. By the time they finish college, most women studying computer science have faced a technical culture whose values often do not match their own and have encountered a variety of discouraging experiences with teachers, peers and curriculum. Many end up doubting their basic intelligence and their fitness to pursue computing. (Margolis and Fisher 2001: 4)

Michael Kimmel suggests that not only individuals are gendered, but most things – groups, activities, interests, institutions, nations, and fields of study – are gendered, too. He asserts that in male-dominated societies, even when there is an assumption of gender-neutrality, male characteristics are valued and male needs are prioritized in ways that reflect the male-dominated cultural bias of the society. It is important to note that this bias often remains unrecognized because male superiority is taken for granted (Kimmel 2004: 101). In fact, Margolis and Fisher found that most boys who are drawn to computers are White and Asian, which suggests that computer science as a discipline is not only gendered male, but also has specific racial identities attached to it as well. Margolis explains that the stereotypical image of computer scientist that most of us carry in our minds excludes women, and African American, Latino, and Native men;

members of these populations, even when they have interest and ability, often feel that "people like me don't succeed" and the sense that they do not belong is enough for them to drop the subject. One young woman put it this way:

> It's like, "Oh, my gosh, this isn't for me." It's [a man's] hobby. They all start reading machine learning books or robotics books or build a little robot or something, and I'm not like that at all. In my free time, I prefer to read a good fiction book or learn how to do photography or something different, whereas [computer science is] their hobby, it's their work, it's their one goal. I'm just not like that at all; I don't dream in code like they do. (Margolis and Fisher 2001: 69)

Math and science, among the highest-paying and most prestigious disciplines, are so closely associated with men, that a study by Lori Bakken determined that 71% of female medical students and 95% of male medical students envisioned a male role model when asked to visualize a physician–scientist role model. Stressing the importance of real-world role models, by far the most frequently reported visualized image (72% women, 60% men) was that of a mentor who was a faculty member in the respondent's own department (Bakken 2005). In the absence of living, breathing female mentors, then, most women and men visualize physician–scientists as men.

A study by David Figlio (Asthana 2007) found that young women with "highly feminine" names such as Isabella, Anna, and Elizabeth are less likely to study math or physics after the age of 16 than are young women with the less feminine names of Abigail or Alex. Responding to the study, an elementary school teacher admitted that it was hard not to make prior judgments based on students' names:

> I think most people get an image in their head when they hear a name. If you treat a child differently because of their name, then they will behave differently. That is why the issue for every teacher is to look beyond their name. (Stebbings 2007)

Feminine names are not only a disadvantage in math and science, but also in law. Named after the Shakespearian character who disguises herself as a man in order that she might be a lawyer, the Portia Hypothesis refers to gender biases in the legal profession. In their 2009 study, Coffey and McLaughlin found evidence of the Portia Hypothesis based on the degree of masculinity in the first name. Changing the unambiguously female name of Elizabeth to a more gender-neutral name such as Kelly increases a woman's odds of becoming a judge by five per cent. A change from a feminine name to one used predominantly by men, such as Cameron, triples the odds of judgeship; and an exclusively male name such as Bruce increases the odds of being a judge by five times.

According to Bourdieu's theory of habitus, women internalize the objective reality that "people like them" are not likely to succeed in these prestigious and lucrative areas. Therefore, rationally calculating their chances for success, women are unlikely to develop aspirations and ambitions that they predict, in the current social context, will have a high risk of failure. Unlike men, women do not take for granted the "connection between effort and reward" in the areas of math, science, and law (MacLeod 1995: 15). In Mead's words, by internalizing the "role of the generalized other" represented in language, and in the low incidence of female images and a preponderance of male images, women develop a sense of self and an identification with other women that dictates: "this just isn't for me." Therefore, success in male-identified realms not only threatens women with social nullification (invisibility) and lack of support – even animosity – but also threatens to undermine their feminine identification. Women who engage in areas associated with men are often perceived as unfeminine, overly aggressive, and unattractive. Combined with the high likelihood of failure, losing their feminine identification is too high a price for most women to risk participation in male-dominated realms. Those who attribute success simply to the talent and hard work of individuals, while claiming that opportunities are equally open to all, are often content to conclude that the penury of women in math, science, and judgeships indicates that women are generally not competent in these areas.

Stereotypes about business leadership

Similar to the assumption that males make the best mathematicians and scientists, one of the most long-standing and pernicious stereotypes is that men are business leaders and women are not (Porter and Geis 1981; Heilman, Block et al. 1989; Valian 1998; Miller, Taylor et al. 1991; Eagly and Johannesen-Schmidt 2001; Martell and DeSmet 2001; Ridgeway 2001; Kimmel 2004). Thirty-five years ago, a study of gender stereotypes revealed that among those associated with women were "dislike of math, not skilled in business, and rarely act as leaders" (Broverman, Vogel et al. 1972). A decade later, not much had changed. In their article "Women and Non-verbal Leadership Cues: When Seeing is not Believing," Porter and Geis (1981) found that sex-role stereotypes trump situational cues when determining leadership. Specifically, they found that when undergraduate students were shown images of business people seated around a table in same-sex groups, the person seated at the head of the table was consistently deemed to be the leader. However, in mixed-sex groups, even when women were seated at the head of the table, they were not consistently seen as the leaders. This is a demonstration of the fact that women are less likely to be granted the deference that situational indicators such as clothing and positioning provide for men. This social reality continually undercuts women's confidence in the connection between effort and reward. In fact, according to our inter-judge coding of interviews, 61% of the minority women entrepreneurs we interviewed said they initially lacked confidence in their ability to become entrepreneurs.

Stereotypes about the difference between masculine and feminine gender characteristics parallel those about leaders and followers (Porter and Geis 1981: 42). Leaders are high-status, commanding, aggressive, confident, competent, rational, and independent. Followers are low-status, inexperienced, cooperative, deferential, emotional, and gentle. Porter and Geis remind us that

> Leadership is a social phenomenon. Becoming a leader depends on acting like a leader, but even more crucially, it depends on being seen by others as a leader. In our society, people do not become leaders by their own individual fiat. (Porter and Geis 1981: 39)

Ridgeway (2001) found that gender status beliefs shape the assertiveness of both women and men, the attention and evaluation their performances receive, the ability attributed to them on the basis of performance, the influence they achieve, and the likelihood that they emerge as leaders. Additionally, Ridgeway found that when women's resistance to the current system of gender status took the form of increased assertiveness, the result was the further reduction in women's ability to lead, because of lack of compliance with their directives. Similarly, Rudman and Glick found that agentic women were discriminated against in hiring practices because they are perceived as "insufficiently nice" (Rudman and Glick 2001: 743).

Women are consistently rated lower than men on many of the characteristics seen as typical for successful managers, and even women who are described as *successful* managers are seen as having less leadership ability than successful managers who are male (Heilman, Block *et al.* 1989). According to Pugh and Wahrman (1983), only when women's performance is superior to men's are women's performances deemed equal to men's.

Yet, even when women's performances are superior to their male counter-parts, their performances are often ignored. In the study, "Selection of a Causal Background: Role of Expectation Versus Feature Mutability" (1993), Ann McGill examines the context of comparisons between female and male competency and discovers that by comparing women who fail to men who succeed, the assumption of male competency and female inadequacy obtains. McGill writes:

> These findings suggest that the comparisons that people make for successful and unsuccessful performance may reinforce negative beliefs about the capabilities of women, especially with regard to traditionally male-oriented tasks. Only when women fail are they compared with men, a comparison that suggests that women are not as capable as men. When women succeed, they are compared with other women, a comparison that suggests that successful women are unusual among the gender, but that reveals nothing about the relative capabilities of men and women. Women who succeed are not compared with men who failed, thus precluding attributions that might address the superiority of women. Men, by contrast, are con-sistently compared with other men, succeeding or failing on the basis of their own relative capabilities. To the extent that men are perceived as generally more capable than women, such within-gender comparisons are unlikely to alter this nega-tive perception of women. (McGill 1993: 706)

As mentioned, most studies examining how ascriptive characteristics affect power and authority focus only on one status characteristic: either on race or on gender. However, Elliott and Smith (2004) found that dis-criminatory treatment affected White women and women of color (African American and Latina women) differently. They found that White women were disadvantaged relative to White men in being promoted to positions of power due to lack of work experience. Women of color were disadvan-taged relative to White men based on lack of education. However, when White women accumulated work experience, they fared worse rather than better relative to White men (Elliott and Smith 2004: 384). Similarly, in their article "When What You Know Is Not Enough: Expertise and Gender Dynamics in Task Groups" (2004), Thomas-Hunt and Phillips also found that women were less influential when they possessed more expertise, and having expertise actually decreased the degree to which others per-ceived them to be leaders and experts. Conversely, having expertise was relatively positive for men. Given that the accumulation of work experi-ence and expertise – the very grounds on which women are often found wanting – creates more disadvantage for White women, Elliott and Smith hypothesize that if Latinas and African American women become more educated, not only will they continue to face discrimination, but it might actually increase. Because additional education will contribute to the ability of women of color to compete in the workplace, as in the case of White women, discrimination toward educated Latinas and African American women might become more pronounced.

James Weldon Johnson explains that though Whites might help Black people in the servant class, they will ignore Black people who are educated:

> I concluded that if a colored man wanted to separate himself from his white neighbors he had but to acquire some money, education and culture . . . For example, the proudest and fairest lady in the South could with propriety – it is what she would most likely do – go to the cabin of Aunt Mary, her cook, if Aunt Mary were sick, and minister to her comfort with her own hands; but if Mary's daughter, Eliza, a girl who used to run around my lady's kitchen, but who has received an education and married a prosperous young colored man, were at death's door, my lady would no more think of crossing the threshold of Eliza's cottage than she would of going into a bar-room for a drink. (Johnson 1912: 36)

Differences in education and experience might be able to explain the disparities in power and authority over a matter of decades, but not the entrenched persistence of disparities in power and prestige over centuries. The superficial complications and complexities of real life can distract us from identifying deeper and more pervasive patterns of interactions among dominant and subordinate groups evident in language, perceptions of reality, and the sociopsychological formations of gendered and racial identity. Examining why affirmative action in education has made little difference in the wage gap, Barbara Reskin points out the basic underlying principle of competition: dominant groups write the rules in such a way that they remain dominant: "so that eliminating race differences in education is unlikely to reduce racial inequality in income because Whites will find another way to maintain their income advantage" (Reskin 1997: 215). In their article "Flattery Will Get You Everywhere (Especially if you are a Male Caucasian)," Westphal and Stern (2007: 267) report that directors increased their board appointments at other firms by using ingratiatory behavior towards peer directors. However, ethnic minorities and women were rewarded less for such behavior. Further, though male Caucasian directors also increased their board appointments through "low levels of monitoring and control behavior, minorities were punished more for such behaviors" (Westphal and Stern 2007: 267). Elliott and Smith also found that "superiors, regardless of their race and sex, tend to fill power positions they oversee with ascriptively similar others . . . they engage in what Kanter calls 'homosocial reproduction'" (Elliott and Smith 2004: 384). Since there are more White men in powerful positions, one way that White men reproduce their social and economic advantages is by (consciously or unconsciously) promoting individuals with similar race and gender characteristics – people like them. In this way, White males continue to make up the mythical norm.

Summary and notes on next chapters

This chapter presents both an overview of sociological theory and specific empirical data that explains how sociology uncovers non-obvious explanations of persistent inequality. Chapter 3 discusses how long-standing systems of discrimination can be and have been changed.

3

Challenging and changing inequality

Astounding turnarounds

Social values are the context of both our external reality and our internalized sense of self. All members of society depend heavily on social values and standards – even when those values and standards do not reflect our own individual self-interest. We tend to preserve our group membership by acquiescing to shared values, often without even realizing it. In a male-dominated culture, women's deviation from maleness means that both men and women come to undervalue women's efforts: "In a culture that reserves virtues for men . . . men's activities are typically valued above women's regardless of their content or importance for group survival" (Reskin 1997: 217). In the context of a male-dominated, White-dominated society, minority women's "failure" is a socially defined phenomenon that does not reflect their theoretical capability, but is a predictable, practical result of reduced social status. This lower status and the attendant expectations are often internalized by minority women, thereby undermining their confidence and negatively affecting their performance.

However, frames of reference and attendant associations can be challenged and are being changed. The 1995–2000 study by Margolis and Fisher sponsored by Carnegie Mellon University resulted in changes to the computer science curriculum, leading to a sixfold increase in the number of women majoring in computer science there, from 7% to an astounding 42%. Computer science at Carnegie Mellon is no longer just male territory.

This increase belies the notion that males have a "natural" propensity for computer science based on chromosomes, brain structure, or other biologically determined male sex characteristics. Such biological explanations draw on the authoritative power of science, presumed to transcend social and political influences, but often used to cloak social expectations and norms that protect the current power dynamics.

Frames of reference can be changed in any area. In chronicling the assumption that only men could master certain musical instruments because they were biologically more competent, Malcolm Gladwell writes:

> The world of classical music – particularly in its European home – was until very recently the preserve of white men. Women, it was believed, simply could not play like men. They didn't have the strength, the attitude, or the resilience for certain kinds of pieces. Their lips were different. Their lungs were less powerful. Their hands were smaller. That did not seem like prejudice. It seemed like fact, because when conductors and music directors and maestros held auditions, the men always seemed to sound better than the women. (Gladwell 2005: 249)

Gladwell goes on to explain how, over time, musicians – especially White women and men and women of color – began to scrutinize the audition process. They demanded that musicians be allowed to audition behind a screen so that their ascribed characteristics would not be known to the judges. Musicians were not identified by name, but by number, and if any identifying details gave away the gender or race of the player, he or she would be given a new audition. Gladwell describes the result:

> As these new rules were put into place around the country, an extraordinary thing happened: orchestras began to hire women. In the past thirty years, since screens became commonplace, the number of women in the top U.S. orchestra has increased fivefold. "The very first time the new rules for auditions were used, we were looking for four new violinists," remembers Herb Weksleblatt, a tuba player for the Metropolitan Opera in New York, who led the fight for blind auditions at the Met in the mid 1960s. "And all the winners were women. That would simply never have happened before . . . I remember after it was announced that the four women had won, one guy was absolutely furious at me. He said, 'You're going to be remembered as the SOB who brought women into this orchestra.' " (Gladwell 2005: 250)

Another judge remarked: "I've been in auditions without screens, and I can assure you that I was prejudiced. I began to listen with my eyes, and there is no way that your eyes don't affect your judgment" (Gladwell 2005: 251).

Even observations of the most seemingly straightforward, established scientific phenomena can be skewed based on social and cultural assumptions. Beldecos, Bailey *et al.* claim that: "Narratives of fertilization and sex determination traditionally have been modeled on the cultural patterns of male/female interaction leading to gender assumptions being placed on their cells and their components" (Beldecos, Bailey *et al.* 1988: 61). Emily Martin also claims that the interpretation of the interaction between egg and sperm is depicted as "a romance based on stereotypical male and female roles" (Martin 1991: 489). She writes:

> At its extreme, the age-old relationship of the egg and the sperm takes on a royal or religious patina. The egg coat, its protective barrier, is sometimes called its "vestments," a term usually reserved for sacred, religious dress . . . It is holy, set apart, the queen to the sperm's king. The egg is also passive, which means it must depend on the sperm for rescue. Gerald Schatten and Helen Schatten liken the egg's role to Sleeping Beauty: "a dormant bride awaiting her mate's magic kiss, which instills the spirit that brings her to life." Sperm, by contrast, have a "mission," which is to move through the female genital tract in quest of the ovum. One popular account has it that the sperm carry out a "perilous journey" into the "warm darkness" where some fall away exhausted. Survivors assault the egg, successful candidates surrounding the prize. (Martin 1989: 489)

Martin demonstrates that cultural stories influence interpretation of empirical data. This becomes even clearer as assumptions regarding the roles of egg and sperm were tested by biophysicists at Johns Hopkins University:

> They discovered, to their great surprise, that the forward thrust of the sperm is extremely weak, which contradicts the assumption that sperm are forceful penetrators . . . In fact, its strongest tendency, by tenfold, is to try to escape by prying itself off the egg. Sperm, then, must be exceptionally efficient at *escaping* from any cell they contact. And the surface of the egg must be designed to trap the sperm and prevent their escape. Otherwise, few if any sperm would reach the egg. The researchers at Johns Hopkins concluded that the sperm and egg stick together because of adhesive molecules on the surfaces of each. (Martin 1991: 492-93 [emphasis in the original])

Though the research at Johns Hopkins was completed in 1984, and Martin wrote her article in 1991, the image of the warrior-like sperm competing with his brothers to penetrate the demure, passive egg still largely dominates both lay and scientific descriptions of the interaction. The egg and sperm interpretation remains one of many examples of how empirical fact is filtered through scientific minds influenced by powerful cultural assumptions. (See Tuana 1988; Turkle 2007; and Ruth Hubbard's [1988, 1990, 1995] many contributions to this literature.)

Stereotype threat: Claude Steele

To explain the psychological and social effects of negative stereotypes, Claude Steele introduced the concept of "stereotype threat." Stereotype threat is the experience of being viewed as incompetent in some area, such as standardized test-taking, because of race, gender, or other group characteristic, and then the fear of acting in a way that confirms that incompetence. Steele describes it as "the social–psychological threat that arises when one is in a situation or doing something for which a negative stereotype about one's group applies" (Steele 1997: 614). Moreover, Steele found that only those who identify with the domain enough to experience this threat would have their performance undermined by the pressure and anxiety caused by the stereotype.

However, in a stunning turnaround, Steele was able to demonstrate that the long-standing discrepancy in SAT scores between African American students and White students could be reduced merely by introducing the test to African American students as "academically insignificant" (Steele 1997). Similarly, women performed worse than men on standardized math tests when they were told that the test reproduced gender differences, but equal to men when the test was introduced as insensitive to gender (Steele 1997: 619-20). Steele used subjects who identified with the domain in question; for instance, women were selected because they were very good at math (entering test scores in the top 15% of the Michigan student population) and reported being confident about their math aptitude (Steele 2003: 117). Additionally, Steele found that the performances of students who do not identify with the domain are not affected by stereotype threat: "[We] had selected Black students who identified with verbal skills and women who identified with math. But when we tested participants who identified less with these domains . . . none of them showed any effect of stereotype threat whatsoever" (Steele 2003: 120).

The concept of stereotype threat is so powerful because it demonstrates that the enduring, socially embedded problems of racism and sexism do not have to be solved in order to create environments where the negative effect of stereotypes is dramatically diminished. Steele has demonstrated that performance can be manipulated by techniques that are readily available and easily replicated. His research demonstrates that though societal stereotypes change slowly, niches that neutralize stereotype threat can be created almost instantly (Steele 2003: 130). He also notes that negative stereotypes about one's own group can be internalized and create self-loathing. This was illustrated in the Clark doll studies when African American children associated negative characteristics with Black dolls more than did the non-African American participants (Steele 1997: 621). However, in those situations where Black participants did not have to worry about a stereotypic perception of themselves, they valued things that were associated with African Americans more than non-African American participants did (Steele 1997: 621).

Since stereotype threat is situational and social rather than individual and internal, it can be immediately changed by changing the environment. Steele writes:

> Thus, the gender-difference conditions (the normal condition under which people take these tests) could not have impaired their performance by triggering some greater internalized anxiety acquired, for example, through prior socialization. Rather, this condition had its effect through situational pressure. It set up an interpretive frame such that any performance frustration signaled the possible gender-based ability limitation alleged in the stereotype. For these women, this signal challenged their belongingness in a domain they cared about and, as a possibly newly met limit to their ability, could not be disproven by their prior achievements, thus its interfering threat. (Steele 1997: 620)

Further, double-minority status can magnify stereotype threat and its negative consequences on performance. Gonzales, Blanton *et al.* (2002: 667) found that in the context of math competency, Latinas are at greater risk for gender-based stereotype threat than are White women.

Solidarity and the neutralization of stereotype threat

'Our initial idea . . was to blame the students . . . we were basically wrong'
(Treisman 1992: 369)

As a graduate student in mathematics, Uri Treisman set out to discover why African American and Hispanic students at the University of California, Berkeley, were struggling in calculus while Asian students were especially strong. In a ten-year period, 60% of the African American students had received grades of D or F, and in no year did more than two Black or Hispanic students earn more than a B– (Treisman 1992: 364). Treisman asked his colleagues for theories about the low calculus grades of Black and Hispanic students on the one hand and the high grades of Asians on the other. When faculty members were surveyed about the performance discrepancies, four widely held beliefs emerged:

1. A motivation gap between strong and weak students

2. Inadequate high school preparation of African American and Hispanic students

3. Lack of family support in the case of weak students

4. An income discrepancy among the families. (Treisman 1992: 364-65)

Though it was not one of the four most common explanations, some of the faculty members surveyed suggested that racial heredity and "genetic inferiority" of Blacks played a role.

In order to compare the ethnic group associated with the worst grades with the one associated with the best, Treisman and his research team picked 20 African American students and 20 Chinese students. After studying each variable in turn, it was still not clear that there were any salient differences. The African American students were clearly motivated and had made great sacrifices during high school to earn acceptance at one of the premier research universities in the United States. They had families that were uniformly supportive; Treisman writes:

> We came to appreciate quickly that many of the parents had decided before their children were ever born that their sons and daughters would go to college. These kids were, in large part, at the university because of the concerted and organized efforts of the adults who cared about them. (Treisman 1992: 366)

The explanation of poor academic preparation did not fit either: among African Americans, the best high school math grades and SAT scores correlated negatively with college calculus grades. In fact, Treisman found that "Many of the 'strongest' students failed early. Black men with high SATs often faced academic dismissal. The few successes, on the other hand, came from students who, on paper at least, appeared to be of middle ability" (Treisman 1992: 366). Income was the only factor that positively correlated with low calculus grades because most of the parents of African Americans were either public employees or unemployed.

Frustrated by lack of answers and unable to explain the discrepancy in grades, Treisman decided "literally to move in with the students and videotape them at work" (Treisman 1992: 365). He found that there were some similarities in study habits: both groups studied alone for approximately eight hours a week, and both turned in every assignment on time. However, that is where the similarities ended. Treisman discovered that after studying alone, the Chinese students then got together and socialized. Over meals, groups of Chinese students would talk about calculus, compare answers, edit one another's work, test each other, work problems from old exams, and generally learn from interacting together. According to Treisman, "They had constructed something like a truly academic fraternity" (Treisman 1992: 366). Meanwhile, Black students always worked alone rather than with other students, rarely interacted with the professor and did not use university services that were designed to help them – though by Treisman's own account, the services were not very effective (Treisman 1992: 367).

Treisman found that part of the problem was the well-intentioned but misguided approach that Berkeley directed toward minority students. He writes:

> Many Black students are suspicious of appeals made to them based on race. These students also dislike the idea of remediation. They see themselves as the tutors, not the tutees. When the university sends a letter as ours did, "Dear Minority Student: Congratulations on your admission to Berkeley. Berkeley is a difficult institution. You are going to need a lot of help and we are here to help you," the [African American] students disregard it . . . They do not choose to come to a Berkeley because they want to learn about being Black. They choose it because they believe in the institution's ideals and elitism. (Treisman 1992: 367-68)

Without realizing it, Berkeley had triggered a reaction to stereotype threat in its African American and Hispanic students. Chinese students, also

minorities, were not vulnerable to the stereotype of poor academic performance, especially in math – a subject often positively associated, however
stereotypically, with Asians – and therefore, their performance did not suffer. Davies, Spencer *et al.* write: "The social identity that is most salient to
an individual's functioning in a given situation is often determined by society's attitudes toward certain identities in that setting" (Davies, Spencer *et
al.* 2005: 278).

At the time, African American students made up such a small percentage
of the students taking calculus that the negative stereotype about poor
academic performance was magnified by social isolation and the seemingly
irrefutable evidence that the lack of Black students in calculus proved that
Black students were not talented in math. The small numbers also seemed
to substantiate the stereotype that African Americans were academically
inferior. Black students did not seek help, in part because they were separated from a race cohort, and in part because asking for help would have,
in their minds and perhaps in the minds of their instructors, confirmed the
stereotype that they were inadequate to the task. Those African Americans who had been the strongest math students in high school, and thus
most invested in the domain, were also the most vulnerable to stereotype
threat, so they failed at a higher rate than students who had been in the
mid-range in high school.

For Chinese students, it was just the opposite: the stereotype associated
with Chinese students is positive for academic achievement, and therefore
the stereotype gave them a social identity that bolstered rather than diminished their confidence. This identification with strong math performance
was intensified and reinforced by solidarity within the Chinese student
cohort. Socializing together as a context for studying calculus both refined
their math skills and strengthened their competency. Like White and Asian
males in computer science, Chinese students claimed calculus as their territory – they identified with the subject and the subject came to be associated with them. Solidarity normalizes a domain. In other words, group
identification, habitus, claims normative status for a group and dominance
in a given territory. Therefore, solidarity is a remedy for stereotype threat.

Treisman and his team devised a plan wherein the study groups that
endogenously occurred within the Chinese student population were
institutionally replicated for African American and Hispanic students. In
response to the "debilitating isolation" experienced by these groups, Treisman set up an "anti-remedial" program that emphasized group learning and
community (Treisman 1992: 368). The anti-remedial program automatically
granted African Americans and Hispanics normative status – they were no
longer considered deviant, outsiders or "strangers." Treisman writes:

> The results of the program were quite dramatic. Black and Latino participants . . . substantially outperformed not only their minority peers, but their White and Asian classmates as well. Black students with SAT scores in the low 600s were performing comparably to White and Asian students whose math SATs were in the mid 700s. Many of the students from these early workshops have gone on to become physicians, scientists and engineers. One Black woman became a Rhodes Scholar, and many others have won distinguished graduate fellowships. (Treisman 1992: 369)

Treisman was instrumental in setting up similar programs for the University of Texas at Austin and City University of New York (CUNY). As a result, the grade point average (GPA) for minority students became higher than that of non-minority students and higher than the class average. At the University of Texas, minorities earned a 3.53 compared to a 1.66 average GPA for non-minority students, and at CUNY, minorities earned a GPA of 3.2 compared to the 1.8 class average (Treisman 1992: 371-72).

Challenging and changing interpretive frameworks

What is the mechanism evidenced in the astounding turnarounds described by Margolis in computer science, Steele in standardized test results, and Treisman in calculus grades? How can alternative "interpretive frames" be created that allow performances to be unencumbered by stereotype threat? One explanation is that the stereotype defines the participant as deviant in the domain – so in the case of Steele's experiments with standardized tests, the stereotype defines African American men and women of all races as stigmatized or deviant, and thus inferior, test-takers when compared to their White male counterparts.

Stereotypes such as "women are poor at math" subvert what Steele refers to as women's "belongingness in a domain" (Steele 1997: 620). Merely introducing the math test as one that is insensitive to gender has the effect of neutralizing the stereotype because it changes the interpretive framework, the social context, in which women perceive themselves and other women. The change can be described as women shifting identification from belonging to a group of people considered deviant and incompetent, to belonging to a group that is recognized as normative and competent.

This phenomenon of identifying with the normative, dominant group is what Steele calls "identity safety" (Steele 2003), and is the opposite of stereotype threat. For those invested in a domain, identity safety can override stereotype threat when the skill is simply reframed as one neutrally or positively associated with the gender and race identities of the participants. The skill itself is less important than whether the participant identifies with the domain and accepts the authority of the social context. This is evident in Ruth Milkman's research on the shift in gender demographics of factory workers in the United States during World War II. Milkman writes: "Idioms of sex-typing can be flexibly applied to whatever jobs women and men happen to be doing" (Milkman 1982: 50).

Women, business leadership, and entrepreneurial activity

'It's like a good family – they never kick you out'

It is obvious that participation in the paid labor force generally, and in entrepreneurship specifically, has very real economic implications for the well-being, even survival, of minority women. Stereotypes that dictate expectations for individuals based on various ascribed characteristics, such as gender, race, and ethnicity, however, remain largely unexamined. Since the economic and social consequences of stereotypes are not always easy to recognize, systems of dominance are reproduced with relative ease and often without serious challenge from those affected. This acceptance may be understandable for those who benefit from stereotypes that cast them as most likely to succeed, but it is also true for those who suffer under a set of social assumptions where they are stigmatized as incompetent, aberrant, and undesirable (Reskin 1997: 215). Levin reminds us that social control works so well because most members of a society internalize social values and identify them as their own (Levin 1994: 375). The seeming naturalness and sheer familiarity of social order, coupled with the pervasive sense in societies emphasizing free agency that values are chosen rather than imposed, cause people to be unaware of their exploited position and the coercive tactics necessary to reproduce systems of dominance (Levin 1994: 375, 105). The very real economic consequences of negative stereotypes include a persistent wage gap: in 2005, U.S. women earned US$0.76 for every dollar that men earned (Fronczek 2005: 6), and rates of unemployment are twice as high for African American women than non-Hispanic white women (McKinnon 2003: 5).

In addition to discrimination evident in hiring and promotion, economic disadvantages experienced by minority women also obtain in entrepreneurial enterprise initiation. Referring to the Global Entrepreneurship Monitor (GEM), Minniti, Arenius *et al.* (2005) report that a

> strong positive and significant correlation exists between a woman's belief of having the knowledge, skills and experience required to start a new business and her likelihood of starting one . . . and a strong, negative and significant correlation exists between fear of failure and a woman's likelihood of starting a new business. (Minniti, Arenius *et al.* 2005: 13)

Given their position in the social stratification, women are understandably more likely to have negative perceptions about entrepreneurship opportunities, and about whether they have sufficient skills to successfully start a business; therefore, they fear failure more than men do (Minniti and Bygrave 2003: 23). GEM data suggests "that fear of failure is highly correlated to [lack of] entrepreneurial activity" and more than 30% of women who feared failure did not attempt entrepreneurship (Allen, Langowitz *et al.* 2006: 31). Further, Eagly and Johannesen-Schmidt (2001) found that women have a more negative self-assessment of their leadership skills than do men because women are faced with greater role incongruity in leadership positions. Despite higher levels of anxiety about failure and more negative self-assessment, however, Allen, Langowitz *et al.* found that in high-income countries "there is no difference in the survival rates of women's businesses versus those of men" (Allen, Langowitz *et al.* 2006: 9).

In yet another example of the reversibility of stereotype threat, after viewing TV commercials that depicted negative female stereotypes, Davies, Spencer *et al.* (2005) found that women's leadership aspirations were depressed. However, women who watched the commercials and then read the following sentence were no longer vulnerable to stereotype threat: "There is a great deal of controversy in psychology surrounding the issue of gender-based differences in leadership and problem-solving ability; however, our research has revealed absolutely no gender differences in either ability on this particular task" (Davies, Spencer *et al.* 2005: 281). By increasing women's sense of belongingness and identity safety, their vulnerability to negative female stereotypes was reversed. This study establishes that media models do have the power to influence a viewer's behavior and sense of self.

But can this type of turnaround happen in the context of business leadership and ownership as well? There is evidence that, under the right circumstances, it can. In our interviews with minority women 75% reported that being an entrepreneur increased their awareness and acceptance of minorities in management and leadership positions. Additionally, all of them reported feeling that they were contributing to a shift in social awareness that minority women could be successful business leaders.

There is further evidence that women-centered business training can affect the ability for women to be business leaders. In an attempt to increase the number of women entrepreneurs, the Women's Business Center (WBC) movement, and federal funding of many Women's Business Centers through the Small Business Administration (SBA), emerged in the 1990s. These centers provide training in the form of business classes and one-on-one counseling to women entrepreneurs, especially women who are socially and economically disadvantaged. Between 1997 and 2002, women-owned businesses increased at more than 150% the national rate; about 13% of those businesses were owned by women of color (Coughlin 2002). Women's Business Centers have been part of this growth.

Though the WBC movement has persisted for over a decade, until recently few studies had been conducted to ascertain how many centers exist, the demographics of clients, how successful WBCs are in assisting women in business formation, what pedagogical techniques are used and what challenges these centers face. In 2005, exploratory research on WBCs was conducted to answer some of these questions (Langowitz, Sharpe *et al.* 2006). Approximately 105 WBCs were identified across the country, and about half of the center directors completed surveys and participated in focus groups. This research revealed that:

1. Women's Business Centers work with a relatively disadvantaged population of women; 67% have a household income under US$50,000; 43% identify as minority women; 49% have no college education; and 6% have less than a high school education (Langowitz, Sharpe *et al.* 2006: 172)

2. As non-profits, women's business centers operate on lean budgets as well as with lean organizations. Annual budgets range from a low of US$25,000 to a maximum of US$3.1 million, with an average budget of approximately US$745,000 per year. The centers average five full-time and two part-time employees, and service, on average, 1000 clients annually. (Langowitz, Sharpe *et al.* 2006: 171)

Despite the constraints detailed above, Women's Business Centers are astonishingly successful in their mission. Compared to the general rate of entrepreneurship among U.S. women of 8.2%, the average center in this research reported that more than 60% of their clients were managing a start-up business, and 34% of those entrepreneurs were managing a start-up that was more than three years old.

In focus groups and on surveys, Women's Business Center directors attribute the success of WBC programs to specific educational strategies, as well as to aspects of the general culture of WBCs. For instance, directors report that they intentionally tailor educational and training programs to women's needs: classes are scheduled around the family responsibilities that many women have, and geared to women's business interests (as ascertained by surveys distributed by WBCs to their clientele), which focus disproportionately on service industries, specifically: retail, food service, childcare, arts, entertainment, and recreation. Additionally, introductory classes at WBCs assume that clients have no business knowledge. For example, one director offered that given the high population of clients in her center who have recently immigrated and are in the process of learning English, she begins by first explaining the meaning of the word "income."

Women's Business Centers use a "relationship" orientation in teaching classes and in one-on-one counseling. Long-term relationships between clients and center staff are strongly encouraged; this priority is manifest in staff training, staff accessibility, and the policy of numerous follow-up contacts between centers and their clients. Almost half of the staff members interviewed for the study had once been WBC clients themselves. The gendered nature of Women's Business Centers is stressed such that directors and female clients (87% of WBC clients are women, and WBC staff members are also predominantly women) overwhelmingly use the word "safe" to describe the atmosphere of the centers (Langowitz, Sharpe *et al.* 2006: 175). Clients made the following comments about the atmosphere at WBCs:

> Everyone is just themselves. You can feel comfortable here. Not embarrassed about anything. Free to learn.
>
> There is unconditional loving support here.
>
> We genuinely care about each other. It is a whole continuum of care – not just business. (Godwyn 2009c: 7)

Though the main characteristic of solidarity at WBCs was gender, race was also mentioned:

> Counseling support for us minorities is amazing. They just keep going and going. Once you come here they keep you excited. It is like a good family – they never kick you out.

> It is hard to have trust when you are in the Spanish community. But, now I tell people to come [to WBCs]. If they come, they don't leave. (Godwyn 2009c: 7)

Directors said that clients often commented that compared to gender-neutral organizations that offer business training and networking opportunities, such as the Service Corps of Retired Executives (SCORE), the Small Business Development Centers (SBDCs) and Chambers of Commerce, female clients report the learning environment at WBCs makes them feel more comfortable and less intimidated. Finally, centers supply networks and mentorship for women. Refuting the conclusion of Lee and Rogoff (1998) – that women might need more business training than men, but not business training that addresses the gender differences between men and women – the research on WBCs established that support and training targeting women's gender-specific needs is powerfully effective in creating entrepreneurship, especially among economically and socially disadvantaged women (Langowitz, Sharpe *et al.* 2006).

Building on the research from the last two decades (Eagly and Johannes-en-Schmidt 2001; Minniti, Arenius *et al.* 2005; Porter and Geis 1981; Heilman, Block *et al.* 1989; Miller, Taylor *et al.* 1991; Valian 1998: 110-14,125-34) a further attempt was made to ascertain if training from a Women's Business Centers affected clients' views on women's business leadership ability and authority in the workplace. In this 2008 study, an image-based survey was given to 44 WBC clients and 44 undergraduate business students (Godwyn 2009c). The images were pictures of women and men of various races (Caucasian, Hispanic, Asian, and African American) in workplace settings. Respondents were asked to identify who was in charge and how they knew. The surveys tested the respondents' ideas and assumptions about how authority is distributed along the lines of gender, and how people are valued in society and in the workplace.

Not surprisingly, and consistent with previous research, both female and male undergraduate business students interpreted men as being leaders more often than women (Godwyn 2009c). However, unlike the business students, when asked to interpret who held authority in a group of business people, WBC respondents interpreted women as being in charge more often than men – 19% more often (Godwyn 2009c). In all other surveys conducted over the last 30 years testing perceptions about the relationship between gender and workplace authority, employability, and competence, no other tested population has perceived women as being in charge more often than men (see Valian 125-31 for literature review). Women trained at WBCs start businesses at almost four times the U.S. national rate for women, and their perceptions about who has leadership ability and authority in the workplace are reflected in their success. They simply see the world differently from most people and work from the learned assumption that women are business leaders.

Women's Business Centers fit Claude Steele's model: committing to a female-centered culture, WBCs allow women to have identity safety (Steele 2003) through optimistic teacher–student relationships, affirmation of domain belongingness, valuation of multiple perspectives, and the provision of role models and self-efficacy (Godwyn 2009c). If the population of economically and socially disadvantaged women who compose the clientele of WBCs could learn to view women as dominating business leadership, might selective training and the experience of identity safety also affect female undergraduate business students in a similar way?

Babson College is a co-ed business school in a western suburb of Boston. For the last 14 years, Babson has been named the top entrepreneurship college in the United States by *U.S. News and World Report.* Babson has also been named the number one business college for young women by *The Princeton Review, Cosmo Girl,* and *Seventeen* magazine. Most U.S. undergraduate liberal arts institutions have more female students than male students, but perhaps because of the current assumption that business is primarily a male domain, at the time of this research, the student population at Babson was approximately 65% male and 35% female. The asymmetry is slightly more pronounced in the faculty: Babson has 265 tenured and tenure-track faculty: 32% female and 68% male. Of the 48 full professors, only 19% are women and 81% are men. Reflecting societal assumptions regarding business leadership, and similar to computer science courses, student interest in entrepreneurship classes tends to be skewed toward White men generally – even in student populations where White males are not the majority. Purdue University reports that over 75% of the students who register for the "Certificate in Entrepreneurship and Innovation" are White males, 23% are women, 6% are Asian, 6% are African American, 3% are Hispanic and 0.2% are Native American (Duval-Couëtil 2007).

Babson, however, is the only business school to have a Center for Women's Leadership (CWL). For the past three years, the CWL has sponsored approximately 20 female students a year as Women's Leadership Scholars. In addition to the standard business curriculum, these female students receive gender-specific training that includes mentorship from a female entrepreneur, career development advice, internships, and admission to a speaker series focusing on women entrepreneurs. Women's Leadership Scholars also have regular dinners and meetings, and receive a scholarship award. If the Women's Leadership Scholar program offers female students the same type of gender solidarity and identity safety that WBCs offer clients, then the expectation is that Women's Leadership Scholars, unlike undergraduate business students generally, would be more likely to perceive women as being business leaders and as having more authority in the workplace than do men.

And in fact, when given the same image-based survey that had been administered to WBC clients and to undergraduate business students, Women's Leadership Scholars identified women as leaders more than twice as often as they identified men as leaders (67% versus 33%). Women's Leadership Scholars were significantly more likely to perceive women in charge than even WBC clientele. Perhaps this is because Women's Leadership Scholars have benefited not only from gender-specific training, increased gender solidarity and neutralization of stereotype threat, but also from the increased social status a prestigious business college degree provides.

Summary and notes on next chapters

This chapter reviews empirical studies demonstrating that prejudicial and discriminatory frames of reference can be changed and that lifting the burden of stereotypes and stereotype threat has a marked and often immediate impact on perception and performance. Chapter 4 describes the origin of the racial, class, and gendered nature of classical economic theory and the attendant conventional business practices.

4
Where did business-as-usual come from?

A sociological examination of the origins of typical business practices

The minority women interviewed for this study practice business in a radically different way from the entrepreneurs often described in entrepreneurship texts and business case studies. Their most notable business innovation is that they bring multiple objectives to their business decisions that include, but do not prioritize, profit. The other considerations described by minority women and held in equal importance to profit include environmental concerns, social and community responsibilities, and being able to express their creativity and self-identities through their business. Consequently, the entrepreneurial process is guided by self-reflection and negotiated through ongoing consideration of moral concerns, and personal and community values. The entrepreneur merges her active construction of self with her decisions about business policies, products, and services. This process happens in the context of gender identity and minority status, and differs from conventional entrepreneurial goals, assumptions, and methods. Chapter 5 will discuss some specific business innovations of the minority women interviewed for this study, but first, it is important to understand how business came to be associated with a race and a gender – how the process and objectives of business came to be identified with and by White men. The following is a brief explanatory overview of the sociology and history of entrepreneurship within a capitalist economic context.

Business-as-usual: the role of self-interest in economic theory

Deeply embedded in conventional explanations of entrepreneurship is the assumption that businesses are primarily a means to make money, and that entrepreneurs are those who are motivated by the desire to accumulate material wealth (Banks 2006: 457, 461). This assumption is often traced to an interpretation of Adam Smith's concept of enlightened self-interest described in the famous quotation from *The Wealth of Nations:*

> It is not from the benevolence of the butcher, the brewer, or the baker, that we expect our dinner, but from their regard to their own interest. We address ourselves, not to their humanity but to their self-love, and never talk to them of our own necessities but of their advantages. Nobody but a beggar chuses to depend chiefly upon the benevolence of his fellow-citizens. (Smith 1776: 24)

Though Smith advocated a marketplace regulated by social norms and informed by morality, his words have been used by many to legitimize the solitary pursuit of self-interest through commercial enterprise, and have further been interpreted to mean that public good should be addressed primarily through the promotion of self-interest. Here is evidence of a common underlying principle of economic theory: that individual self-interest on the one hand, and public good and social benefit on the other, are two distinct and separable categories. For instance, the economist Milton Friedman famously declared that "the business of business is to make a profit, not to engage in socially beneficial acts" (Reich 2007: 173). Indeed, Robert Reich writes that even those businesses that launch corporate responsibility initiatives do so only to the degree that such social responsibility results in shareholder value and increased profit:

> All these steps may be worthwhile but they are not undertaken because they are socially responsible. They're done to reduce costs. To credit these corporations with being "socially responsible" is to stretch the term to mean anything a company might do to increase profits if, in doing so, it also happens to have some beneficent impact on the rest of society. Taken to the logical extreme is the textbook economics argument that whenever a company increases its profits it has a positive effect on society because it thereby utilizes assets more efficiently, releasing those that are no longer needed to

be used more efficiently elsewhere. In this sense, all profitable companies are socially responsible. (Reich 2007: 171)

Accordingly, corporate social responsibility initiatives are not a repositioning of business decisions within the sphere of social values or the balancing of stockholder earnings and community considerations, but a continuation of the primacy of profit for the company. The interpretation seems to be that taking care of private interests is, in some ill-defined way, the same as addressing the public good. A key assumption of this interpretation and of Smith's injunction to observe self-interest is that there is some minimal degree of equality and mutuality among trading partners. Though Smith intended to endorse capitalistic exchange as a revolutionary doctrine that would replace feudalism by defeating the privileges of the landed gentry and mercantile interests, **he mistakenly assumed the very equality and mutuality he thought would be established through capitalistic exchange**. Even in the case of dramatic inequality – when one person is a beggar – Smith emphasized the idea that the logic of the trading process is primarily mutual exchange rather than one-sided altruistic giving or the exploitation of the weak:

> Even the beggar does not depend on [the benevolence of his fellow citizens] entirely. The charity of the well-disposed people, indeed, supplies him with the whole fund of his subsistence . . . But . . . The greater part of his occasional wants are supplied in the same manner as those of other people, by treaty, by barter and by purchase. (Smith 1776: 24)

Perhaps because he situated this example within the context of moral sentiments, Smith glossed over the fact that beggars do indeed *depend* primarily on the charity of the wealthy. It is only surplus material that they trade "in the same manner as those of other people." Moreover, in many real-world instances, the lack of mutual exchange is glaring. There are whole populations of people, such as children and the infirm, and entities, such as endangered species and layers of the earth's atmosphere, that are, in a sense, beggars. They are not in a position to offer immediate and obvious benefit to the self-interest of trading partners. In fact, in many situations there is no obvious and direct ability to trade at all. Therefore, insofar as the self is conceived as an isolated being, and self-interest is defined through singular and direct experiences of instrumentally motivated exchange that at most can extend only to the span of the individual's lifetime, then long-term investment in the environment, in the community or even in one's own progeny, does not make rational sense.

However, when the boundaries of the self include identification with community, with one's children and with the ecological balance of the earth, then self-interest is defined by a wide range of concerns that transcend the direct experience and even the lifetime of any single person. To make use once again of Morrie Schwartz's distinction: it is the difference between conceiving the self as a wave or as part of the ocean.

Sociological interpretations of self-interest and the meaning of wealth

The sociologist Max Weber argues for the primacy of cultural values rather than those of self-interest as the motivation behind human behavior. Like Smith, he situates the guiding principles of commerce within a social context. However, for Weber, self-interest was not merely a characteristic of isolated individuals applying instrumental rationality; rather it reflects the social values emblematic of the cultural and religious context in which capitalism became firmly established. In other words, in an oxymoronic twist, this particular social context encouraged militant individualism.

In *The Protestant Ethic and the Spirit of Capitalism,* Weber theorizes that capitalism began in the West, meaning the United States and Western Europe. He argues that entrepreneurship with the goal of accumulating capital to reinvest in the business was not the consequence of greed or avarice, and not merely rational, "smart business." Instead, the accumulation and reinvestment of capital resulted from a religious belief that wealth was evidence of a connection to the divine. In this context, labor was seen by some Christians (primarily members of several early Protestant sects) as a calling, a duty; and material affluence was an indication that God guided the laborer. Quoting Puritan church leader Richard Baxter, Weber writes:

> Hence, the faithful Christian must follow the call by taking advantage of the opportunity. "If God show you a way in which you may lawfully get more than in another way (without wrong to your soul or to another) . . . you may labor to be rich for God, though not for the flesh and sin" . . . Wealth is thus bad ethically only insofar as it is a temptation to idleness . . . But as a performance of duty . . . it is not only morally permissible, but actually enjoined . . . To wish to be poor was, it was often argued, the same as wishing to be unhealthy. (Weber 1904: 162-63)

Weber also quotes the Methodist minister John Wesley, who writes: "we must exhort all Christians to gain all they can, and to save all they can; that is, in effect, to grow rich" (Wesley 1904: 175). Accordingly, Weber found that there exists "a direct parallel between the pursuit of wealth in the Kingdom of Heaven and the pursuit of success in an earthly calling" (Weber 1904: 268). Quoting Johannes Hoornbeek, a Dutch Puritan, Weber illustrates the belief that wealth was an indication of God's favor: "Everything is the work of God's Providence, but in particular He takes care of his own" (Weber 1904: 269).

As material wealth became an indication of membership in God's chosen elite, emotional attachments, charitable work and earthly sentiments were denigrated. For this group of Protestants, asceticism and the denial of sensual pleasure went along with the spirit of capitalism. Believers were told to eschew enjoyment and earthly delights. Money earned was not to afford leisure, comfort, beauty, or luxury, but accumulated in the name of God and therefore remanded back to the business. This orientation created a clear distinction between Protestant and Catholic doctrine. Whereas for Catholics, charity towards others and kindness on earth would help secure a place in heaven, the Protestant sects associated with ascetic capitalism believed that good works were irrelevant. Instead, those chosen to go to Heaven were distinguished only by true belief in God and by economic success – that is, by the accumulation of material wealth.

The suppression of art and music was one result of the prioritization of paid labor and the strict prohibition against "wasting" time in any other pursuit, especially those that elicited emotions and sensual enjoyment. Again quoting Baxter, Weber chronicles the prohibitions of Puritanism and the subsequent cultural effects: "Novels and the like should not be read; they are 'wastetimes' " (Weber 1904: 272). Weber writes:

> The decline of lyric poetry and folk-music, as well as the drama, after the Elizabethan age in England is well known . . . But very striking is the decline from what seemed to be a promising musical beginning . . . to that absolute musical vacuum which we find typical of the Anglo-Saxon peoples . . . (Weber 1904: 272)

and:

> We may recall that the Puritan town government closed the theatre at Stratford-on-Avon while Shakespeare was still alive and residing there in his last years. Shakespeare's hatred and contempt of the Puritans appears on every occasion. As late as 1777, the City of Birmingham refused to license a theatre because it was conducive to slothfulness and hence unfavorable to trade. (Weber 1904: 274)

Though Weber situated capitalism within a religious/cultural context, he acknowledges that: "the religious roots died out slowly giving way to utilitarian worldliness" (Weber 1904: 176). And Banks comments, "economics were initially embedded in social relations and shaped by moral values, but Modern, formal economic institutions emerged as an autonomous sphere governed by instrumental rationalization and separate from moral purpose" (Banks 2006: 461). A critical examination of religious beliefs and cultural assumptions exposes a social matrix for reproducing gender, race, and class inequality that held sway even within the ostensible commitment to equal opportunity and democratic principles that characterizes the United States. The resulting social and economic value system based on the tenets of classical economic theory and the complementary religious dogma serve as thinly disguised justifications for wealth to be concentrated in the hands of the few. Weber writes:

> The impersonality of present-day labor, that, from the standpoint of the individual, is its joyless lack of meaning, still has a religious justification [in the United States]. Capitalism at the time of its development needed laborers who were available for economic exploitation for conscience' sake. (Weber 1904: 282)

Anthropologist Helena Norberg-Hodge observes that the Western cultural assumptions on which our economic system is founded have "grown so widespread and so powerful that [Western culture] has lost a perspective on itself; there is no 'other' with which to compare itself" (Norberg-Hodge 1991: 3). The scarcity of critical examination of the basic tenets that undergird economic theory continues to characterize contemporary business and entrepreneurship texts. Norberg-Hodge writes that we assume "human beings [are] essentially selfish, struggling to compete and survive, and that more cooperative societies [are] nothing more than utopian dreams" (Norberg-Hodge 1991: 2). Yunus agrees. In his 2006 Nobel Prize acceptance speech, he put it this way:

> I am very unhappy about the conceptual restrictions imposed on the players in the market. This originates from the assumption that entrepreneurs are one-dimensional human beings, who are dedicated to one mission in their business lives – to maximize profit. This interpretation of capitalism insulates the entrepreneurs from all political, emotional, social, spiritual, environmental dimensions of their lives. This was done perhaps as a reasonable simplification, but it stripped away the very essentials of human life ... We have remained so

> impressed by the success of the free market that we never
> dared to express any doubt about our basic assumption. To
> make it worse, we worked extra hard to transform ourselves,
> as closely as possible, into the one-dimensional human beings
> as conceptualized in the theory, to allow smooth functioning
> of free-market mechanism. (Yunus 2006)

This set of assumptions about human nature, business, and entrepreneurship ensures that crucial environmental, social, and ethical concerns will
be secondary to competitive processes manifest in the narrow goal of making money that is often given primacy in business and entrepreneurship
studies.

Using sociology to interrogate contemporary business assumptions and entrepreneurship education

In an attempt both to capture and to avoid the fundamental contradic-
tion within economic theory, John Cassidy has coined the term "rational
irrationality" (Cassidy 2009: 30). This oxymoronic phrase means "behavior that, on the individual level, is perfectly reasonable, but that, when
aggregated in the market-place, produces calamity" (Cassidy 2009: 31).
Unlike the discipline of economics that recognizes some behavior as both
individually rational and collectively irrational, sociology does not recognize a pre-social self, thereby problematizing the distinction between the
individual self and collective society. That is to say, sociology challenges
the notion that any behavior can be defined as reasonable if it imposes
systems of discrimination that result in widespread inequality, or benefits
individual, private interests in the short term but jeopardizes the survival
of the community in the long term (please see the discussion in Chapter 6 regarding different types of rationality). Though the disciplines of
economics, psychology, and management address entrepreneurship as a
phenomenon, only sociology and social psychology are theoretically and
methodologically equipped to examine the social status characteristics of
entrepreneurs and the ways these characteristics affect the availability of
opportunities, the entrepreneur's perception of opportunities, her decision-making processes, and her performance.

Additionally, sociology provides an unparalleled theoretical depth and
critical perspective on the power of privilege. In most business case studies and representations of entrepreneurs, it is not only minority status that
remains invisible and outside of analytical consideration: majority status and its attendant privileges also remain largely unacknowledged and
unexamined. We use sociological theory to understand why women are

not given the recognition they deserve, explain how this can change, and describe what we can expect from a future that acknowledges the value of women entrepreneurs.

A critical examination of entrepreneurship textbooks

Economic theory suggests that business ventures – and entrepreneurship, insofar as it is included in the business realm – must exploit opportunities, and pursue primarily economic goals (profit) in order to remain competitive in the context of market forces and survive over the long term. Entrepreneurship education often delivers to this expectation by adopting the self-interested and self-serving individual unit, the "economic man" of classical economic theory (Crittenden 2001: 67); by focusing on White, educated, male business owners (Ogbor 2000: 265); and by glorifying large-growth enterprises while disdaining lifestyle ventures (Timmons and Spinelli 2007: 87-88).

Resonating with ascetic capitalism, contemporary entrepreneurship textbooks and entrepreneurial training in business school settings exalt "equity-minded" and "high potential, high-growth ventures" (Timmons and Spinelli 2007: 115) that yield remarkable monetary wealth relatively quickly and then are sold, or "harvested" (Timmons and Spinelli 2007: 87).

Celebrating this emphasis on wealth accumulation, in the seventh edition of their popular entrepreneurship textbook, *New Venture Creation: Entrepreneurship for the 21st Century* (2007), Jeffrey A. Timmons and Stephen Spinelli write:

> This overall search for high potential ventures has become more evident in recent years . . . Hundreds of thousands of college students now have been exposed to these concepts for more than two decades, and their strategies for identifying potential businesses are mindful of and disciplined about the ingredients for success. Unlike 20 years ago, it is now nearly impossible not to hear and read about these principles on television, in books, on the Internet, or in a multitude of seminars, courses and programs for would-be entrepreneurs. (Timmons and Spinelli 2007: 87)

Additionally, small businesses or so-called "lifestyle businesses" – those intended to maximize the quality of life rather than the quantity of profit – are unfavorably compared to high-potential businesses:

> For many aspiring entrepreneurs, issues of family, roots and location take precedence. Accessibility to a preferred way of

> life, whether it is access to fishing, skiing, hunting . . . can be
> more important than how large a business one has or the size
> of one's net worth. Others vastly prefer to be with and work
> with their family or spouse . . . Yet couples who give up suc-
> cessful careers in New York City to buy an inn in Vermont to
> avoid the rat race generally last only six to seven years. They
> discover the joys of self-employment, including seven-day,
> 70–90-hour workweeks, chefs and day help that do not show
> up, roofs that leak when least expected, and the occasional
> guests from hell. The grass is always greener, so they say. (Tim-
> mons and Spinelli 2007: 87-88)

Moreover, "entrepreneurs" are counseled to think "big" because it leads
to the advancement of their personal wealth. In the quotation below, Timmons and Spinelli write that those who are "wedded" to their business are
"enslaved" by their commitment. Such business owners are depicted as
hard-working, but not that bright – they don't think big enough, and they
aren't going to get rich:

> Time and again the authors have observed the classic small
> business owner who, almost like a dairy farmer, is enslaved
> by and wedded to the business. Extremely long hours of 70,
> 80, or even 100 hours a week, and rare vacations, are often the
> rule rather than the exception. And these hardworking own-
> ers rarely build equity, other than in the real estate they may
> own for the business. One of the big differences between the
> growth- and equity-minded entrepreneur and the traditional
> small business owners is that the entrepreneur thinks *bigger.*
> Longtime good friend Patricia Cloherty [venture capitalist and
> past president of Patrioff & Company] puts it this way, "It is
> critical to think big enough. If you want to start and build a
> company, you are going to end up exhausted. So you might
> as well think about creating a BIG company. At least you will
> end up exhausted and *rich*, not just exhausted!" (Timmons and
> Spinelli 2007: 115 [emphasis in the original])

The emphasis on building "BIG" companies and getting "rich" demonstrates
that the following illustration from Weber still applies: "the leading dry-
goods man of an Ohio city" who, while his wife and daughter read together
in the evening, schemes to make his store front bigger. His European son-
in-law wonders, "Couldn't the old man be satisfied with his $75,000 a year
and rest? No! The frontage of the store must be widened to 400 feet. Why?
That beats everything, he says" (Weber 1904: 283). Weber writes that in
the young man's opinion, his father-in-law was needlessly obsessed with

making his business bigger – he was already wealthy – while ignoring his family and intellectual pursuits. Similarly, Timmons and Spinelli counsel entrepreneurs not to identify with their business or become too attached – not to be "wedded" and "enslaved" by their ventures. Work is not portrayed as a meaningful or fulfilling end in itself or as a way to define and express oneself, but rather as a means to equity and wealth. It is the size of the business and the profit it produces that matter. Ideally, the business will be sold, "harvested," and the entrepreneur will be rich.

Though entrepreneurial textbooks commonly devalue lifestyle businesses, it is important to note the critical necessity of small, entrepreneurial enterprise to the growth of the U.S. economy. Small businesses, those the U.S. Census Bureau refers to as "nonemployer businesses," (meaning no paid employees, usually family businesses, often referred to as "Mom and Pop," and/or home-based ventures) make up 70% of the businesses in the United States (U.S. Census 2006). In 2003, these small businesses generated US$830 billion dollars, up from US$586 billion in 1997. The growth rate in non-employer businesses between 2002 and 2003 was 5.7%, the largest since 1997, the year the Census Bureau began releasing statistics on non-employer businesses. In 2003, there were 18.6 million non-employer businesses in the United States, and 5.3 million businesses with fewer than ten paid employees. Firms with fewer than ten workers employed 15.9 million people (U.S. Census 2006).

According to the National Small Business Association (NSBA), a Harris Interactive Poll on the *Confidence of Leaders of Major Institutions* reported that 54% of adults expressed a great deal of confidence and trust in small business owners; in fact, small business owners have ranked in the top two highest spots in inspiring the public's trust since 1973 (NSBA 2008). Correspondingly, a 2008 study sponsored by American Express found that small businesses give much more generously to charities than do large companies. On average, small businesses give 6% of their earnings to charity, and 80% of small companies with profits between US$250,000 and US$1 million gave to charities. Only 69% of businesses with annual earnings over US$1 million are philanthropic (Preston 2008). Finally, the NSBA reports that in the last 15 years, small businesses have created 21.9 million jobs, while large businesses have created only 1.8 million. Therefore, extolling large-growth business and disdaining small business might be less about job and wealth creation for the many and more about wealth creation for the few.

As mentioned earlier, Babson College in Wellesley, Massachusetts, is a high-ranking U.S. business school specializing in entrepreneurship. It makes substantial contributions to the standards by which entrepreneurship education is judged, both in U.S. schools and internationally. Given the dominant themes in entrepreneurship texts, it is not surprising that in a 2006 survey answered by 53 Babson College students, 14 of those students, or a little over 25%, reported that "profit" or "making money" was an important or the most important aspect of successful entrepreneurship (Godwyn 2009a).

Yet, in the same survey, students and faculty members also reflected critically on the meaning and emancipatory power of entrepreneurship. Representative student comments include:

> Babson doesn't always stress the part about finding something you love to do.

> Babson's idea of success is measured in money. It should attract students who do not just want to make money, but want to make a difference in the world.

> Many students here are driven by money, and though money is great, that is not everything. We need more classes concerning ethics, not just a one day discussion. Ethics should be taught to all and not just those who decide to take those classes.

Representative business faculty member comments:

> I think that . . . entrepreneurial success is most often measured by revenue and profit growth. We do not get really excited about businesses that are sustainable, but are not growth engines in some form or fashion.

> My impression is that we go very little beyond money, and in fact little beyond technology-based entrepreneurship. The radical answer is that it should be instilled in our core programs, in the very vision of entrepreneurship we provide our students from day one. A more moderate possibility would be to include coverage of the expanded view of entrepreneurship in some part of our core curriculum, and preferably not only in the ethics component. The idea is to get the students to understand that this is not just a moral injunction, but an avenue for personal fulfillment and often for financial success too.

Though business school course material and entrepreneurship textbooks emphasize rapid-growth business and rapid accumulation of profit, some students and faculty members reject this paradigm. They continue to look for meaning in work and assert the need for social values, ethics, and morality as the larger context in which businesses are situated.

Perhaps in response to these entreaties, Timmons and Spinelli, who for a time both served as entrepreneurship professors at Babson, extol and promote the "Timmons Model of Entrepreneurship." According to the schematic, the Timmons Model includes, among other things, the founder, the team, opportunity, resources, uncertainty, and capital market context – but all these entrepreneurial elements are entirely built on a foundation of "Sustainability: For Environment, Community and Society" (Timmons and Spinelli: 2007: 89). According to the book index, however, "sustainability" is mentioned only once in the entire text – on the schematic. Somehow, a discussion of the very foundation of entrepreneurship is omitted.

Though entrepreneurship texts often claim that entrepreneurship is more than business ownership – that it is a "mindset" (Kuratko and Hoggetts 2007: 5) or even "a way of life" – there is little evidence that entrepreneurship instruction substantiates these claims (Godwyn 2009b). In an effort to create an interface between business and social values, the philanthro-capitalistic model of giving is routinely touted at business schools. This model reflects the notion that entrepreneurs will make their millions (or billions) by first successfully implementing the instrumental rationality emblematic of classical economic theory, and only afterwards might they turn their attention to social issues such as education, health, and justice. Of the 642 pages in *New Venture Creation*, only three, pages 624-26, mention the term "social responsibility." This social responsibility discussion is entitled "Beyond the Harvest" and notes that after accumulating monetary wealth, many entrepreneurs donate money to college endowments, symphony orchestras, and museums and donate time to community activities such as voluntary, civic associations; also noted was that entrepreneurs often invest in "new companies" (Timmons and Spinelli 2007: 625). But beyond a cursory and superficial exhortation to "Give back to the community and society" (Timmons and Spinelli 2007: 625), the message in much of the entrepreneurship instruction – not only from Timmons and Spinelli – is geared towards maximizing profit.

In their article "Towards Integration: Understanding Entrepreneurship through Frameworks," Morris, Kuratko *et al.* (2001) explain that a diversity of resources is required for successful entrepreneurship, but their attempt to define the field differs very little from a typical business manual:

> Resources have been grouped into six categories: physical (e.g., buildings, equipment), relational (e.g., customers, distributors, networks), organizational (e.g., structures, processes, systems), financial (e.g. cash, debt capacity), intellectual and human (e.g., sales capabilities, R&D skills), and technological

> (e.g., patents, licenses, access to particular technologies).
> These resource categories can be captured using the acronym,
> "PROFIT." (Morris, Kuratko *et al.* 2001: 43)

A brief review of another major entrepreneurship text reveals a similar orientation. *Entrepreneurship: Theory, Process and Practice* (2007) is a popular college-level entrepreneurship text that, like *New Venture Creation,* is also in its seventh edition. Co-authors Donald Kuratko and Richard M. Hoggetts are seminal figures in entrepreneurship scholarship. Kuratko, a professor at the University of Indiana, has authored over 160 articles and 22 books on entrepreneurship. Kuratko and Hoggetts distinguish entrepreneurs from small business owners primarily by the size of their ambitions; that is to say, in their estimation, entrepreneurs focus on rapid growth and profit generation:

> The terms entrepreneur and small-business owner are sometimes used interchangeably. Although some situation encompass both terms, it is important to note the differences in the titles. Small businesses are independently owned and operated, are not dominant in their fields, and usually do not engage in many new or innovative practices. They may never grow large, and the owners may prefer a more stable and less aggressive approach to running businesses. In other words, they manage the business by expecting stable sales, profits and growth . . . On the other hand, entrepreneurial ventures are those for which the entrepreneur's principal objectives are innovation, profitability and growth . . . Entrepreneurs and their financial backers are usually seeking rapid growth and immediate profits. (Kuratko and Hoggetts 2007: 4)

Small businesses, then, are characterized by lack of "dominance," lack of "aggression" and lack of "innovation." However, because this definition of entrepreneurship only recognizes innovation directed towards and resulting in "rapid growth and immediate profits," the minority women's business innovations showcased here would not count as innovations at all. The encouragement of high stakes, risk-taking behavior, the warnings against being "enslaved" by or "wedded" to one's business and the emphasis on achieving "dominance" and using "aggression" to build big business with rapid growth all mark these texts as rewarding gendered characteristics and using imagery typically associated with men. Similarly, the discouragement of emotional ties and attachment to family, along with the subordination of quality of life issues in favor of calculated self-interest and instrumental rationality, characterize some of the central texts in entrepreneurship literature. These values affect our collective understanding of social status, inform current business practices, and influence gender, race, and class identity.

Women and minorities in capitalist economies

The Protestant ethic taught individuals to secure their own grace rather than to be concerned with others (Weber 1904: 133); to wit: "Loveless fulfillment of duty stands higher than sentimental philanthropy" (Weber 1904: 270). It is easy to imagine the grave disadvantage this orientation to work and wealth imposes on women and minorities. If the subtext of the Protestant ethic was that one's connection to God – and in Durkheim's estimation, God is simply the representation of cultural values and ideals – was determined by economic success, then women and disenfranchised minorities were relegated to the ranks of the damned. The accumulation of wealth through labor in order to demonstrate that "prosperity is the reward of a godly life" (Weber 1904: 269) is the exclusive prerogative of those who have access to highly paid work.

Meanwhile, until the early 20th century, U.S. women could not hold property or public office; they were barred from higher education, could neither vote nor serve on juries. In fact, women could not accumulate wealth systematically through labor: any wages they earned belonged to the male head of household, and their domestic work on behalf of their own families was not considered work at all because it was unpaid. In the 21st century this tradition continues, as college-educated women in the United States are secluded in the domestic sphere, providing unpaid labor to their families to a higher degree than are most of their peers in other industrialized nations (Crittenden 2001: 17). The devaluation of care-giving work and emotional attachment has consistently characterized the U.S. economic system and tax structure. Consequently, a college-educated woman in the U.S. gives up over US$1 million in salary and benefits if she becomes a mother – the so-called "mommy tax" (Crittenden 2001: 89). The social imperatives of childcare and domestic work, major contributors to the production and reproduction of human capital, are largely provided by private resources (often women's unpaid or underpaid labor). This is an example of private work with a huge social payoff, except to the women themselves, whose efforts are denied social prestige and economic compensation.

In his commentary on the new democratic nation, Alexis de Tocqueville describes the surprising degree to which American women were saddled with "social inferiority," "extreme dependence," and confinement "within the narrow circle of domestic life" (Crittenden 2001: 49). Early on, women's low social status was codified in tax policies and economic definitions. For instance, in Alexander Hamilton's 1791 *Report on Manufactures*, only goods that could be sold for profit were included in the "total produce" of society and thus the domestic labor women provide their own families has *never counted* as a positive contribution to the economy (Crittenden 2001: 47). Instead, women's labor continues to be considered a "labor of love," and those mothers, unpaid and laboring at home, are not recognized as productive citizens; they are "dependents" who must be supported by a "working" member of the household. Crittenden writes:

> For men was reserved the world of money, commerce and industry. For middle- and upper-middle-class white women, the ideal was to become the embodiment "of pure disinterested love, such as is seldom found in the busy walks of a selfish and calculating world." (Crittenden 2001: 47)

Women continue to be largely responsible for the very emotional attachments and good works that were denigrated in the creation of capitalism. For middle- and upper-middle-class White women, those who were in the class and race position to offer the most direct economic competition to White men, the rationale was that women were too delicate, too sensitive, and too moral for the rough-and-tumble world of paid labor:

> Under this doctrine of "separate spheres," the "true woman" was the upholder of private morality and the caring sentiments. She would never stoop to ask for any monetary compensation for her labors. She was put on a high pedestal, but asked to carry a very heavy load. (Crittenden 2001: 48)

Given the cultural and religious association between being wealthy and being blessed, the poor were often held accountable for their own failings. The lack of empathy and cavalier condemnation of fellow human beings set the context for the abominations of U.S. history such as the enslavement of African peoples, the genocide of Native peoples, and the indentured servitude and inhumane work conditions visited on immigrants and refugees. The ideology used to keep men and women of color from accessing the economy was that they were lazy, unintelligent, and dishonest:

> The analogy between the unjust (according to human standards) predestination of only a few and the equally unjust, but equally divinely ordained, distribution of wealth, was too obvious to be escaped . . . poverty [was] very often [considered] a symptom of sinful slothfulness. (Weber 1904: 281)

If middle- and upper-middle-class White women were too moral and uninterested in personal gain to pursue wealth, racial and ethnic minorities were not moral or godly enough to deserve it. The result is that business, finance, and wealth remain associated with and largely controlled by White men.

Gender and minority status in psychosocial development: relational and individuated selfhood

In addition to the works of Marx and Weber, sociological literature is rich in admonishments that the devaluation of emotional ties, continuation of economic inequality, and exploitation of workers and natural resources are the inescapable consequences of capitalist economies, but only a few discuss how the domination system of capitalism specifically affects the self-development of women and minorities. For our purposes here, women are a subset of minorities (Hacker 1951). Therefore, though what follows focuses on female development and attendant gender behaviors, we apply the analysis to minorities broadly. One of the first to draw a clear connection between women's psychosocial development and women's social subordination in capitalist economies was Nancy Chodorow. Her analysis of the relational self can also be extended to aspects of minority identity beyond gender as well.

Chodorow locates women's social and economic subjugation in the fact that childcare responsibilities fall disproportionately on women's shoulders. She points out that capitalism depends on this asymmetrical parenting to create gendered personalities and behavior traits in both women and men. Chodorow writes:

> Women's mothering is tied to many other aspects of our society, is fundamental to our ideology of gender and benefits many people . . . It created heterosexual asymmetries which reproduce the family and marriage, but leave women with needs that lead them to care for children, and men with capacities for participation in the alienated work world. It creates a psychology of male dominance and fear of women in men. It forms a basis of the division of the social world into unequally valued domestic and public spheres, each the province of people of a different gender. Women's mothering is also a crucial link between the contemporary organization of gender and the organization of production. It produces men with personality characteristics and psychic structure appropriate to participation in the capitalist work world. (Chodorow 1978: 219)

The social and psychological consequences of women as primary parents include adult women who identify and develop their selfhood *in relation to* others, and adult men who establish their masculine identity *through separation from* others:

> Feminine personality comes to define itself in relation and connection to other people more than masculine personality does (in psychoanalytic terms, women are less individuated than men; they have more flexible ego boundaries). Moreover, issues of dependency are handled and experienced differently by men and women. For boys and men, both individuation and dependency issues become tied up with the sense of masculinity, or masculine identity. For girls and women, by contrast, issues of femininity, or feminine identity, are not problematic in the same way. (Chodorow 2001: 175)

Because most children are cared for by women, girls and adult women learn to identify themselves and act according to the nurturing, empathetic, cooperative, and interdependent behaviors that operate in care-giving. Men and boys, on the other hand, must struggle to separate themselves from these caring characteristics and behavioral responses in order to differentiate themselves from women, in order to establish their masculine identity. According to Chodorow, this is not merely role playing or learned behavior: socially constructed gendered characteristics (and here this argument can be extended to aspects of minority identity as well) are internalized over time and become a largely unconscious aspect of responding to and understanding the world. In this context, male attempts to differentiate themselves from women lead men to devalue women, sometimes with violent consequences; to denigrate emotional attachments in general; and to assert their dominance in the public sphere where legal, economic, and political institutions operate:

> Women's mothering in the isolated nuclear family of contemporary capitalist society creates specific personality characteristics in men that reproduce both an ideology and a psychodynamic of male superiority and submission to the requirements of production. It prepares men for participation in a male-dominant family and society, for their lesser emotional participation in family life, and for their participation in the capitalist world of work. (Chodorow 1978: 181)

Chodorow concludes that having such a large proportion of childcare performed by women is bad for men and bad for women and children. Women and children suffer when women are primary parents because they can be too merged with their children:

> My view is that exclusive single parenting is bad for mother and child alike. As I point out earlier, mothers in such a setting are liable to overinvest in and overwhelm the relationship. Similarly, I think, children are better off in situations where love and relationship are not a scarce resource controlled and manipulated by one person only. (Chodorow 1978: 217)

Men also suffer when women are primary parents because though it guarantees them "sociocultural superiority over women, [they] always remain psychologically defensive and insecure" about their masculine identity (Chodorow 2001: 186). In order to maintain their superior position, men compromise their ability to have intimate, caring relationships – those relationships most frequently associated with women – and in order to distinguish themselves from those female subordinates, they disparage and malign all things associated with feminine characteristics including cooperation, emotional ties, nurturing behavior, interdependence, and mutuality.

Men opt instead for hierarchical, impersonal, and competitive interactions – these are all indications of masculinity, and because the public sphere containing economic exchanges and political decisions is gendered male, typical masculine characteristics and behavior have higher social status. Indeed, Chodorow cites the dangers of ultra-rigid ego boundaries manifest in masculine behavior that include the extreme individuation associated with the Protestant work ethic:

> The argument can be made that extremes in either direction are harmful. Complete lack of ego boundaries is clearly pathological, but so also, as critics of contemporary western men point out . . . is individuation gone wild, what Bakan calls "agency unmitigated by communion," which he takes to characterize, among other things, both capitalism based on the Protestant ethic and aggressive masculinity. (Chodorow 2001: 186)

Chodorow also points out that:

> Women's work in the labor force tends to extend their housewife, wife, or mother roles and their concern with personal, affective ties (as secretaries, service workers, private household workers, nurses, teachers). Men's work is less likely to have affective overtones – they are craft workers, operatives and professional and technical workers. (Chodorow 1978: 180)

For Chodorow, shared parenting would create more balanced adult women and men, temper the gender binary constructed around polarized characteristics and result in a greater degree of social and economic parity.

Co-parenting clearly has benefits for gender equality, for parents and for children. Summarizing cross-cultural anthropological data, Michael Kimmel writes, "These two variables – the father's involvement in child rearing (often measured by spatial segregation) and women's control of property after marriage – emerge as among the central determinants of women's status and gender inequality" (Kimmel 2004: 59). However, what is underemphasized in Chodorow's analysis is that the relational aspect of women's psychosocial personality development is not a shortcoming that can and should be corrected through co-parenting; rather, it is a *strength* that can and should be encouraged and actively developed in both women and men. Because of the highly affective ties between parents and children, which can at times be symbiotic, parenting is perhaps the most powerful crucible in which to develop a relational self.

We argue this relational self is the key to better ways of doing business. In fact, one universal characteristic of the minority women entrepreneurs interviewed for this study is that they have merged with their businesses. In other words, they make no distinction between themselves and their enterprise; they see themselves in and express themselves through their businesses. As Pauline Lewis says, "I am my company." And Najma Jamaludeen comments on being an entrepreneur: "I love it. It is a part of me . . . It is how I relate to freedom." Barbara Manzi declares, "If it has my name on it, it **has to be correct**." Maryam Jamaludeen adds, "I learned that being in a family is the same as being in a business. Same thing." Judi Henderson-Townsend remarks that businesses reflect the character of the entrepreneur: "who you are, what your values are, and what you represent."

What this also means is that the minority women in this study identify with clients, customers, and employees. Their lack of individuation and their flexible ego boundaries create relationships governed by mutuality and empathy such that they see themselves in others. Their gender and minority identifications support the valuation of merging with community, family, and environmental concerns.

This type of relational selfhood is more available to women and minorities (and this holds for the range of minority identities including race, ethnicity, religion, class, sexual orientation, disability, and others) because these groups tend not to develop the individuated selfhood characteristic of empowered majorities. As Chodorow notes, those with "sociocultural superiority" always remain "defensive and insecure" about their identity (Chodorow 2001: 186).

This defensiveness and insecurity leads to the domination model as those in the majority struggle to maintain sociocultural and economic superiority. In *Capital*, Marx writes that the "capital relation" is apparent not only in capitalism but is generally characteristic of relationships in capitalistic societies:

> The capitalist process of production, therefore, seen as a total connected process, i.e. a process of reproduction, produces not only commodities, not only surplus-value, but it also produces and reproduces the capital-relation itself; on the one hand the capitalist, on the other the wage-labourer. (Marx 1887: 724)

Therefore, in practice, capitalist societies operate primarily on the principles of "domination" rather than on the mutuality embodied in the "partnership" model (Eisler 2007). In order to protect their privilege, those in majority positions – positions of power – are more likely to develop individuated selfhood and defend the boundaries of their group affiliations from those devalued "others." As a result, people lose their identification with other human beings (they become dehumanized) and begin to identify only with their own individual interests. Marx writes:

> In estranging from man (1) nature, and (2) himself, his own active functions, his life activity, estranged labor estranges the *species* from man. It changes for him the *life of the species* into a means of individual life. First it estranges the life of the species and individual life, and secondly it makes individual life in its abstract form the purpose of the life of the species, likewise in its abstract and estranged form. (Marx 1844: 76 [emphasis in the original])

In Western cultures, the characteristics of high individuation and competitiveness are generally valued. These majority traits are clearly gendered, but they also have race and class associations as well: the White race and the middle class (in the United States) are considered normative. This demographic becomes the referent for the generic "human." Therefore, most White, middle-class men do not identify in solidarity with a specific race or class community. In fact, David R. Roediger quotes James Baldwin's strident declaration that there is no White community: "The crisis of leadership in the white community is remarkable – and terrifying – because, there is, in fact, no white community" (Roediger 1994: 13). Roediger continues, "It is not merely that whiteness is oppressive and false; it is that whiteness is *nothing but* oppressive and false . . . Whiteness describes, from

Little Big Horn to Simi Valley, not a culture but precisely the absence of culture. It is the empty and therefore terrifying attempt to build an identity based on what one isn't and on whom one can hold back" (Roediger 1994: 13 [emphasis in the original]). One way, then, that normative positions and the attendant advantages are competitively maintained is through lack of empathy with and caring about others.

There is empirical evidence that those who uncritically hold majority perspectives and benefit from them – people in power – have less ability to see the world from the viewpoint of others. In four separate experiments, Galinsky, Magee *et al.* (2006) found that those people with high power status had a harder time than people with low power status in spontaneously adopting another's perspective. They write that those in powerful positions are "less likely to take into account that others did not have access to privileged knowledge suggesting that power leads individuals to anchor too heavily on their own vantage point" (Galinsky, Magee *et al.* 2006: 1068). In their article "Power and Perspectives not Taken" they asked participants to draw the letter "E" on their foreheads. Those participants with "high-power" were more likely to draw the E in a self-oriented direction rather than in a way that others could read it. High-power participants were also less able to read the facial expressions of others: "suggesting a power-induced impediment to experiencing empathy ... Across these studies, power was associated with a reduced tendency to comprehend how others see, think and feel" (Galinsky, Magee *et al.* 2006: 1068).

Highly individuated personalities resonate more with rule-driven systems and abstract principles than they do with emotional attachments and relationships. In her groundbreaking study of gender differences in moral decision-making, Carol Gilligan found that women tend to make moral decisions based on an idea of responsibility towards others while men tend to emphasize the idea of individual rights:

> [Women's] conception of morality as concerned with the activity of care, centers moral development around the understanding of responsibility and relationships, just as [men's] conception of morality as fairness ties moral development with rights and rules ... the morality of rights differs from the morality of responsibility in its emphasis on separation rather than connection, in its consideration of the individual rather than the relationship as primary. (Gilligan 1982: 19)

Again, our position is that self-identity and behavior are culturally and socially rather than biologically driven. As mentioned, in many non-Western cultures, highly individuated selves in either men or women are virtually unknown. Primary identification is with one's community, clan, ancestors, land, and deities. Behaviors associated with gender and race, then, are far from biological destiny. It is not uncommon for individuals to act outside of norms; however, there is also powerful pressure to conform. Normative behavior pertaining to gender and race changes over time, across cultures and often depends on the economic class, age, religion, sexual orientation, and even political affiliation of the individual. Therefore, while social expectations for behavior are constructed *in response* to certain physical characteristics – for example, secondary sex characteristics and skin pigmentation – behavior itself is not biologically ordained.

Given the history of gender development and racial positions in a Western cultural milieu, White men are more likely to be isolated and self-interested, behaving like the so-called "rational" actors. Consequently, the rules of classical economics, which emphasize individual over community interests, provide a welcoming context to their business acquisition, development, and goals. However, these rules are neither a familiar nor a comfortable fit for minority women entrepreneurs.

Regardless, the Henry Higgins refrain persists: women are routinely admonished to act more "like men" and not to "care" about others in order to successfully compete in the business world. In 2010, popular blogger and consultant Clay Shirky published "A Rant about Women." The rant garnered national coverage and was featured in media outlets such as NPR. As an adjunct professor at New York University (NYU), Shirky noticed that his female students were not being offered the best jobs. He felt that this was because "not enough women have what it takes to behave like arrogant self-aggrandizing jerks" (Shirky 2010). He lamented that women were less inclined to lie about their accomplishments and be as shamelessly self-promoting as his male students routinely were:

> There is no upper limit to the risks men are willing to take in order to succeed, and if there is an upper limit for women, they will succeed less. They will also end up in jail less, but I don't think we get the rewards without the risks. (Shirky 2010)

His advice to women? Simply adopt the characteristics associated with masculinity, with male behavior:

> [Women] aren't just bad at behaving like arrogant self-aggrandizing jerks. They are bad at behaving like self-promoting narcissists, anti-social obsessives, or pompous blowhards, even a little bit, even temporarily, even when it would be in their best interests to do so. Whatever bad things you can say about those behaviors, you can't say they are underrepresented

among people who have changed the world. Now this is asking
women to behave more like men, but so what? (Shirky 2010)

According to Shirky, those people who make so-called rational choices,
choices that promote short-term self-interest, succeed because they do
not "care" about the reaction of others, and "not caring works surprisingly
well" (Shirky 2010). Shirky later admitted that he neglected to mention that
women who act "like men" usually do not get the best job offers either. Perceived as being overly aggressive and presumptuous, or as Rudman and
Glick (2001: 743) put it, "insufficiently nice," these women, too, are often
passed over.

But before blaming women for their lack of economic success, we should
turn a critical eye on a *system* that rewards "self-promoting narcissists and
anti-social obsessives." Moreover, this is not merely about women and men,
but also about traits and social responses. Therefore, we need to separate
the sex (female or male) from the set of gendered traits (feminine relational
selves versus masculine individuated selves) and the social response (positive for individuated males, negative for individuated females and positive
for relational females, negative for relational males). Traits can be and are
appropriated by anyone, but social responses reserve rewards for specific
behavior from specific populations.

We also have to remember that the common manifestation of the capitalistic economic system is an example of a domination system. That is
to say, for the system to work, *only some* of the participants are allowed
to be predominantly antisocial and self-interested. The rest of the participants *must* be pro-social and community-oriented, or communities would
not exist. Randall Collins writes, "If people acted on a purely rational basis,
they would never be able to get together and form a society at all . . . The
world would consist of isolated individuals eternally suspicious of each
other" (Collins 1992: 9,11). Rather than a code of conduct towards which
women and others should be encouraged to aspire, rational self-interest
and narcissistic antisocial behavior are merely characteristic of those
who have heretofore ruled the domination system that typifies capitalism.
They can only dominate by subordinating others. These behaviors, and
the values that support them, must be critically examined as contribu-
tors to social and economic inequality, the profusion of unethical business
practices, and the exploitation of environmental resources.

Though the values, assumptions, and perspectives of classical economic
theory have underwritten many businesses and largely dictated social status, they provide only one narrow paradigm or worldview. As mentioned,
these values work best for certain populations – namely, the mythical

norm: "White, thin, male, young, heterosexual, Christian and financially secure" (Lorde 1984: 116). These values are so familiar, they can seem natural, self-evident, and all-encompassing, such that we cease to question them and cannot imagine another way of doing business. In fact, those who do business differently are criticized and admonished to act according to the norm, or as Shirky said, "behave like men."

Yet, given the current exigencies of increasing poverty, growing environmental damage, and lack of sustainable energy, the progress made under conventional Western economic policies and business practices is beginning to reverse itself. For the first time since the Great Depression, children born in the United States are not expected to have a longer lifespan than their parents (Olshansky, Passaro *et al.* 2005). As Norberg-Hodge stated, we have lost perspective on our ways of doing things; there is no "other" with whom we can compare ourselves (Norberg-Hodge 1991: 3). The economic and ecological catastrophes resulting from current business practices can be viewed as an opportunity and an impetus to explore other models, and the minority women entrepreneurs interviewed here provide a different perspective. They demonstrate how to standardize pro-social and community-oriented policies making these policies normative and central to doing business, rather than marginalized and exceptional.

Summary and notes on next chapters

This chapter argues that classical economic theory, and the practices associated with traditional capitalistic enterprise and commonly endorsed in entrepreneurship textbooks, do not reflect a neutral position but instead have their origins in psychosocial perspectives with a race, class, and gender bias towards wealthy, White men. The next three chapters will focus on specific minority women within the interrelated areas of business innovation, partnership, and community membership. It is important to note that these areas are interrelated and mutually informative: the business innovations initiated and employment policies adopted by minority women entrepreneurs are often an outgrowth of their identification with, and loyalty to, community members.

PART 2

5
Minority women as business innovators

As we have said, the business innovations initiated by the minority women in this study are not primarily directed towards increasing the profitability of their businesses. The innovations, like the enterprises themselves, are reflections of the gender identification and minority status of the entrepreneur. Because the innovations distinguish these businesses from others, they make them unique and advance their viability. They are the result of a high degree of empathy and identification with others, a commitment to social and environmental causes and a vision for a better life. These innovations are quintessentially entrepreneurial because they represent a new conceptualization of business. This level of entrepreneurial innovation is referred to as "history-making" (Spinoza, Flores *et al.* 1997: 2).

History-making is the combination of "how entrepreneurship practices, the practices of virtuous citizens, and the practices of solidarity cultivation" come together such that the innovation "changes the way in which we understand and deal with ourselves and things" (Spinoza, Flores *et al.* 1997: 2). It is worth repeating another quotation from these authors in this context:

> The entrepreneur does not have faith in and commitment to herself, but rather to an intuition or an idea that has struck her as requiring the giving up of the self as she knows it for a new life in a new world that everyone will share (Spinoza, Flores *et al.* 1997: 44)

This "giving up of self" is a reference to the giving up of the construction of self as individual, isolated and separate from larger social concerns. It is identification with the social significance of one's actions, as these actions are informed by an understanding of how an innovation provides value to self and others. It is the movement from identifying as a single wave to identifying as part of the ocean.

Reconceptualizing business

History-making, then, can be viewed as the process in which perceptions and assumptions change, in which we detach "from our traditions and habitual forms of life" (Spinoza, Flores *et al.* 1997: 6) and create a shared vision through mutual appreciation of desirable innovation, improvement, and progress. The minority women-owned enterprises studied here invite us to conceive of business in a new way. Before proceeding, it is helpful to review the current typology of business to understand why and how their ventures are different than established definitions. Chapter 4 explores the history, sociology, and theoretical underpinnings of profit-maximizing businesses (Yunus: 2007a: 21): that is, for-profit ventures based on the tenets and assumptions of classical economic theory. Though there are many other kinds of business, for the purposes of this discussion we will examine three additional types: social entrepreneurship, social business, and socially responsible business (i.e., corporate social responsibility programs).

Social entrepreneurship

Though there is no one commonly agreed definition of social entrepreneurship, some aspects commonly associated with social enterprises are that they are non-profit, have a social purpose and/or social mission and attempt to eliminate a need. For instance, the Grameen Bank, though a for-profit business, lends money to impoverished women with the goal of making poverty disappear. Though the minority women-owned businesses featured in our research certainly have a component of social entrepreneurship, they might or might not formally codify that responsibility in a mission statement, and none of them report that they are attempting to make a need disappear. A broad definition of social entrepreneurship is "any innovative initiative to help people" whether economic or non-economic (Yunus 2007a: 32). So in that broad sense, each interviewee in this study is a social entrepreneur; yet the minority women interviewed (with the exception of Rita Chang) do not overtly represent their businesses as social entrepreneurship, nor do they identify themselves as social entrepreneurs.

Social business

Social business is another designation for businesses that are not profit-maximizing ventures. The Grameen Bank would also fit in this category. Yunus writes:

> The company itself may earn a profit, but the investors who support it do not take any profits out of the company except recouping an amount equivalent to their original investment over time. A social business is a company that is cause-driven rather than profit-driven with the potential to act as a change agent for the world. A social business is not a charity. It is a business in every sense. It has to recover its full costs while achieving its social objective. (Yunus 2007a: 22)

The designation "social business" also captures some of the aspects of the enterprises owned by the minority women described here; however, there are notable differences. Though these minority women entrepreneurs create products and policies that respond to social needs, most also run their businesses for profit and not all the profit is turned back to the business. Their profits provide sustenance for themselves and their families, not only sustenance for the business. These women balance making profit with contributing to the social good. Their businesses are not *either* cause-driven *or* profit-driven; they are *both* cause-driven *and* profit-driven. The balance is an active process evident in the general attitude, assumptions, and culture that inform their business decisions, and this balance is also manifest in ongoing, situation-specific negotiation. The subsequent narratives show that in the for-profit companies discussed here, neither the cause nor the profit can be sacrificed to the other and still allow the business to retain its character or its purpose.

Corporate social responsibility or the socially responsible business

To the degree that corporate social responsibility (CSR) has been instituted in for-profit companies there is little dispute that social responsibility is a distant second to profit. Rejecting corporate responsibility as a solution to social problems, Yunus puts it this way:

> CSR takes two basic forms . . . "weak" CSR has the credo: *Do no harm to people or the planet (unless that means sacrificing profit)* . . . [and] "strong" CSR says: *Do good for people and the planet (as long as you can do so without sacrificing profit.)* (2007a: 15 [emphasis in the original])

> Occasionally, through a happy accident, the needs of society and opportunities for high profits happen to coincide. But what happens when profit and CSR do *not* go together? What about when the demands of the marketplace and the long-term interests of society conflict? What will companies do? Experience shows that profit always wins out. (2007a: 17 [emphasis in the original])

Yunus explains that the reason profit invariably wins out is because of the fundamental logic behind business. In other words, the very conceptualization of business practices dictates that when immediate, short-term profit for a private company is at odds with social interests (whether those interests are long-term or short-term), those who make the business decisions are judged as being "irresponsible" if they choose public good over private profit:

> Since managers of a business are responsible to owners or shareholders, they *must* give profit the highest priority. If they were to accept reduced profits to promote social welfare, the owners would have reason to feel cheated and consider corporate social responsibility as corporate financial *irresponsibility*. (Yunus 2007a: 17 [emphasis in the original])

One irony of this model is that it assumes shareholders are not affected by the social impact of the company in which they hold stock. It is as if shareholders are not also people. In this traditional model, shareholders can be compared to truculent diners who insist that their peas not touch their potatoes, ignoring all along that the food goes into the same stomach and will be used to fuel the same body. The dichotomy between private and public interests is similar – the peas might not touch the potatoes for a while, but in the end, we have one planet, one atmosphere, and one set of limited resources. Shareholders might enjoy higher stock prices if a company cuts corners and pollutes waterways, but the same shareholders might also have to drink the water, or watch their taxes increase when the state initiates a clean-up. Even polluting waterways far away can cause unanticipated harm: pollutants from the industrial Midwest of the United States give rise to acid rain on the east coast.

Shared natural resources, whether water, air, or human capital, are part of complex systems that connect all people and interests together over time. Short-term profit-maximization of private interests at the expense of social, cultural, and environmental considerations ignores the social basis of identity – in other words, it ignores our humanity. Yunus writes: "Mainstream free-market theory suffers from a 'conceptualization failure', a failure to capture the essence of what it is to be human" (Yunus 2007a: 18). The corporate social responsibility model does not fit the entrepreneurship practiced by the minority women interviewed in this study. In their businesses, profit simply does not take precedence over social responsibility.

However, during interviews, these entrepreneurs rarely identify their approach to doing businesses as being distinctive – it is as if they are so close to their businesses that they do not understand how different they are. Additionally, there can be some conservatism in the way minority women describe themselves. They do not generally represent themselves as radicals or rebels bent on changing the world. Reasons for this are many. We speculate they might be reluctant to emphasize their status as deviant, as outsiders, thereby inviting additional marginalization. They might be trying to avoid the association with fringe groups, such as environmentalists, or with negative stereotypes of women being unable to handle money, not having an understanding of proper business behavior or being too soft and emotional to make tough decisions. For instance, Pauline Lewis of oovoo design (featured prominently in Chapter 6) reports that "every day" she has to "defend" her decision to have her manufacturing done in Vietnam against pressure to become bigger and move to China where she could increase profits.

To the degree that these entrepreneurs have applied specialized nomenclature to identify their businesses, they have referred to their ventures as "green," as "responsible," and as "progressive." But the phrase that seems to truly capture what sets these businesses apart was coined by Judi Henderson-Townsend. She calls her business "socially conscious." This term fits so well because these businesses sensitively react to the social environment and maintain both an emotional and a cognitive connection to emerging social needs. This is possible because the entrepreneurs have imbued the businesses with themselves, with their own social consciousness. The term "socially conscious" is applicable to every enterprise in this study. Each entrepreneur has her own unique way of guiding her business innovations, but common to all is that business decisions resonate with gender and minority identity, social values, and moral convictions.

One final point regarding the definition of socially conscious business: it is not only the mission, product, services, or policies that qualify these businesses as socially conscious: it is also the way the entrepreneurs invest their money. The Grameen Bank began lending almost exclusively to women not because women borrowers had a formal social mission or because they were necessarily selling products that were of particular social or environmental merit (though of course some of them were). The bank decided to lend to women because women were investing in ways that resulted in a rapid decrease in poverty for themselves, their families, and their communities. They educated their children, hired employees, and invested in community improvements. They helped each other. As they rose above poverty, these women spread the wealth; they invested in others, and consequently whole groups of people were advanced with unprecedented alacrity.

And it is not just poor women who show this proclivity. A 2009 study on philanthropic giving conducted by Ledbury Research reports that affluent U.S. women give almost twice as much money as do affluent men – women donate 3.5% of their wealth to charitable causes compared to 1.8% for men (Frank 2009). According to a 2005 analysis of IRS data by the Grant Thornton National Tax Office, women also give almost 30% more money to their heirs than do men – US$21.7 billion compared to US$16.8 billion (Ransome 2008).

The rest of this chapter will focus on two representative minority women entrepreneurs and the innovations they introduced: Judi Henderson-Townsend, the owner of Mannequin Madness, and Margaret Henningsen of Legacy Bank. As mentioned, these innovations are not geared primarily towards a rapid increase in profit, but they do provide value to the business and also to the community; specifically, they are making history in that they change "the way in which we understand and deal with ourselves and things" (Spinoza, Flores *et al.* 1997: 2). In fact, these innovations and these entrepreneurs invite us to reconceptualize business.

Judi Henderson-Townsend and Mannequin Madness: 'We have the perfect body for you to buy or rent'

It is rare that the minority women interviewed here describe their business in social terms or identify themselves as anything other than traditional business owners. For some, such as Judi Henderson-Townsend, there is an effort to underscore the fact that the social aspect of their enterprise is thoroughly consistent with turning a profit. As mentioned earlier, these entrepreneurs must establish that they are serious business owners with real businesses.

Henderson-Townsend, an African American women with dreadlocks and an authoritative presence, is a mannequin liquidator. She recycles mannequins from national retailers, then rents and sells them to customers all over the United States and Canada; she describes her innovative enterprise as a "unique business niche." A green business based in Oakland, California, Mannequin Madness has won numerous awards, including those from the Environmental Protection Agency (EPA) and Intel, and has been featured on Cable News Network (CNN) and in *Fortune Small Business*. These endorsements give Mannequin Madness credibility and legitimacy, but Henderson-Townsend explains that she still works hard to compensate for her outsider status:

> So few of our customers are African American. I could probably count on two hands the number I've had in the six years I've been in business. Think about it. In the course of a day, how many Black-owned businesses do you see? . . . you still have a long way to go before an Anglo does business with an African American. You have to be conscious to make it comfortable for them. There can be no question or doubt about your professionalism. I can't make a mistake. White men from Texas can make mistakes . . .
>
> I learned I had to watch my language. I used to call my business "wacky." It has been drilled in my head from an early age that I have to be twice as good as my White counterparts. I had to realize that it's not wacky for me to be the best at what I'm doing.

The minority women interviewed here walk a fine line. On the one hand, they are outsiders, and that's good: what they have to offer is an underrepresented, and therefore novel perspective, product, or service. On the other hand, in order to make clients and customers feel comfortable, they must present themselves as normative, knowledgeable, confident professionals – as insiders. Their business motives are both traditional – most of them use their businesses to generate profit, and also progressive – they generate profit in unique ways that have a positive social effect. During the entrepreneurial process, they remain cognizant of both the social and economic impact of their business decisions. Henderson-Townsend explains:

> I didn't start this business because I am an environmentalist. But I began to understand that there is an important environmental component that needed to be communicated. Many of the mannequins that we have would have been thrown into a

landfill because when stores no longer need them, they just want to toss them out. But first of all, it costs stores money to throw them away because they have to have these big dumpsters. Secondly, it's just not an environmentally sound thing to do, to put something that doesn't biodegrade in a landfill. So that's the message I communicate when I make contact with store staff . . . There is an economic benefit and a socially conscious component as well. And I convey that in a way that I am not begging. That they understand, I am not a charity and "poor me" kind of thing . . . Part of the reason we won the Environmental Protection Award was because we were able to quantify how many mannequins we have saved from going into a landfill, what impact that's having and even to show that people who might never buy a mannequin from us will still benefit from us being in business.

It is common for the minority women interviewed here to be modest about their innovative contributions and also to establish that they are normative business owners, that they are regular people. For instance, although Henderson-Townsend rejects the label of environmentalist, Mannequin Madness is not only a green business, but Henderson-Townsend is very innovative in applying green principles to various aspects of her enterprise. Building on the environmental benefit of recycling mannequins, Henderson-Townsend has branched out and also recycles packing material:

We are also a point where people can drop off their Styrofoam peanuts and packing material. We recycle those, too. People drop them off, and we use them to pack our mannequins. Once again, I started that not because I am so noble, but I was trying to cut costs. It costs a lot of money to buy shipping material. But people are willing to bring theirs here at no cost to us. And [customers] are glad they're doing a good thing.

Here again, Henderson-Townsend attributes her environmentalism to practicality rather than nobility – she wants to cut costs – but what business doesn't? She implements a socially conscious innovation and, like every entrepreneur in our study, seamlessly and successfully couples economic and social benefit.

But what about when there is a conflict between values and profit? The prospect of alienating a big client can be especially daunting to a small venture, and a loss of one or two big clients can mean the loss of the entire business. Henderson-Townsend describes a situation where she had to decide whether to voice her values regarding racial diversity, even if she might offend a client and jeopardize a big sale:

This is something I am very proud of. We had a customer doing a catalogue of lingerie, and they wanted eight mannequins. But all the mannequins they selected were Anglo. Well, I knew for a fact – I have a friend who owns a clothing store, and she sold some of their lingerie, and she's African American. So I suggested to them, "Might you want to have one mannequin of color?" And they hadn't even thought about it. And then, once they were aware, they bought several mannequins of color. And this customer ended up being a great client to me, and it really was a conscious effort for me to mention it to them. Before that my husband said to me, "Look, just take the money. Don't try to tell them how to do business." But they need to at least be aware that we, too, want to be seen as objects of desire, to be represented. Here they're going to do this whole catalogue, and not have one face of color? So they ended up buying an Asian mannequin, an African American and one that looks Latina. But I thought, if I hadn't been there at that moment to say that, they wouldn't have thought about it. So I'm just doing what I can in my own little corner of the world, whether it's being the unexpected person showing up at a technology fair – because who thinks an African American woman with dreadlocks would be there? Or telling people that mannequins come in different colors and sizes.

One reason that Henderson-Townsend made the decision to voice her values and risk the sale was that she did not see it as an either/or choice; she perceived it as a both/and possibility. Her husband's perception of the situation was that she would either prioritize her values or prioritize the money from the sale. His perception is marked by rigid boundaries between two discrepant and discrete outcomes. But Henderson-Townsend thought that she could have both, and that by cultivating a relationship with the client based on her values, she might not only get the money from this particular sale, she might also gain a long-term client – and that's what happened. Because Henderson-Townsend perceives her business as an extension of herself, imagining that both desired outcomes might be merged together and accomplished was easier for her than for her husband. It feels natural to her to integrate her personal and social values with her business practices and create an economically thriving culture that reflects who she is. She is her business, and she describes her business as the relationship among her product, her employees, her customers, and her investors. In fact, Henderson-Townsend believes the tie that binds them all together is the culture she creates through her principles and values:

Sometimes we put a nice little message in the mannequin boxes so when the customer opens them, they read it, and it makes them happy. It's part of our whole culture. That is part of communicating. You're always communicating all the time. The more consistent you are, the better it is for everybody. Customers have a better understanding of who you are and what you stand for. When you get to the point when you have investors, they, too, can see what you stand for. And employees – you know they feel like: "OK, if I'm working for this company, these are some of the principles they stand for." Everything we do should be consistent in that. And not like a canned kind of mission statement. I'm not looking for that. But really something conveying the message of who you are, what your values are, and what you represent.

Matthew Stewart writes, "Anyone who has studied Aristotle will know that 'values' aren't something you bump into from time to time during the course of a business career. All of business is about values all of the time" (Stewart 2006). It is only when we pretend we are not connected to other people, and that larger social concerns do not affect us as individuals, that we allow business decisions their own autonomous sphere.

Margaret Henningsen and Legacy Bank: focusing on the underserved

Named "Financial Services Company of the Year" in 2009 by *Black Enterprise Magazine,* Legacy Bank was founded a decade earlier by Margaret Henningsen (with partners Delores Sims and Shirley Lanier), and is the first bank in the United States founded by African American women. The bank is an imposing, stately, marble building in the heart of Milwaukee, emblazoned with the emblem of an eagle "because they fly over everything," and called Legacy because the "focus of the bank is to create a difference for our children."

When we met in 2006, Henningsen was about to turn 60. An inveterate optimist, her professional demeanor is frequently interrupted by a hearty laugh that she seems unable and unwilling to repress. Henningsen started Legacy Bank in what she describes as "a moment of temporary insanity" prompted by the need for a community bank to serve the central city of Milwaukee and beyond. Legacy Bank's mission is a commitment to "building businesses, increasing home ownership, developing the economic base of the community, and creating wealth, with a focus on the underserved."

When I ask Henningsen why she wanted to start a bank, of all things, she begins by giving me a history lesson. Referencing Bill Dedham's work on racial discrimination by mortgage lenders (a series of articles in the *Atlanta Journal-Constitution* entitled "The Color of Money" that won the Pulitzer Prize in 1989 for investigative journalism), Henningsen explains that the primary reason she founded Legacy Bank was that lending and banking services were being systematically withheld from African Americans:

> I decided after my 50th birthday in 1997 that I would start my own bank and that was driven by my dissatisfaction by the way banks were lending to women and minorities in the city of Milwaukee. [The banks] weren't lending. They were not approving the loans. And a few years prior to that – I had actually been thinking about this during the moment of temporary insanity! – there were several national studies that were done that indicated that Milwaukee led the nation 4 to 1 in denials to minorities who applied for mortgage loans. Even when they compared apples to apples, they found that banks here were not lending to people who were Black . . . So we made the national news, and when I say "we," I mean Milwaukee. For more than a year, every major network covered this: *60 Minutes*, all of the cable news channels. They all talked about Milwaukee incessantly – how the ratio was 4 to 1 that Blacks were discriminated against – and so a consortium was formed of all the banks. The mayor, the governor, the county executive, pulled all the major financial institutions together and said, "You better fix this!" [pause] It wasn't being fixed fast enough for me.
>
> The second thing that happened was that there were several national studies done – and one was done here locally by the University of Wisconsin, Milwaukee – that looked at lending patterns for [loans] to start-up businesses to support entrepreneurs or to help businesses that were in existence and needed an infusion of capital. And one of the studies looked at the top 50 cities in the United States and mapped or graphed out how lending was done by zip codes . . . They had a grid that showed the amount of money that went into each zip code from the worst, or lowest amount, to the highest amount. And we were 50. Out of the 50 cities they looked at, we were 50, as far as capital that was lent in certain areas of the city based on zip codes. Now, I could have saved them all a lot of work, and answered all of these questions and told them all this from my own experience.

Denied mortgage loans, African Americans could not own homes; denied business loans, they could not start enterprises to support themselves. These lending policies were effectively running Blacks out of town.

Sociologist Robert Merton theorized that social expectations dictate our goals and the means to reach them. For instance, in current U.S. society, becoming wealthy is a common objective, and the normative method for acquiring wealth is to go to school, study hard, and secure a well-paid job. But Merton also realized that many individuals, while desiring the same goals, can be denied access to the normative methods of achieving them. For instance, obstacles to education or barriers to employment might not change the desire to be wealthy, but can seriously impede an individual's ability to secure a well-paid job. According to Merton, those individuals who circumvent normative methods to achieve their goals – in other words, those individuals who employ deviant means – are "innovators" (Levin 1994: 393). Technically, Merton was referring to illegal activity – for example, those who rob banks to become wealthy.

But when normative paths are inadequate or unavailable, there are more subtle, and legal, remedies. For instance, in the last example, Henderson-Townsend uses innovation to challenge the perceptions and under-representation of African Americans by introducing clients to the idea of using mannequins of color. Innovation, then, can be defined as behavior that uses atypical methods to achieve normative goals. In the case of Legacy Bank, the innovation is directed towards reducing prejudice and discrimination against African Americans who seek bank loans. Both Henderson-Townsend and Henningsen create "success out of hatred" (Butler 1991: 6). Their commitment to social justice, and their identification with the values of racial and gender equality, along with their undeniable outrage, demands that they personally develop solutions that champion the African American community, and that create available paths to normative success.

Though she is a successful and well-respected citizen of Milwaukee, Henningsen continues to identify with those who have been "underserved" in the larger social and economic systems. Butler notes that there is a tradition of solidarity and mutual identification within racial minorities, and he specifically mentions African American entrepreneurs.

> Because they are grounded in a unique tradition of self-help, their role models, funding for education and aspirations are grounded in their communities rather than in white communities; they support historically black organizations and institutions, even when they live today in integrated communities.

No matter what their achievement in life, they never refer to Afro-American institutions, which were established by Afro-Americans, as inferior. Their positions in life today – which are, for the most part, related to business, the professions (such as doctors, lawyers, professors, dentists, and the like), are the result of the self-help values of their parents, which were passed down through generations. (Butler 1991: 235)

Like Henderson-Townsend and the other minority women entrepreneurs interviewed for this study, Henningsen merges or blends her individual perspective with a community perspective making it difficult to distinguish between the two. Such flexible ego boundaries mark her orientation as communitarian or, in Butler's terminology, as collectivist.

In addition to the general mission of serving the underserved, a specific innovation that characterizes Legacy Bank is the First Accounts Financial Liberty Program. This program targets the "unbanked," those adults who do not have and cannot easily acquire a bank account. Most people without a bank account are low-income earners, and young, ethnic, and/or racial minorities. Without a bank account, many are forced to rely on third-party check-cashing businesses. These businesses often charge exorbitant fees to cash pay checks and provide other financial services, such as short-term loans. These so-called "payday" loan shops are so numerous that according to a 2004 Ford Foundation Report, "there were more payday loan shops in America than McDonald's restaurants" (Stoddard 2007). The First Accounts Financial Liberty Program not only provides a bank account at Legacy, but First Accounts customers are offered financial education and hands-on mentoring. Through this process, customers learn how to manage their money, avoid the high fees associated with payday loan shops and might even be able to improve their credit report. Henningsen explains that many unbanked people never had a bank account, while others had bounced a check or two and landed themselves in ChexSystems, a national database of consumers who have had problems with their checking accounts (Stoddard 2007).

According to Henningsen, "Once someone gets into that system, it is nearly impossible to get out" (Stoddard 2007: 6). Every incident stays on an individual's ChexSystems record for five years from the date the incident was reported. According to Stoddard, most banks now say, "Our bank policy is that we will not open a checking account for you if you have one or more incidents reported to ChexSystems" (Stoddard 2007: 6). While most banks turn away those who have had trouble, Legacy reaches out to them.

The 2004 Ford Foundation Report described the First Accounts Financial Liberty Program as the perfect balance between "high touch" and high tech (Stoddard 2007: 6). Three times a week, Henningsen holds financial education classes at partner social service agencies. There, potential customers learn how to manage check and savings accounts, credit cards, and loans – everything from how to read a bank statement to how to apply for a home mortgage loan. Those who take the classes are not required to open an account with Legacy. These classes contribute to the financial viability of the attendees and help create better customers for any bank (Stoddard 2007: 6). Judy Dunlap, Vice President of Audit and Compliance at Legacy Bank, comments: "Many of our customers were turned away by other banks when they tried to open an account or get a loan. After working with us, and demonstrating their creditworthiness, our customers are sought after by every bank in town" (Stoddard 2007: 7).

The policies of Legacy Bank are not only socially responsible, they are socially conscious: they heal wounds endured by low-income, marginalized people. Grameen Bank reaches out to those people other banks declare uncreditworthy, and Legacy reaches out to people other banks deem untrustworthy. Legacy invests in a socially and economically disadvantaged population, and the risk has paid off. Its customer base and the surrounding community have become stronger, more financially fit and more economically solvent. By giving the underserved access to bank loans, Henningsen is changing the sense of identity in a population of African Americans who have grown accustomed to being discredited: those people who, turned down by banks and effectively kept from attaining the social goals of home ownership and economic independence, lost their confidence and their sense of worth.

As we have seen, the creation of selfhood is a process wherein the cumulative, internalized sense of who we are is continuously created and recreated through interaction with others (Collins 1992). Ascribed characteristics such as race, ethnicity, and gender resonate with social meaning and affect the process of mutuality, social power, and the creation of self and other. In the process of helping others, Henningsen is also transforming her own identity. An African American woman who once suffered in an abusive marriage and was forced to declare bankruptcy herself, she is now in a position to extend economic resources, confidence and self-respect to others:

> They know Legacy is here . . . But people still come with this trepidation. And they'll say it to us. I'll say, "What took you so long to get here?" "Well, I was worried – I thought you'd say no." We hear that a lot, because they have been put in a position for so long where people have said to them, "Your

business will not succeed. You're not bankable. You can't have a second chance. You'll never become a homeowner. Your children won't go to college."

When you keep hearing this over and over again . . . and see, in our country, Blacks have a lot to overcome because we have hundreds of years of being told, "You're inferior." And even people who are full of self-confidence are not full of self-confidence. If you're a minority, some of those things – I don't care how good you are – just never go away, because you experience, on a regular basis, demeaning things. If I walk into a room and nobody knows I'm Margaret Henningsen who started Legacy Bank, I'm subject to get treated the same way as someone who would walk into that room who is on welfare. We experience that all the time. So when our customers come in here they bring experiences with them that are both historical (that they haven't had themselves) and recent, that they have had themselves . . . I don't know that as Blacks, or even as women, that you get 100% away from whatever it is that makes you feel you are just not quite at the same level as that White male . . .

And so I think that what happens is, in our market, we deal more than any other financial institution, except for other minority-owned financial institutions, with people's emotions, whereas it's all cut and dried at the major institutions because it's just about going in and filling out the application. But when [our customers] come here, there's a relationship that develops because the assumption is, you look like me, so I know you know what I'm saying [laughs].

And that's very true because we do know what they're saying . . . We're more likely to see our customers outside of the bank socially, because we may go to the same places. And so, there's just a different kind of relationship that's there. But the common bond between us that makes the banking relationship work better, is the common experiences that we have had over our lifetimes.

On the one hand, Henderson-Townsend and Henningsen demonstrate radical autonomy and self-empowerment: they identify a problem and take decisive action to solve it. On the other hand, they have flexible rather than rigid ego boundaries: rather than directing their energy solely towards the self-oriented goals of wealth and prestige – as would the rugged individualist or instrumental rational actor of classical economic theory – they enable and ennoble the community of people with whom they identify: women and African Americans.

According to Butler, the model of entrepreneurship as individual self-promotion neglects key aspects of solidarity and forgets the non-rational, cultural, religious, and emotional motivations that Weber first identified in entrepreneurs:

> The theoretical preoccupation of scholars with rugged individualism has led to a misinterpretation of the ethnic self-help experience. The collectivist approach, with an emphasis on self-help institutions, stresses the cultural side in explaining the economic stability of ethnic groups, and also brings to bear the idea that these institutions have more of an influence on the development of economic stability through business activity than through the process of assimilation. Collectivism concentrates on the "cultural baggage" of a group as the major explanatory variable. (Butler 1991: 23)

Henningsen's explanation of what drove her to the "moment of temporary insanity" when she decided to embark on the long and difficult process of founding Legacy Bank, resonates with family values, personal experiences, a sense of moral purpose, and, as Butler notes, "cultural baggage":

> So my father looked at my mother and said, "Why would she want *that* job?" And my mother looked at him and said, "Because she thinks she can change the world."
>
> I don't know if everybody should be as drastic as I was and go out there and start a bank. But when I was 19, in the '60s, the civil rights movement was at its height, and I used to visit with my grandmother on a regular basis to keep her up to date with what I was doing. I had my Angela Davis natural and my dashiki and Black power and all that kind of stuff. Sociology and anthropology were two things I loved. And I really wanted to even major in them. So I started telling her.
>
> She said, "Anthropology, what's that?" And I started to explain: "Oh, you know, it's the study of man and how we came out of the ocean," and I was just babbling away in my 19-year-old way. And I looked at Grammar. She was just sitting there. No expression on her face, and she didn't say anything. Finally, she said, "Well, Margaret Jean, that class is a waste of your time and money." And I said, "Why?" She said, "Because we all know God started the world, and he created man and woman." And my 19-year-old mouth went into gear before my brain did, and I said to her, "You know, Grammar, I'm not even sure I believe there is a God." And I actually lived to tell about it! [laughs] But the look on her face told me that I had crossed over into the possible land of the dead. And she said, "Well, why do you say that?" I said, "Because look at all the things that are happening

to Black people. And if there really is a God, then why aren't we having a better life? And why are we being treated so bad? And why isn't He doing something to help us?" And she looked at me and said, "That's why He put you here."

And you know what? I'm telling you, every time somebody asks me to do something, I can hear her saying, "That's why He put you here."

I do know that what finally made me make up my mind [to start a bank] is I just got tired of people coming into my office and saying: "Can you help me? Because I've been everywhere else, and people told me I should come talk to you, and you could help me own a home."

And so because I was real active in the civil rights movement, you get to this point where you go "How dare they treat us like this? And it only has to do with the color of my skin!" Ahhhhhh! [screams in exasperation]. So, you know, now I have my own bank, and I can do whatever I want [laughs]. It doesn't work exactly that way but . . . a lot of things happened [in Milwaukee] that were not given proper attention. And one of them was [lack of bank loans] for people being able to start their own business or purchase a home. And that was my thinking with Legacy Bank. That if major financial institutions did not want to support our community, we had to have a way to support it ourselves. And, thus, the moment of temporary insanity!

Henningsen's goal is to make money, but not primarily for herself. She wants to make money for the Black community in the central city of Milwaukee, a group of people with whom she identifies – she recognizes herself in them. In this way, Henningsen exemplifies the characteristic of "giving up of the self" (Spinoza, Flores *et al.* 1997: 44). That is to say, she does not identify as a separate entity with an isolated biographical past and future; instead, her behavior and decisions are consciously situated within a matrix of connections to a larger culture and history.

The minority women interviewed here take radical steps in the name of social consciousness and take responsibility and ownership for the consequences. However, as mentioned in Part 1, beginning on page 109, their behavior is also a manifestation of flexible ego boundaries – boundaries that traditional psychoanalytic language derogatorily refers to as "weak." Flexible ego boundaries are more common to the formation of a relational self and, in the current context of gendered social expectations, more common to women. Rigid or – to use the traditional language – "strong" ego boundaries are more common to men (Chodorow 2001: 175).

As already discussed, the preoccupation with and accreditation of male development and male personality structure means that the flexible ego boundaries that characterize female gender identity are viewed as potentially problematic: a liability rather than a strength. Chodorow writes:

> The cases I describe suggest that there is a tendency in women toward boundary confusion and a lack of sense of separateness from the world. Most women do develop ego boundaries and a sense of separate self. However, most women's ego and object-relational issues are concerned with this tendency on one level (of potential conflict, of experience of object-relations), even as on another level (in the formation of ego boundaries and the development of a separate identity) the issues are resolved. (Chodorow 1978: 110)

In prevalent cultural definitions of success and desirability, it is common to both psychological and economic theory to applaud the instrumentally rational, isolated actor who possesses rigid ego boundaries that delineate a separate self – in other words, those characteristics more often associated with White men. In contrast, characteristics such as flexible ego boundaries, altruistic behavior, and a merging of self and other, characteristics more often associated with women – especially minority women – are often pathologized. Sociological theory, however, can be used to understand the exultation of the individual self as a cultural artifact, as a means to accommodate the current economic arrangements and as a way to advance the interests of select populations. As long as individual wealth accumulation defines our economic ideals, those who deviate from that mode of behavior might well be seen as unsuccessful, even unstable.

However, given the current state of economic and environmental damage caused by such definitions, we might begin to redefine good business as balancing wealth accumulation with social values. Spinoza, Flores *et al.* write:

> The entrepreneurs worth thinking about are the ones who are sensitive to how the problem that they sense has its roots in our pervasive way of living, our lifestyle, either in our culture as a whole or in some more or less self-contained domain. (Spinoza, Flores *et al.* 1997: 41)

We submit that the entrepreneurs who run socially conscious businesses are the ones worth thinking about.

6

Minority women in partnership with producers, vendors, and customers

Alienated work and the development of gendered selves

One of the biggest challenges to and emancipatory opportunities of entrepreneurship is the potential to reconceptualize the workplace and therefore remedy the alienation that often characterizes the modern relationship between workers and the product of their labor. To quote William Scott Green once again, entrepreneurship can be "an antidote to the alienation that both Marx and Weber saw as the ineluctable trait of capitalist modernity. In some basic sense, the entrepreneur is at one with the enterprise of her or his devising" (Green 2005: 4).

Though many authors have chronicled the alienation experienced by service workers (Hochschild 1983), there is perhaps no greater alienation than is found routinely on a factory floor. Marx was among the first to recognise the effect of the mechanized age on the meaning and experience of work:

> Marx defined meaningful work as work in which the worker maintains control of the creative process . . . He argued that industrial assembly lines would rob workers of their feelings of control over the creative process. There is a big difference between building an entire engine and merely being responsible for turning one bolt . . . Because [the creative process] is

not possible in assembly lines, such work is inevitably alienating (meaningless) to the worker. A worker may need to keep
working at an alienating job because it is the only way to earn
a living, but it becomes a matter of stultifying routine. (Levin
1994: 395)

In *Learning to Labour,* his ethnographic study of young, White, working-
class British men, Paul Willis investigates the formation of masculine
characteristics in response to alienation and class domination manifest,
in part, in factory labor. MacLeod explains that these young men, referred
to as "the lads," achieve their masculinity through participating in factory
work. He writes, "The lads equate manual labour with masculinity, a trait
highly valued by their working-class culture; mental labour is associated
with the social inferiority of femininity" (Willis 1995: 19).

Willis is similar to Chodorow in finding that the psychosociological construction of masculinity is an essential ingredient in the perpetuation of
inequality in capitalist societies. Willis, however, uses a Marxist foundation
to integrate both gender and class reproduction, and unlike Chodorow,
focuses on male rather than female development.

Conceiving gender identity as an interactive, negotiated process where
masculine and feminine behavior are achieved and developed in relation
to each other, Irene Padavic reminds us that "gender is enacted in institutions, one of the most important of which is work" (Padavic 1991: 279-80).
In her study of how gender is created in the traditionally male-dominated
world of factory work, Padavic found that the masculinity promoted and
created in factories is "formal, stylized" and "exists partly as a defense
against the alienation and humiliation . . . implicit in factory work" (Padavic
1991: 280). Ben Hamper, whose memoir *Rivethead* recounts deep ambiva-
lence about his years as a factory worker, describes his first experience
wielding a spot-welder on the assembly line at General Motors:

It took some doing, but within two or three days, I was an
accomplished spot-welder. I found out how to tilt the machine
so that the sparks flew out sideways and not straight down
on my head. There was something very hale and manly about
husking that mean hunk of hell once you got the hang of it. It
gave me a sense of complete reign – King Rat, Ball-Buster Goliath, the hysteric bombardier makin' flame-broiled waffle mince
out of the rib cage of BAD TRUCK POWER. This crunchin' dino-
saur was my bitch. A flame-snortin', black goose Magnum.
(Hamper 1986: 39)

For Hamper, the spot-welder has become what Sherry Turkle calls an "evocative object" (Turkle 2007: 50). Turkle's concept of evocative objects refers to those objects onto which people project their subjectivity – in other words, those objects identified as symbolic representations or physical extensions of self. For instance, Turkle describes technology writer Annalee Newitz as unable to determine where "her laptop ends and she begins" (Turkle 2007: 52). Akin to Newitz's laptop, the spot-welder is a reification of Hamper's male body and masculine self – of strength, power, dominance, all characteristics embedded in the current social definition of manhood.

According to Padavic, the strident opposition towards women entering these factory environments reflects a "fear that masculine turf would be feminized" (Padavic 1991: 280). Yet Padavic also found that the presence of women in predominantly male workplaces "was useful for *confirming* masculinity" (Padavic 1991: 290 [emphasis in the original]). In her own experience as a coal worker, Padavic encountered sexist attitudes, isolation, paternalism, and alienation on the factory floor. She writes, "Men may constrain women to behave and respond in accordance with stereotypes, and gender ideology is perpetuated. More immediately, such treatment produces negative effects which include the instillation of fear and self-doubt" (Padavic 1991: 289). She writes of her own response to her male supervisor's paternalism:

> [My supervisor] described in detail how dangerous the plant was ("if your long hair gets caught in a gear . . ."). He reassured me that if I were in an accident he would take me to the emergency room and wait there "so you don't get scared." Importantly, the result of the dire warnings was that I was jumpy and afraid on the job for the first few weeks. By treating me as if I were a stereotypically feminine woman – afraid of big machinery and liable to be clumsy around it or unable to control it – he succeeded in some respects in turning me into a feminine women afraid of big machinery, which had not been a prominent component of my identity before. (Padavic 1991: 286)

The factory floor, therefore, is not only a site of workplace alienation, but also of class reproduction and the reproduction of gender inequality.

The reconceptualization of factory work

Few of the entrepreneurs in this study manufacture goods; however, Pauline Lewis of oovoo design does. Lewis identifies as Asian American and lives outside Washington DC. She has a quick smile and an infectious laugh. Like all the entrepreneurs we interviewed, Lewis is passionate about her product: handmade handbags that she and a Vietnamese woman design together. A central part of her business mission is to help South-East Asian women, and for Lewis, that means it is not enough that business ownership gives her the ability to be "at one" (Green 2005: 4) with her enterprise; she also shelters her producers from the workplace alienation typically encountered in manufacturing environments and gives them an opportunity to engage in creative processes.

As we have found, relational selves – selves constructed in relation to and connection with others – are guided by a morality of responsibility (Gilligan 1982: 19). Those minority women entrepreneurs who employ others and/or outsource production feel a keen and pervasive responsibility for workers. In addition to Lewis, Barbara Manzi and Margaret Henningsen have businesses large enough to employ full-time workers. These entrepreneurs navigate their role as employer with a great degree of thoughtfulness and sensitivity – so much so that their decisions regarding remuneration and employee benefits would be considered irrational, naive, even foolish, by conventional business standards.

This chapter concentrates on Pauline Lewis and her reconfiguration of factory work as meaningful and creative; therefore, her policies and treatment of workers are the focus here. Lewis's refusal to subject workers to the onus of traditional factory work, her reconfiguration of the typical corporate hierarchy and her challenge to gender constructions within the workplace are not merely employment policies; they are important entrepreneurial innovations that provide sharp contrast to conventional business practices. Additionally, Lewis's business decisions also reflect her identification with and loyalty to communities – specifically to the communities of American and Asian women, and of socially conscious business owners.

Pauline Lewis and oovoo design: *omnia ex ovo* (everything from an egg)

> I want to tell you how I started three years ago. I actually started when I was backpacking across Vietnam, and I was invited to observe a women's cooperative. From the moment I walked in, I was mesmerized. There sat a group of women, about eight to ten women, all sitting in a sewing circle. They had their own

little pieces of embroidery work they were doing. There was soft chatter, and there was tea. They had some children on the side who were being looked after by someone else, and they invited me into their sewing circle. And I thought . . . I need to invite all of America to be part of this sewing circle. It was very peaceful. It was quiet. I wanted to capture that moment for American women. So that's how I started my business three years ago. Since then we've grown to half a million dollars, and we're still growing.

In her catalogue featuring hand-embroidered bags, purses, and wallets, Pauline Lewis playfully asks:

Does oovoo mean something? You bet it does! Oovoo has its roots in the Latin *ovo,* which is the female egg. The O on Oovoo represents the embroidery circles I work with in Vietnam; oovoo is the circle that connects producers, vendors and customers. (Lewis 2008)

Her narrative is a warm embrace of women and womanhood:

We [also] do embroidery work on the inside [of the handbags] because that really represents a woman to me – we're not just pretty on the outside; we're pretty on the inside. So we want to reflect that in our bags.

Lewis shares her company structure and business policies immediately with her customer, who, she imagines, is part of the circle:

I started oovoo because of my love for handcrafted art and a desire to build a business based on positive relationships among women. Oovoo is a collaboration between one woman in Virginia [Lewis] and one woman in Vietnam. This alliance has grown to support hundreds of women in Vietnam: all workers are paid 15% above market rate and given a month's salary as bonus during the Vietnamese New Year. They are also given an annual, all-expense paid vacation in Vietnam. (Lewis 2008)

Certainly Lewis sells bags, but her product is a reification of her personal values, the social mission of oovoo and her vision of how businesses should be run. Like every entrepreneur in this study, Lewis has a personal vision of what the workplace should be like and was motivated to open a business in order to contribute to wider social change (Johnson 2004). The symbol of the feminine, the egg, and the egalitarian circle transplants the typical business imagery of the phallic pyramid and top-down corporate hierarchy. She describes her business as a set of relationships beginning in "collaboration" with a Vietnamese woman and an "alliance" that supports hundreds of women in Vietnam.

Instead of using the "market" value as the standard wage for her employees, or taking advantage of high unemployment rates by undercutting workers to increase profit, Lewis deliberately partners with a factory that pays more than the typical wage, and in addition, awards a month's salary as a bonus in recognition of the cultural importance of the Vietnamese New Year. Not only are employees provided with time off; incredibly, oovoo provides each worker an annual *all-expenses paid* vacation. These policies and others put oovoo in stark contrast to companies that prioritize profit maximization where owners are primarily trying to "get rich" (Timmons and Spinelli 2007: 115), or where being "competitive" is the rhetoric that organizes and drives decision-making. In this way, Lewis is not only a business owner; she is truly an entrepreneur.

The workplace policies at the factory employed by oovoo design simply do not exist in enterprises typically represented in business schools, unless those enterprises are marginalized under the rubrics of "social entrepreneurship," "social business," or not-for-profit businesses – and even then, the attention and respect paid to workers who make the bags for oovoo design is revolutionary.

Though she spoke of oovoo as manifesting her values of fair and just labor relations, of creating products that embody beauty, integrity, and cooperation, and finally, as a source of personal fulfillment and happiness, it is important to note that during our interviews, Lewis did not categorize herself as a social entrepreneur or depict her business as social entrepreneurship. Oovoo is a for-profit company, but it is not primarily profit-driven. Lewis puts profit on a par with other goals and rejects the adversarial, conflict-ridden business model governed by instrumental rationality; therefore, we apply the term "socially conscious business" to her enterprise. Because Lewis includes policies that are not aimed primarily at maximizing profit, within the context of classical economic theory and conventional management practices, these policies – and Lewis herself – would be considered irrational and irresponsible. But that is only because rationality is narrowly defined as instrumentality and responsibility is defined as profit maximization.

Different kinds of rationality

Max Weber makes a distinction between formal rationality and substantive rationality. Formal rationality refers to particular interventions intended to create particular effects. It is linear and precise, with a singular goal. Formal rationality is strategic and instrumental: opening a business to get rich is an example of formal rationality. Substantive rationality, on the other hand, is holistic, reticular, value-driven, and cognisant of the interdependency of interconnected objectives and perspectives. Richard Munch writes:

> Formal rationality is limited to specific causal knowledge about specific means–end relationships and to the realization of a specific end and one substantial value. Substantive rationality has to include many substantial values; it has to look at the whole world as something that should be made better. (Munch 1994: 174-75)

In a business governed by substantive rationality, the entrepreneur's social, personal, moral, and political values are manifest in her business practices, and on a par with the recognition that the enterprise must also make money. Hoping to post US$1 million in sales by the end of 2007, Lewis is also clear that money is only part of her business objectives – in fact, making money is not enough. It is common to hear that businesses must remain competitive to survive, but for Lewis, oovoo not only has to make a profit; the work also has to be emotionally, socially, and personally satisfying. At one point, despite increasing profits, Lewis lost the emotional connection with her company, and she considered shutting down:

> Last year my goal was to make a half million [dollars in sales], and we pretty much did that. Then it was: now what? It's just going to be more work. The goal is a million – and it became very goal-oriented. I lost the feel, the emotion, of why I started the business: what it was all about. And so, I was seriously thinking of closing my business and thinking, "You know what? Maybe I've had fun and it's time to move on."

Lewis got her drive and energy back when she won "Make Mine a Million," a contest created by the entrepreneur Nell Merlino, with the objective of getting a million women to the million dollar mark by 2010. Participating in the contest not only gave oovoo credibility and recognition, but also made Lewis realize how isolated she had become. In order to stay in business, solidarity with other women entrepreneurs was "so crucial."

> I like to cultivate an openness so that we can share information. I happen to know quite a few bag designers who are in the industry, and we share information openly. It is just part of my belief that when you do that you end up getting a lot in return.

So, when we're running a business that can be a very cut-and-dried or very objective-driven [process], it's really making that connection with others that helps spur us on and drives us to that next goal, and helps us achieve that next thing.

To use Turkle's language, Lewis's evocative object is her company; she does not know where she ends and it begins. She articulates the fluid boundaries between herself and oovoo design:

Part of my mission statement is to help other women in South-East Asia and give back to women in South-East Asia. That's part of my core mission and my company's core values. And I say "we" because I am my company. Those two things are very closely intertwined at this point in time.

Born in Malaysia, Lewis has lived in Singapore, Hong Kong, and the United States. An important part of Lewis's self-identity is her identification as a minority woman, which for Lewis means weaving many facets of gender, ethnic, and national identities together:

I have identified myself as Asian American since college really. Prior to that, there was some rejection of the Asian culture and really wanting to be more American, so to speak. [Now] I have a very strong identification with my Asian culture. And I'm very, very OK with it. It's one of those things where I joke about it and it's not something that I am remotely ashamed of. There were times where I have been, but that's not the space where I am right now.

In truth, what really happened is that in college I developed gender awareness. I took a lot of Women's Studies classes, and my last year I took a class on Third World Women and that really opened my eyes . . . but I didn't start to identify [as Asian American] until I went to Oberlin College for a year as a resident coordinator . . . Oberlin has a strong history of Asian American voices. I lived in a place called Asian House, and all the students I worked with were living in Asia House – and that really helped me! I could step back and see what they were going through and then that process was really what helped me identify myself as Asian American.

One of the things I saw at Oberlin that I didn't necessarily see at Hamilton College [her alma mater] was the ability for students to embrace their culture and be very proud of it . . . but still declare themselves Americans – Asian Americans . . . That really brought to my attention this idea that you can have your cake and eat it too, so to speak. That you can really be

proud of your Asian origins and your roots, but still be American and still . . . come out with a voice that is unique and different . . . the Asian American voice.

The stereotype of Asian students – studious, doesn't
cause any trouble, very involved with school work, not very
social . . . I tended to be put in a group when I went to Hamilton, so when I went to Oberlin and saw Asian American students who were loud and not afraid to speak their minds and
really protest and do all those things, I was like: "Wow! This
is kinda cool!" . . . and it allowed me to understand that there
was another way to be Asian in America and that was Asian
American. I didn't have to be just Asian and have no voice and
be demure and be quiet and be studious. There was a whole
other voice that I could speak with.

Like her experience being a racial minority in college, as a minority woman,
Lewis was also unusual in corporate culture:

I was in the corporate world for ten years. I worked in marketing research . . . and the normative voice – all my clients –
tended to be White males. We did high-level reporting to the
board or CXO level. Even in Asia, there is a tendency for it to be
White males, or at least males, and that was the norm.

In Oberlin College there was a normalization of Asian identity; at the
Women's Business Center of Northern Virginia, where Lewis got her entrepreneurship training, there was also a normalization of women business
owners. Lewis talks extensively about how important it was for her to see
other women who are successful entrepreneurs:

So when I decided to leave the corporate culture, the corporate environment, and start my own business, I was so lucky
to even think of the Women's Business Center as the first place
to go. That little seed of starting my own business was cultivated here because [it was] the norm – it was just women,
and I had role models here. There were women here who had
already started their business who I could identify with and
say, "Yes! That could be me in two years or in three years." And
that's what really gave me the confidence and the inspiration
to really take that seed and grow it.

This is a fantastic time for women to start what they've
always dreamed of starting, and I think the reason for that
is we have examples out there now. Back in the 1960s and
'70s, it was really hard to find. These women were few and far
between. Now we have women at the board and CXO level. We

have women who have been doing this for seven to ten years, and we can see them. They're visible, and we are talking about them, and that is making all the difference in the world to have other women that you can look at and say, "Yes. If she can do it, I can do it." And I know it goes as far as being able to call her up . . . and I'm going to call her and ask her for her help.

Despite the normalization of women entrepreneurs at the Women's Business Center and the increasing presence of women in high-level corporate positions, women are still a minority in business, especially in manufacturing, and Lewis ran into resistance from male factory owners in Vietnam.

She describes the process of finding a manufacturer for her bags as being both a challenge and an opportunity:

I already knew that I pretty much wanted to do handbags . . . So I went to Vietnam with the understanding that I was going to meet bag manufacturers. And I met quite a few . . . all of whom were male. They owned their own manufacturing company or factory. And the factories I visited were much like a lot of factories you would see across Asia. Just sort of, you know, lots of machines, very noisy inside. And that wasn't what I wanted. Plus, they really didn't take me seriously. They probably saw this American woman who looked bored and was probably using her husband's money or something. And that's when I really said to myself, "Well, if the men aren't going to take me seriously, where are the women? Let me see if I can find a couple of women to take me seriously in Vietnam." And I did!

I found a woman who said, "Yeah, I'll work with you, and yes, we have a factory." Her factory is zoned in an area where you can have light industry as well as homes, and she is actually in a four-story sort of house situation where there are sewing machines on the first and second levels, and there are people who put the hardware [Lewis points to the clasps on the handbags] together on the third level and then there's packing on the fourth level. So even though it's a factory, it's quiet. It's not loud, humming with constant machinery. It's a great environment to work in.

For Lewis, the challenge was to recreate the workspace, and the construction of self, specifically of gender, that attends factory work. She approached this task as a responsibility to her own personal and social identities, values, and business mission. In this process, Lewis negotiated her identity as an Asian American women entrepreneur, and she deliberately took other women with her. Her enterprise is constructed in a matrix of political, social, and moral values, and her products reflect her ability to see herself in other women: those with whom she works, those who buy her bags, and those aspiring entrepreneurs.

A true entrepreneur, Lewis defied and discarded stereotypes about her gender and her ethnicity, about who should start a business and what policies make a business successful. Similar to the young women in Margolis's study who found ways to become computer science majors at Carnegie Mellon, Lewis's innovations include reconfiguring the meaning of interaction with the physical world, the world of material. She rejects the stereotypical factory setting with its big, noisy machines, and the sweatshop, assembly-line mentality that prioritizes routinization and uniformity of goods at a low cost.

Because the embedded power dynamics of top–down, hierarchal organization have long been concretized on the typical factory floor, many have suggested that the hyper-masculinity associated with factory workers is a type of false consciousness meant to mitigate the demoralization and alienation workers often experience (Willis 1977; Padavic 1991; Hamper 1986). Instead of accepting the current state of manufacturing, Lewis persists in her loyalty to her emotional, personal, and cultural ties, and to the range of women involved in her enterprise; she devises ways in which she can create products that reflect her values.

Consistent with the descriptions of ethnic minority entrepreneurs supplied by John Butler (1991), Lewis's business connects her to the economy, but it does even more – it introduces her voice as a minority business owner into the larger cultural discourse. In this emancipatory process, she continues to carve out an identity that recognizes and integrates multiple aspects of self as she develops her personal and professional mission. By contributing to the emancipation of herself and others, Lewis employs an entrepreneurial vision striking in its contrast to the narrow focus on self-interest and profit-maximization:

> It gives me a sense of personal satisfaction to help other women to get to the place they want to go. And I'm not saying the same space where I'm at right now, but wherever they're meant to [be], to be able to say to them, "You can do it! What's the first step? Take it!"

This is really the time for women who want to lend a hand to others and pull them up along with them.

7

Minority women entrepreneurs as community members

The important role of data-gathering: who is counted?

As already evident from data presented so far, it is impossible to discuss minority women entrepreneurs without also discussing their commitment to their communities – yet here, too, the behavior and values of minority women are not generally represented in entrepreneurship literature or found in workplace research. In fact, in their review of work-life literature, Eby, Casper *et al.* identify the "virtual omission" of non-work factors such as community involvement and volunteer commitments (Eby, Casper *et al.* 2005: 182, quoted in Ozbilgin, Beauregard *et al.* 2009: 8). Critics of workplace studies point out that research is usually tailored to represent majority populations, or even directed towards idealized rather than real situations. Noting the assumption of traditional nuclear families where the husband is in the paid labor force and the wife is unemployed, Ozbilgin, Beauregard *et al.* suggest "bringing life back to work-life research" (Ozbilgin, Beauregard *et al.* 2009: 9). In real life, only 17% of U.S. married couples have an employed husband and a non-employed wife, whereas 26% of all households are headed by single women and 5% by employed wives and non-employed husbands (Ozbilgin, Beauregard *et al.* 2009: 9). In addition to ignoring time spent on community commitments and the variety of family configurations, diversity in gender, race/ethnicity, sexuality, health, and disability are also largely absent from work-life samples (Ozbilgin, Beauregard *et al.* 2009).

This lack of research and discourse in the work-life literature not only means that challenges and opportunities experienced by a range of people will not be addressed in workplace practices, but also ensures that excluded populations will struggle to participate in and identify with work experiences. In this case, the lifestyles and values of minority women are often left out of workplace considerations and policies – in effect, minority women are excluded from work communities. They don't count. Ozbilgin, Beauregard *et al.* (2009: 18) write:

> We contend that individuals who do not conform to the White, able-bodied, heterosexual mainstream, and whose work-life experiences are not acknowledged by either work-life research or literature or the human resource management policies derived from it, are disadvantaged in terms of status, mutual understanding between social groups and positive self-concepts . . . membership in social categories accounts for a significant component of an individual's self-concept contributing to people's sense of self-esteem. (Ozbilgin, Beauregard *et al.* 2009: 18)

Work-life research is similar to entrepreneurship literature in representing and serving a narrow range of workers: married, White, able-bodied, heterosexual. Not surprisingly, those who are represented in work-life literature are the most likely to feel that workplace policies are fair and equitable. This sense of fairness correlates with high morale and retention rates:

> Recognizing the imbalance in the work-life literature, Casper, Weltman and Kwesiga (2007) . . . revealed that employees with traditional family structures perceived greater equity . . . and that perceptions of inequity were associated with reduced commitment to the organization and increased intentions to leave the organization. (Ozbilgin, Beauregard *et al.* 2009: 19)

Discrimination by omission, then, is a very effective way to drive people out of workplace communities.

As mentioned, women and minorities – those people who are positioned as out-groups, as "strangers" – are more likely to report turning to entrepreneurship as a response to workplace discrimination. Gender and racial discrimination manifest in wage gaps and lack of promotion has been widely documented, but more subtle exclusion from community membership and workplace research is less acknowledged. As Barbara Manzi of Manzi Metals reports, she was told she "was just not their kind." In conscious recognition of loyalty and community membership, the minority women entrepreneurs interviewed here often report that the reason they started their businesses was to serve the minority communities with which they identify. Minority women might open a business as a constructive response to feeling unwelcome in the workplace, as well as a way to help others who have been similarly ill-treated. By creating alternative environments in which they and other members of their community thrive, minority women reject and resist environments that do not value them.

Community loyalty as evidence of outlier status

As business owners, each entrepreneur interviewed in this study engaged in what Susan Murray refers to as "motive talk" (Murray 2000: 138). That is to say, each entrepreneur articulates her motives for going into business. Murray contends that motive talk is necessary when the intentions behind and/or meanings of behavior are unclear. Business may be seen as gendered male, associated with being White and educated and often touted as a circumscribed, separate sphere where rational decision-makers eschew emotional attachments, considerations of family loyalty, or solidarity with community. Consequently, entrepreneurship might be interpreted as "an undesired, untoward, and therefore questionable choice of employment" (Murray 2000: 138) for minority women. In fact, even as minority women entrepreneurs encounter prejudice in conventional workplaces, they must also demonstrate that their status as entrepreneurs does not diminish their minority identity and commitment to community values.

In addition to motive talk, minority women also give "accounts" of their business decisions and experiences as entrepreneurs. Murray (2000: 142) explains the concept of accounts through the work of Scott and Lyman, as "a linguistic device employed whenever an action is subjected to valuative inquiry. Such devices are a crucial element in the social order since they prevent conflict from arising by verbally bridging the gap between action and expectation . . ." (Scott and Lyman 1970: 343-44). As discussed in Chapter 5, minority women walk a fine line. On the one hand, in order to establish credibility and legitimacy in the majority community, they have to give accounts that reflect their normative status. For instance, Margaret Henningsen comments:

> Banking is a male-dominated field, so the major challenge was convincing regulators and potential investors that three Black women in their fifties could start a bank and make it success-

> ful. It took us three times as long to raise the needed capital as our White counterparts who started banks before, during or after us.

On the other hand, as outliers, minority women also give accounts that reflect their identification with their gender and minority communities. Therefore, to "bridge the gap between action and expectation," minority women must counter the expectation that as entrepreneurs they strictly adhere to profit-maximizing, self-interested, instrumental behavior. To establish gender identity and community loyalty, they must dispel the notion that they are conventional business owners. Typical "actions" of minority women entrepreneurs, including balancing profit with respect for social concerns or cultivating flexible boundaries among a range of responsibilities and values, are behaviors that are highly inconsistent with conventional business discourses and expectations. The communities these entrepreneurs are loyal to might be the larger natural, ecological community; a community of others similar in gender, race, ethnicity, religion, or physical disability; or a community comprised of their own extended and immediate families. Accounts of the valuation of community membership arise from the understanding of these entrepreneurs that the choice to own a business is not one usually understood by others as consistent with their allegiances and social values. These factors create a context in which minority women entrepreneurs feel they have to explain themselves and their choices. The decision to go into business, therefore, necessitates a complex "account" where minority women explain how their motives for being business owners are not necessarily directed towards rapid growth and high profit, how their business decisions do not always conform to the rules of business-as-usual and how they manage their identities as entrepreneurs while also maintaining their identities as minority women.

Many workers enter the paid labor force because they need money, and therefore create "economic" accounts even for low-paying jobs. For example, "the benefits are really good" was an account given for employment as a childcare giver (Murray 2000: 144). Although the minority women interviewed here sometimes create accounts based on economic imperatives, theirs are overwhelmingly what Murray refers to as "affinity" accounts (Murray 2000: 144): accounts that reflect their identification, community membership, and loyalty along the lines of gender, race, ethnicity, class, religion, family, or social value systems. Minority women therefore justify their position as entrepreneurs and participants in the competitive, capitalist marketplace through their emotional connections to others, and this is obvious as they explain their business innovations – innovations that are not separable from community commitments, and personal and social values. Being a business owner, an entrepreneur, therefore, does not necessarily indicate surrender to the values of individualism and profit-motivated capitalism; entrepreneurship, including for-profit business ownership, can also be motivated by and sustained through a pro-social, community-based, political agenda.

Perhaps because minority women are rarely associated with or trained for business ownership, only three of the entrepreneurs interviewed here – Rita Chang, and Najma and Maryam Jamaludeen – attribute their entrepreneurship to innate predisposition or socialization rather than personal choice. The next two sections belong to them.

Rita Chang and Classroom Encounters: teaching innovation

Rita Chang identifies as a minority entrepreneur in myriad ways: as an Asian American, a woman, and perhaps the most unusual, a teacher. Chang reports that being both a teacher and a business owner "is virtually unheard of." After working for 20 years in entrepreneurial public health, public service, and public science positions, Chang eventually became the Executive Director of the Center for Health and Global Environment at Harvard Medical School, but she now teaches earth science in a suburban high school. Married, the mother of two daughters and a consummate multitasker, she is also the founder of Classroom Encounters, a nonprofit company.

Chang decided to enter teaching as a second career knowing that teachers "do not make a lot of money." But for Chang, teaching is "a calling." A self-identified "activist at heart" with a "pioneering spirit," Chang has always believed in empowering individuals through knowledge and a deeper understanding of their connection to the world (McGee 2007: 15). Classroom Encounters represents an important dimension of Chang's community involvement; it is an activist project. In an effort to give students an opportunity to discover more meaningful connections between their lives and the real world, between science and life outside of academics, Chang developed Classroom Encounters as a curriculum innovation to teach and learn science. When asked why she started her business, she replies:

> I guess I still wasn't satisfied [even after starting to teach earth science]. There was a part of me that felt that what was really essential was changing the minds of the young people . . . I went to where I thought the action was going be.

To engage young people in the same passion she has for science, Chang chose to focus on global climate change – a problem that lends itself to a wide range of scientific inquiry and intervention. She then invited leading global-change scientists from diverse fields into her classroom to conduct experiments, or "learning encounters," with high school students. Chang devised ways to film and produce DVDs of the scientists' classroom visits in order to save and share the experiences and to motivate and engage students emotionally, intellectually, and creatively. Student, scientist, teacher, and filmmaker came together in a groundbreaking collaboration. Classroom Encounters was born (McGee 2007: 15).

Students participate in the productions at every level: they research the scientific concepts in pre-production; they are filmed conducting experiments in the classroom; they interview the scientists for special segments; they provide art and music in post-production; they help to create free web-based teaching resources (including films of their own); and a student camera crew works with professional film-makers to facilitate the shoot. Classroom Encounters has received national recognition for innovation and exemplary content from *Booklist*, *Library Journal*, the Public Broadcasting Service (PBS), and the National Science Teachers Association.

Demonstrating how difficult it is to integrate and harmonize her gender identity, her identity as a teacher, and her identity as an entrepreneur, Chang mentions that being a business owner is "very lonely," and that she often feels like "a fish out of water." Because of her business, Chang says she "doesn't fit the model of being a teacher." There is an assumption that teachers, especially female teachers, should choose their profession primarily because of emotional satisfaction rather than economic benefit. In fact, in her article "Getting Paid in Smiles," Murray argues that the gendering of care-giving as women's work, especially when the work involves caring for children, is primarily manifest in low pay and high emotional fulfillment (2000).

When discussing her colleagues, Chang becomes thoughtful and a bit tentative. She chooses her words carefully. As a result of the alienating influence her business has on other teachers, Chang says she usually keeps the details of Classroom Encounters to herself; she feels she must "keep a low profile" because she doesn't "want to make anybody's nose out of joint." Despite the nonprofit status of her social entrepreneurial venture, other teachers and some parents do not approve of her business and have voiced suspicions that she is using students to make money. The reputation of business as opportunistic, unethical, and non-humanitarian is a distinct liability for Chang. She says that insofar as business is associated with private profit and self-interest, and teaching is based on selflessly serving the public good, there is a "fundamental conflict" between a business model and a teaching model. Yet Chang wants to do both simultaneously – and thinks she can, especially because her business is a socially conscious business. She states unequivocally, "As a teacher, I'm not comfortable with a profit-oriented business. There was never any expectation of making any money; there was an expectation of making something of social value."

Regardless of her motives and her account of her business, Chang feels that when she is around her teaching colleagues, the entrepreneurial dimension of her life must be kept quiet; she must remain a "closet creator." This can be difficult, because Chang believes that being an entrepreneur is part of her personality – not just a career decision, but a congenital characteristic and foregone conclusion:

> It's in my nature so it just happens. It's a way of thinking about how to get things done, a way of doing and problem-solving, and a way of making things happen, and it's a way of unleashing some creative energy in others and yourself since everything is unknown. It's exhausting, demanding, and never-ending – at least during start-up. To say I like being an entrepreneur would seem strange; it's more my nature, and I feel aligned with myself when I'm able to chart my own course because I usually don't see things the way others do. I don't feel frustrated, and I don't feel held back, and I don't feel that I have do things I don't like or think right because someone else less qualified, less collaborative, or less imaginative is in charge. I feel some pride that I'm a person who isn't afraid of taking risks, and who has a lot of creative energy.

Chang certainly is creative, passionate, and as Green said, "at one with the enterprise of her devising" (Green 2005: 4). When asked how she feels about her business, Chang replies, "I feel like I'm creating art, and it's art that uses lots of different people and interactions and caring about something, which in this case is the planet, learning, and good science." Though Chang attributes being an entrepreneur to her individual nature, she does not adopt an individualistic and self-interested motivation for opening a business, nor does she make use of rationales provided by classical economic theory. In fact, Chang is the only entrepreneur in our study to self-identify as a social entrepreneur. Chang volunteers her time, energy, and money to Classroom Encounters, and she counts on others to volunteer their help:

> Most of the money for this has come out of our own resources. We had the desire to create something of social value, not

> really for profit. We had very little money. We certainly had no money in the beginning at all. What happened is that people wanted to help . . . It was goodwill; it was meant to share what had been created in this process.

Rather than seeking personal gain, Chang provides an account of her business innovation that emphasizes serving several communities – teachers, students, and the larger ecological environment:

> I wanted to make a contribution [to teaching]. I think too often students don't have an idea what science is all about, how it's done and they don't have great role models.
>
> Our changing planet challenges our imagination and creativity and problem-solving skills as never before. Classroom Encounters creates classroom-friendly media for teachers so they can improve how science is learned, taught, and communicated. We do this by bringing teachers, world-class scientists, students, and media-makers together in a collaborative and participatory learning environment (the "encounter") – in an actual classroom – and modeling the learning process "live."
>
> A professional camera crew teamed with students captures the interplay. We have focused on global-change science content and how this dynamic science is done in the real world since changes to our planet are intellectually and emotionally engaging, relevant, and compelling to young people. Global-change science is driven by discovery, current research, big questions, and inquiry. When this science-rich content can be captured in media that teachers can use in their lessons, labs, and activities, teachers have new tools at their fingertips to teach the national science standards in ways that can inspire and motivate young people. They can also model the innovative thinking and problem-solving skills needed in the 21st century. It's a really good product idea; I mean, it's a real innovation that's not out there. It has tremendous value to me and to society.

Through her commitment to her students, to the environment, and to teaching and studying science, Chang is forging a new model of business: a community-based model that is not *in conflict with* public good, but rather *a tool used for* public good.

Najma and Maryam Jamaludeen:
'being in a family is being in a business – same thing'

If Chang was born an entrepreneur, the Jamaludeens had entrepreneurship thrust upon them. Sisters, best friends, serial entrepreneurs, and inventors, Najma and Maryam Jamaludeen talk about being raised as entrepreneurs. Both young women identify as Muslim African Americans and were brought up in a highly entrepreneurial family. In the neighborhood where they grew up, theirs was the only family that owned a business. As children, they worked in the family's perfumery. They also opened businesses of their own: Maryam, who loves culinary arts, made desserts and egg rolls every Friday to sell to neighbors; and Najma, who now has her degree in fashion design and merchandising, had her family and friends as her first customers.

Najma and Maryam are currently involved in several businesses including Temsah, a shea butter line of lotions and creams, and Basketmate, an invention by Najma which features a flexible attachment to laundry baskets that increases basket capacity and ease of handling. In 2007, Najma pitched Basketmate for Oprah Winfrey's "Next Big Idea," in an attempt win a spot on the QVC trade show.

Najma is the mother of three children and Maryam has four. They explain how the decision to be entrepreneurs reflects their family identity. Najma says:

> It's really just part of our lifestyle. My mother got married to my stepfather when I was five, and he operated a perfumery business. He made incense and perfume products. And so we kind of just got dragged into that. I worked pretty much from the time I was seven. It's not like child labor or something – well, it was, but . . . [they both laugh] sometimes I think about [why we are entrepreneurs] and I guess you're a product of what you were raised with.

Maryam agrees:

> We have a business mindset because we were raised as entrepreneurs. It was ten of us kids: three children by my father and seven with my stepfather. I remember when we walked away from [my stepfather's] business we went to the University of Detroit business school, and all we could think of was what else can we make to start our own business? We just can't get it out of our systems. People wonder about us. We have worked [for other people], but we can't keep our jobs longer than a few years because we are just entrepreneurs.

Working for their stepfather was part of their lifestyle as they grew up, but it was also clear to them that entrepreneurship was a lifeline, a connection to the economy. Najma explains that after she and her siblings no longer had a relationship with her stepfather, it was clear that the older children would have to support the family:

> I have a lot of brothers and sisters who don't have a father. It's either [open a business] or "What am I going to be? A doctor?" It's just that there are ten kids and then we have [our own] kids and – you know – my income . . . Maybe because my parents didn't raise us to go to college . . . If they had, then all ten of us would have been raised to get a degree and get a good job. But it has always been a communal kind of thought with us. It's like: I have a business and then my brothers and sisters can work for me, and my kids can work for me. They won't have to wonder about where they're going to get a job from or what they're going to do.

Maryam adds:

> Our main focus was our seven brothers and sisters because we didn't want them to work like we worked. We worked long hard days as children. Like I said, we were the workforce. If we hadn't been working so much, we would have had more opportunity. And that's the responsibility our parents put on us. We were home-schooled so we didn't have the exposure of seeing what was out there and being exposed to scholarships and stuff like that. We were thinking – how can we get some money so that [our brothers and sisters] can go to college? . . . We did all go to college. We all have our degrees. And we did make it possible for our younger brothers and sisters to go to college, whether it was moving in with us or working and giving them what [money] we made. We wanted them to have more opportunities than we had.

Given their relative isolation, Najma and Maryam's family has always been their community. The sisters are astonishingly close and affectionate towards each other. They often finish each other's sentences. Home-schooled as children, they worked together on schoolwork and in their stepfather's factory; now they are business partners and collaborators. Both wear the hijab, and their religious practices are central to their identities and family solidarity. Najma explains that even as an adult, she has remained closest to her family members:

We are Muslim, and we were very cloistered. I don't want to say Amish, but it was close [laughs]. And so, you know, when I think about reaching out to other businesses, there wasn't much reaching out. Even now, my friends are my family because that's all who was ever around. But honestly even to the point that my daughters have said, "Mommy, you don't have any friends." It's weird: I don't have any.

Maryam interjects: She has me.

Najma smiles: Yeah! [both laugh].

Similar to the other entrepreneurs interviewed for this study, Najma and Maryam do not make a distinction between business values and personal values, between their emotional commitments and their economic responsibilities. A relational self (see discussion in Chapter 4) is evident as they describe a perceived merging with their enterprises. They develop and express selfhood through their entrepreneurial activity, and do not distinguish their business interactions from those involved in personal and intimate relationships. In fact, Maryam contends that being in business and being in a family are the same thing:

In the entrepreneurship class I took last semester, I wrote my paper on my marriage. I learned that being in a family is the same as being in a business – same thing. The same concepts and the same principles that go along with family go along with business. And that's being committed, sacrificing, being determined, being a leader, being a follower. And those things go along with being a good entrepreneur. And having a good team is very important. And we have an excellent team. We know each other from a business standpoint. We can do business together, and we're very close. We help each other out, so, great opportunity and great team are the two most important things.

Not just a passion, entrepreneurship was a necessity: Najma and Maryam simply had to provide for themselves and their siblings. Maryam recounts:

We loved it. We loved the challenge. It was fun, at first. And then when we *had* to do it; it was like: this is your food, clothing and shelter. [My stepfather] didn't say that, but we kind of knew. When we left the business and walked away, he told us, "We're cutting off the lights, cutting off the food."

And Najma adds:

> We were good kids, and we did what we were told to do. And then we always refined it. We didn't just do it. We did a good job and refined it ourselves. Even when [my stepfather] was talking about automation, he said, "You guys are faster than any machines could work." There was no other money. We were the money that was coming in. That was the income. We knew that. We had seven other kids and we weren't going to leave them without anything. We still never have.

Despite the tremendous need to bring in money, the Jamaludeens primarily give affinity accounts rather than economic accounts of their own entrepreneurial processes. That is to say, profit is necessary, but not adequate. It is also the identification with the process of being entrepreneurial, innovative, and inventive and the dedication to creating work for themselves and their family members that are essential to their enterprises. Najma explains this sense of ownership of ideas and the thrill of implementing and sharing them with others:

> It is really fun to make something and think someone else might like it. And put it out there. We talk incessantly and so the ideas are always flowing through constantly. So that's like the adrenaline rush, so when you get an idea that you think might be good . . .
>
> *Maryam finishes her thought:* You want to make it.
>
> *Najma adds:* You want to get it together and work it out. I guess we're really good at looking at something and seeing potential in it. We have a good eye for design.

Recognizing their economic drive and need to make money, do they prioritize making a profit? Their answer is complicated. They acknowledge that money is important, but they do not subordinate the quality of the product or their identification with their product in order to make a sale. In fact, it is their social identity, their reputation, which emerges as a central aspect of the entrepreneurial process. They maintain that they can always make money, and certainly they have been employed by others, but earning a living through their entrepreneurial businesses is better because they get paid for doing what they love. The key to their entrepreneurial endeavors is that these endeavors are self-expressive; entrepreneurial activities are an extension of their selfhood and their personal identity in the community:

Maryam: No, we never cared about profit like that. The reality is when you're an entrepreneur, it's in your blood; it's not about the money.

Najma: Well, it is . . . But we wouldn't cut corners. Whatever we present – definitely, absolutely – whatever we present has to be perfect. Your presentation and how you are portrayed [by customers and others in the community] – but not in a fake way – your reputation is paramount.

Maryam: Yes. It has to be perfect. The money doesn't matter because we know we can make money. It's just very high standards. It's like a thought process and a way of being where you feel . . . like, if I settle for less, who am I? I can't settle for less and I don't want anybody else to settle for less. When we put a product out there, we think the same way. We like it so much.

Despite being in desperate economic straits, being young and relatively isolated, and perhaps most important, shouldering the responsibility for their seven siblings, Najma and Maryam Jamaludeen's narratives are consistent with the other minority women interviewed here. They have a strong personal identification with their product – Maryam asks, "If I settle for less, who am I?" They also have a strong identification with and responsibility towards their own family ("Our main focus was our seven brothers and sisters") and with their customers as well ("It is really fun to make something and think someone else might like it," and "I don't want anybody else to settle for less"). They do not pit the valuation of profit against quality, even though they really need the money. They simply do not make that trade-off. Rather than the typical "either/or" zero-sum construction found in conventional business explanations, the Jamaludeens adopt a "both/and" understanding of the entrepreneurial process. They merge themselves and their relationships in their businesses so that they do not make a distinction between their intimate emotional ties with family and their behavior in their business.

Self-identification with the business, the lack of clear boundaries between personal, social, and professional identities, and the devotion to supporting a community are all common elements of the minority women entrepreneurs in this study. As evident from the narratives of Rita Chang, and Najma and Maryam Jamaludeen, some minority women feel they were destined to be entrepreneurs: entrepreneurship is something they cannot help; it is "in their blood." For other minority women entrepreneurs, the commitment to social advancement for a particular community inspires a very conscious and deliberate decision to own a business; in these circumstances, entrepreneurship is explained as a personal and political choice. This is the case for Nancy Stevens and Kathy Deserly, and their narratives follow.

Nancy Stevens: Motivational speaker, turning 'I wish I had' into 'I'm glad I did'

Blind since birth, Stevens twice won the world triathlete championship, gained three gold medals in the 1998 Olympic trials and is a long-distance cycler – she has logged over 3000 miles across the United States. Stevens qualified for the cross-country Paralympics team, and in 1985 she was an alternate for the downhill ski team. Stevens is such an accomplished athlete, and seemingly fearless individual (downhill ski racing is terrifying in itself – imagine doing it blind), that it is hard to believe that she might ever have lacked confidence. But right before making the cross-country team, Stevens remembers she hit a wall of discouragement:

> I had tried so many different sports [bike racing, power lifting, and speed skating] and I finally thought, OK, maybe I'm not meant to do this. It just didn't seem like anything was working out. Then when I was asked to try out for the Paralympics cross-country ski team, I thought, here I go again; I'm going to try this again! It was a difficult week of skiing. It was pretty cold. I was skiing with someone I didn't know, and it was a lot of work. Then I finally made the cross-country ski team. It was such a huge goal in my life and huge accomplishment for me because I had almost given up so many times.

Stevens describes herself as "a ham at heart," who loves to sing and act, and though she had worked for organizations, she decided that the best use of her skills would be as a motivational speaker to help inspire others to reach their goals. In 1998 she started a business that, as she says, is "very originally" named NancySpeaks.com. In creating a program around the concept of "Jump Start Your Heart," she aimed to help others like herself take chances:

> So finally when [I made the ski team], I started thinking about how many people wish they could do something or tried for something, whether it's a degree or a career they've always wanted, or a sport . . . I thought, I wonder if I could somehow inspire others to reach for their goals. So I started my speaking business . . . My speech actually didn't have a name for a

couple of years – I'm not good with names. Then one morning I
woke up at three in the morning and just thought, I know what
my speech is going to be called: "Jump Start your Heart: CPR
for your Dreams."

Stevens recounts that right after opening her business, a friend of hers told
her that public speaking is the single activity that people fear the most.
Stevens comments, "She said, leave it to you to come up with a profession
that is the scariest for everybody else."

The ability to inspire others and help them pursue their goals and
dreams is the motivation behind Stevens's decision to become an entrepreneur. She recalls that during the four years leading up to the Paralympics
she trained between 15 and 20 hours a week, while still working full-time.
Because she is blind, Stevens cannot just ski or run alone; she has to find
someone to go with her. Her athletic success depended on a large team of
people who helped her train:

I had a really wonderful team of people who helped me. I had
senior citizens who skied with me. And high school students.
Amazing, the people who would come out! And I had runners
in the summertime. There were so many hurdles and so many
times that I learned something from the experience, and I
thought, this is why I want to do something to inspire other
people.

Stevens believes that working for herself offers a better service to the community than working for someone else. Using music, humor, and songs,
Stevens gets her audience to take risks they never thought possible.

I talk about creating a vision, staying persistent, and taking the
risks in order to accomplish the goal – whatever it might be. I
tell stories; I act them out sometimes. I sing. It's a whole experience, so if people don't relate to a story, they might relate to
a song or a quote. I'm very stubborn and very determined. I
had so much support, and that's what kept me going. So when
I give talks, I make it interactive with the audience. It's like I'm
building a workshop, and I'm not just doing a keynote presentation. I'll get people to talk and interact with each other and
with me.

Charismatic with a sharp wit and a self-deprecating manner, she is pretty
irresistible. Stevens recalls during one event, she was on stage and, even
before her first joke, the audience laughed uproariously. She realized then
that she had been facing the wrong direction. Rather than being embar-

rassed or feeling foolish, she simply turned, faced the audience, and kept going. Her target audiences are women's groups, nonprofit organizations, and government agencies.

In 2006, Stevens became a certified Life Coach. She works with people who are newly disabled, or those who have had a disability since birth and who want to find ways to develop independence or to stay independent. Nancy has also done advocacy work in Mexico for blind people. She coaches people who have heard her talk and want to continue with a program to reach their goals:

> I decided to get certified as a Life Coach because so often people came to me after I was done speaking and would say, "Wow, I'm so inspired to write my book, or I'm so inspired to try for X," whatever it might be. So I wanted to be a support to them in another way.

As an athlete, Stevens learned both to keep her hopes high and also to cope with inevitable disappointments. She counsels clients to approach setbacks by saying, "OK, it didn't work out this way so maybe something else is going to come up." She has developed summer camps that train women with various levels of physical ability to compete as triathletes, and she has worked with city governments to increase accessibility for people with disabilities. Living alone and traveling extensively with her guide dog, one focus is transportation facilities:

> Another challenge is when I go to a city I don't know [for speaking engagements]. Just getting around can be hard. I have to ask people to show me where the room is. I travel alone, usually with a seeing-eye dog. If I am traveling for business it is easier, because people are usually so excited to escort the speaker.

Stevens comments that people are always surprised at what she, a blind woman, can do. She says, "If there is something I want to do, I really strive to make it happen. I want to live my life without regrets." But she does not just focus on herself. In common with the other minority women entrepreneurs in this study, Stevens is a champion for people with whom she identifies. As an advocate, she also tells their stories. For instance, she mentions that over 70% of blind adults are unemployed, and that this figure has "sadly not changed much" since the passage of the Americans with Disabilities Act (ADA) in 1990. Stevens wants to help other people, especially those who are disabled "do the things they think are impossible." She found that she could help people become independent. Stevens knows how it feels to be pitied and to be afraid: "Some people look at me and say: "Oh gosh, poor thing. How can you even get out of bed?" But I like to show people how to turn 'I wish I had' into 'I'm glad I did.' "

Kathy Deserly: advocating for Native children

A striking woman with a regal bearing, Kathy Deserly has a warm smile and a soft voice. As a child welfare advocate for over 30 years, she has seen both the joy of families together and the desolation of families pulled apart. Deserly consults on issues related to foster care, adoption, and various aspects of child welfare. For instance, working through a Federal contract from the Bureau of Indian Affairs, Deserly spent last summer 2006 assessing child welfare programs for Native people by visiting tribes in Texas and New Mexico. Her job takes her to different states around the country, and she also regularly works with tribes, state agencies, and national child welfare organizations throughout the state of Montana, where she resides.

Deserly, like Margaret Henningsen and Nancy Stevens, is a repository of the stories of those whom she represents, and their stories become hers. Though she realizes she cannot solve all their problems, Deserly carries the memories of families around with her and treats these memories carefully, as part of the larger story of Native American history and culture. Having worked for state organizations for most of her career, she has been a business owner and private consultant for the last five years. She explains her business:

> The work I do really stems from the federal law, the Indian Child Welfare Act that was passed in 1978 to try to stem the flow of children out of Native families. Many had been placed in foster care and with adoptive parents, and often these children never returned to their Native communities because of the way the child welfare system worked. You know, it's a bureaucracy wherever you are, and once you get into that system . . . children are placed in foster care, and for a variety of reasons, sometimes kids don't get returned to their families. When Native children are placed with non-Native families, it is [not in] compliance with the Indian Child Welfare Act. So one of the things the Indian Child Welfare Act also promotes is the recruitment of more Native foster families to be available for children in the system.

Deserly explains that though the current Bureau of Indian Affairs is now in charge of preserving Native families, there is a long history in the United States of taking Native children from their families of origin. In this process, Native cultures have been disrupted and communities have been dispersed:

> The Bureau of Indian Affairs is the agency most people are familiar with because they were given the charge of handling "Indian Affairs." They are part of the Federal government and go way back – over one hundred years. [The Bureau of Indian Affairs was initially formed in 1824, and has had a variety of names. It was first a division of the Department of War, and in 1849, the Bureau was transferred to the Department of the Interior.] One of the things the Bureau was responsible for was the development and operation of boarding schools. These were schools where Native children were housed 24/7 – all year around. These institutions were set up for education, but at the same time, these children were taken from their families for such long periods that they really were changed forever as a result of that experience.

Deserly grew up in Southern California, and identifies as Hispanic with Guatemalan and Choctaw Indian roots. When asked how she became involved in the preservation of Native families, she explains that when she was a child she saw Native children being kept behind a fence at a boarding school. The sight confused and disturbed her. At the time, there was no active political movement protesting the treatment of these Native children; in fact, despite the high population of Native people in Southern California, few talked about or even knew about the boarding schools. Growing up in California, Deserly remembers seeing children behind a fence:

> I remember all during my childhood seeing small children at boarding school. This wasn't a high school – this was little kids, and they were behind a fence. They were fenced in there and one time when we drove by, I asked my Mom, "Why do those kids have to be there? You know, why do those little kids have to be behind that fence? What kind of school is that?" And I learned it was a boarding school. But I had no idea that these kids were coming from Arizona and other places to go to school and that they were staying there year-round . . . It's really interesting because even though there are quite a number of Native Americans on reservations in Southern California as well as urban Indians – it has one of the highest populations of urban Indians in the country – a lot of people just didn't

have a clue about the history of so many Native children being removed from their families, and why we would need a law to protect them.

Deserly's decision to become involved in preserving Native culture is also informed by the experiences of her own family members. She explains that her father knew he was part Indian, but never knew for sure which tribe his ancestors were from. Adopted by non-Natives, he lost his family history and spent his life feeling unmoored, that he did not belong:

> My family is kind of a mix. Like a lot of American families, we have a variety of backgrounds. My grandmother was from Guatemala, and came to this country as a child because her mother died. My grandfather, her husband, was from Scotland, so he comes from a White, Anglo background. My Dad was adopted himself. He said he knew he was part Indian, part Choctaw or Chickasaw, he didn't know which, but he knew he was part Indian. After I started working in foster and adoption care, I wanted to talk to him more about it before he passed away. He said he felt like a black sheep, is how he put it. And I don't know that it was because he was part Indian. I think it was more because he was adopted and not born to the family he was raised in. He didn't feel like he quite fit in. I just remember him talking about the feeling of being a black sheep.

As Deserly mentions, most people have never heard of the wide use of boarding schools for Native American children and do not know the extent of what she refers to as the "historical trauma" endured by Indians. When asked to explain the rationale behind the boarding schools, Deserly links it to ongoing prejudice towards Native Americans:

> Why were Native children taken from their families? That's a good question. I think all you have to do is watch TV or movie Westerns, and you see this whole cowboy and Indian thing. And if you take that to another level, to a historical and political level, nobody knew what to do with the Indians. Native Americans were the first people who were here from the beginning. From where you come from, from the East [Deserly is referring to Massachusetts on the east coast of the U.S.], it was the Indian people who rescued the European immigrants and helped them survive those first winters. But then, you know, as more [European] people started encroaching on Native territory, then the battles began. The U.S. government said, "We need this land for our people. We need to do something with

the Indians. We need to move them away or we need to edu-
cate them. We need to teach them how to be farmers."

It just really became this issue of what to do with Native
people, and at some point it was decided the best way to handle this situation was to start with the kids. We can assimilate
Native children into American society where they learn our
ways, our language, learn to read and write. The thought was
they'd learn to assimilate into mainstream culture, and that
never really worked. It never really worked anywhere . . .

So there's just a really long history of abuse of Native people, and you hear the term "historical trauma." And [Native]
people today who are raising their children or trying to make
it in this world experience this historical trauma because it's
so recent, and it's something that has impacted maybe themselves, their parents, their grandparents.

Deserly cites the alarmingly high percentages of Native children in the
child-welfare system and explains the obstacles to placing Native children
in Native families:

Today here in the state of Montana probably 35–40% of the
children in foster care are Native children, and yet the Native
people only represent about 6% of the state population. In
South Dakota, 60% of the children in foster care are Native,
and in Alaska 60% are Native, so there are some huge numbers
out there . . .

Though child-welfare agencies try to support the interests of Native children, Deserly believes that at the same time some of the more bureau-
cratic rules undermine the ability of Native families to provide foster and
adoptive care. She points out that there are not enough Native families
that qualify as foster or adoptive homes: not because these families do not
wish to participate, but because they are far away or lack resources:

There are not enough relatives used to provide care. It's
sometimes easier to place children in a licensed home that's
available rather than really seek out possible family members
who could help. Maybe they're not nearby. Maybe they are in
another state . . . One thing I have to say, though: on a reserva-
tion there tends to be many more relatives who are willing to
step up to take care of the children, but there's also an issue
of payment for these families, because if they don't become
licensed by going through a really rigorous licensing proce-
dure, they cannot access a higher foster care range and take
care of the children. And a lot of the families I talk to – it's

really interesting – a lot of them will say, "I don't want to take
the money. This is my [niece or nephew or cousin]. I just want
to take care of them." But for any family, even a family that's
earning significant income, it's a burden to bring in another
child, let alone two or three. So people really do need that
extra help.

Because the government bureaucracies operate with rules that reflect
the perspective and mentality of majority populations, Deserly calls into
question their ability to manage the welfare of Native children fairly and
judiciously. She makes it clear that it is not just the cowboy and Indian
portrayals, nor even the use of names like "Braves" and "Warriors" for
sports teams, that marginalize and caricature Native people; there is also
active and direct prejudice towards Indians that she has both witnessed
and experienced:

The greatest slur that I have heard that's being used, and it
goes on at places like high school basketball games, is when
non-Indian teams are playing Indian teams from nearby. When
people are getting mad about something, they'll refer to Indians as "prairie niggers." . . . My point is when that sort of environment is there, and it's allowed, these are some of the same
people with the power to take children from their parents,
whether it's people on the police force or social workers or
court workers. These people from these communities are making the judgment about whether children will be permanently
removed from their families. These people who potentially
have this kind of history and can make decisions based on
that history or not, because while there is historical trauma
for Indian people, there is also a history of non-Native people in terms of being adversaries of Indians. It's just this kind
of trickle-down that comes through history that you have to
acknowledge.

With short black hair and brown eyes, Deserly's appearance is ethni-
cally and racially ambiguous, which she says "works" for her because
she "doesn't stand out in any way." Like all of the minority women in this
study, Deserly feels comfortable being with majority populations, but she
strongly identifies as a minority woman, and she especially identifies with
Native people:

I do identify as a minority because of how I was raised and
where I've lived. I sometimes feel unique. While I identify as
a minority person, at the same time I feel that I can maybe
more easily walk into a meeting of, say, White people – for lack

of a better word – and basically feel like I fit in. I can be comfortable. But I find myself much more comfortable in Native communities. I think for some people there is one place where they feel at home and nowhere else, but I guess I sort of walk a line.

Deserly navigates the boundary between majority and minority communities in her personal, political, and professional decisions. This puts her in a particularly good position to represent a range of interests and to empathize with many different views. It is therefore not surprising that her business is dedicated to mediating between the experiences of tribal members and the construction of laws and agencies that govern the welfare of Native children. Deserly comments that she is "only now beginning to realize how few people have my experience in my particular field." She is proud to report that in one state she is helping to develop a tribal-state collaborative to bring tribes, state agency workers, and private non-Native agencies together to try to address pressing issues in child welfare. She comments, "It has been very difficult at times, but it has also been good; it's even been great, and it's getting better, but there is a long history of difficult relations."

Deserly, like the other minority women interviewed here, has a business that is inseparable from her personal identification with and dedication to a community. Her consulting business does not exist apart from her identity as a minority woman and her commitment to Native families. Though the money generated from her business supports her and her family, money is clearly not the *raison d'être* of the business. The same is true for each of the other minority women in this study; they live through their businesses on multiple levels: materially, emotionally, politically, professionally, and ethically. They are not looking to harvest their ventures and move onto the next, nor are their decisions calibrated toward rapids growth, expansion, and profit. Their businesses, and the emergent entrepreneurial processes, are a representation and extension of self in a larger social context.

PART 3

8

Minority women entrepreneurs: challenges and opportunities

The feminization and denigration of altruism

Samuel Johnson famously said, "No man but a blockhead ever wrote, except for money." While we send clear messages to men that maximizing profit is reasonable and valuable, women often get the message that work, regardless of remuneration, is a vital social contribution that is expected of them. In fact, women contribute the vast majority of unpaid labor (Crittenden 2001: 77). In effect, then, we define those who don't prioritize money, many of whom are women, as blockheads. And if men prioritize social good over money (unless they do so in a high-risk, daring, thrill-seeking way), they might very well meet with an even worse reception than women do. In fact, cynicism towards do-gooders is rampant, and motives that are not immediately self-serving or profit-generating are highly suspect.

Reporting on Paul Wagner, a man who donated a kidney to a stranger in need, Larissa MacFarquhar documents that his offer was met, in part, with public hostility. Wagner was the subject of an angry article in the Philadelphia *Daily News,* and he even received death threats in the hospital while recovering from the surgery. MacFarquhar writes:

> Most people find it uncomplicatedly admirable when a person risks his [*sic*] own life to rescue a stranger from fire, or from drowning. What, then, is it about saving a stranger by giving a kidney . . . that people find so odd? Do they feel there is something aggressive about the act, as though the donor

were implicitly rebuking them for not doing it, too? . . . Or perhaps it's that organ donation . . . is conceived in cold blood,
and cold-blooded altruism seems nearly as sinister as cold-
blooded malevolence. Perhaps only the hot-blooded, unthink-
ing sort can now escape altruism's tainted reputation, captured
in the suspicious terms for what people are really engaged in
when they think they're helping (sublimation, colonization,
group selection, potlatch, socialism, co-dependency – the list
goes on) . . . What was "altruism" after all? A motive so much
in conflict with primary instinct had to represent some kind
of pathology. Was it masochism? Unresolved guilt? Altruistic
donors . . . were "not to be trusted," "screwballs." "These people must be abnormal – to do such a thing," one transplant
surgeon said. Donating an organ to a stranger was not just
not admirable, doctors felt – it was perverse, it offended the
conscience. It was against human nature. (MacFarquhar 2009:
40,43)

Reflecting on this tendency to understand and define human nature as
essentially selfish and in constant, fierce competition for survival, Helena
Norberg-Hodge writes:

Mainstream Western thinkers from Adam Smith to Freud and
today's academics tend to universalize what is in fact Western
industrial experience. Explicitly or implicitly, they assume that
the traits they describe are a manifestation of human nature,
rather than a product of industrial culture. (Norberg-Hodge
1991: 2)

Reacting against this "mainstream Western" assumption, Yunus said,
"Human beings are a wonderful creation embodied with limitless human
qualities and capabilities. Our theoretical constructs should make room
for the blossoming of those qualities, not assume them away" (Yunus
2006). How can the assumption that humans are selfish and self-interested
explain that women do so much unpaid labor? Or spend more on others
than on themselves? Those who cling to the notion that human nature
is essentially selfish and competitive, and therefore consistent with lais-
sez-faire capitalism and traditional profit-driven enterprise, not only deny
the enduring gendered division of labor, but also ignore the fact that the
numerical majority of people – women – are human.

Working for social good has been denigrated as feminine self-sacrificing,
pathologized as masochistic, and penalized with poverty. Yet we could
not survive socially or economically without those who do this. They are
the "life-blood" of families and communities, and the "very heart of the

economy" (Crittenden 2001: 8). Human nature, then, is not necessarily competitive and self-interested; even the nature of business, insofar as it is defined as the exchange of goods and services, need not be essentially profit-driven. The characteristics that we have come to associate with business are merely the characteristics of the current dominant business culture, the values and representations of those in the majority. Those who differ, even insofar as they offer alternatives that resonate with social good, are all too often marginalized, ignored, and dismissed.

Assumptions about human nature that complement and support free-market economics define "rational" behavior as instrumental, strategic, and self-serving at the cost of relationships with others. For instance, game theories such as the Prisoner's Dilemma are sometimes used to predict and model individual responses to financial markets. In this game, players are told that they and a partner have been arrested and charged with a crime. The police, who have insufficient evidence to convict, question the suspects separately. Though the game has many variations, the general idea is this: if each remains loyal to the other and denies the crime, both will get a reduced sentence, such as one year apiece. If both betray their partner by telling the police of the other's guilt, then they each get the same sentence of five years (ten years collectively). But if only one partner betrays the other, and one remains loyal, then the betrayer is released and the loyal partner is given the longest jail time – say 15 years.

Using game theory to explain the "rational irrationality" that makes capitalism so prone to crashes, John Cassidy writes:

> The optimal joint result would require the two of you to keep quiet, so that you both got a light sentence . . . But you know that you're risking the maximum penalty if you keep quiet because your partner could seize a chance for freedom and betray you . . . Hence, the rational strategy for both of you is to confess and serve ten years in jail. In the language of game theory, confessing is a "dominant strategy," even though it leads to a disastrous result. (Cassidy 2009: 33).

According to Cassidy, the logic behind these models is "the same logic that applie[d] to the decisions made by Wall Street" (Cassidy 2009: 31) that ultimately led to the crash of 2008. In this case, it meant banks placed their bets against sub-prime mortgages even as they encouraged their clients to buy them. In the case of the Prisoner's Dilemma, this logic means reducing one's own jail time, even at the cost of the relationship with a partner. In both cases, prioritizing partnership before individual considerations is defined as irrational and unreasonable. The game itself produces and rewards this result. The results are, of course, a reflection of the values of those who make the rules of the game. They reflect a conventional understanding of rationality within economic theory: an understanding that valorizes self-interest and betrayal at the cost of cooperation and relationships.

Even when the "dominant strategy" leads to a "disastrous result," resistance to changing the conventional mode of doing business remains strong. For instance, each entrepreneur in this study describes, sometimes bitterly, how her minority status incurred prejudice and discrimination. Minority women have had to contend with abuse and invective, in part because they do not fit the usual demographic for business leaders, but also because they have the temerity to resist standard business practices, at times replacing competitive policies with cooperative ones. Like the altruistic organ donors, business owners who prioritize quality, community values, mutuality, and social good rather than profit alone are often disparaged and maligned.

The minority women in this study demonstrate that business does not have to operate as a separate economic sphere outside the context of human social values. In fact, the values by which profit-driven, self-interested business owners operate are not "business" values: **they are social values applied to business.** The entrepreneurs featured here draw attention to the fact that the tactics of business, even if commonly concealed under explanations of human nature or the perceived need to be competitive, are always within the purview of human choice and are always a manifestation of personal and cultural value systems. In other words, there are no economic inevitabilities that are beyond the scope of human intervention; business practices are not a product of rapacious, uncontrollable human nature intent on individual survival at any cost. That is a convenient myth used to justify the emphasis on short-term self-interest. These entrepreneurs remind us that selfless caring for others is just as central to human nature as is self-interest. More surprisingly, they demonstrate that caring for others is eminently compatible with lucrative, sustainable business enterprises. These stories, and so many others like them, challenge the notion that it is beyond human capacity to balance business concerns with social good.

In fact, researchers have found evidence that people are happiest when they use their money for *social* rather than *individual* ends. In their study, "Spending Money on Others Promotes Happiness," Dunn, Aknin *et al.* tested a representative sample of 632 Americans and found

> that spending more of one's income on others predicted greater
> happiness both cross-sectionally (in a nationally representative

survey study) and longitudinally (in a field study of windfall spending). Finally, participants who were randomly assigned to spend money on others experienced greater happiness than those assigned to spend money on themselves. (Dunn, Aknin *et al.* 2008: 1687)

They write, "Ironically . . . the mere thought of having money makes people less likely to help acquaintances, to donate to charity, or to choose to spend time with others, precisely the kinds of behaviors that are strongly associated with happiness" (Dunn, Aknin *et al.* 2008: 1687). However, given that those people who primarily pursue money are routinely thought of as devoid of sentiment and emotional attachment – as "solitary and selfish" (Bennett 2009) – it is not at all ironic that thoughts of money make people less likely to help others; it is predictable.

Dunn, Aknin *et al.* found that respondents were doubly wrong about the impact of money on happiness, with the majority predicting that personal spending (i.e., money spent on themselves) would make them more happy than pro-social spending (i.e., money spent on others) and that US$20 would make them happier than US$5. Therefore, to the degree that individuals think about money within the context of individual self-interest, they are reducing their ability to be happy. Yet we continue to assume and teach that the primary goal of business is profit, and the primary reason for making money is to advance individual self-interest. The conventional goals, then, of having a lot of money (getting rich) and spending it on oneself (instrumental rational action) are not the goals most likely to deliver happiness.

But if spending money on others leads to happiness, why isn't there more pro-social spending? In fact, pro-social spending is more the norm for women than for men; as we have seen, women donate a higher percentage of their income to charity, give more money to their heirs and spend more money on the care and welfare of children. Crittenden quotes economists Hoddinott and Haddad:

> It is supported by a mass of case study material that, relative to women, men spend more of the income under their own control for their own consumption. Alcohol, cigarettes, status consumer goods, even "female companionship" are noted in the literature. (Hoddinott and Haddad 1993 quoted in Crittenden 2001: 121)

Crittenden cites an impressive amount of empirical evidence that supports Yunus's observation that while men are more likely to indulge in personal spending, women are more likely to spend on others, especially on goods that benefit children. Here are some examples:

- In Kenya and Malawi, the more income controlled by women the greater the household caloric intake, whatever the overall household earnings

- In Jamaica, female-headed households consume foods of higher nutritional quality and spend a larger share of their income on children's goods

- In the hands of a Brazilian woman, US$1 has the same effect on child survival as US$18 in the hands of a man

- In Guatemala, the higher the share of total household income earned by a child's mother, the better nourished the child. Extrapolating this data, US$11.40 per month in a mother's hands would result in a child achieving the same weight gain as US$166 earned by the father

- A study of 14 typical poor villages in South India found that the men retained up to a quarter of the earnings for their own personal use – five to six times the proportion of their own income that women spent on themselves

- Jan Pahl, a sociologist at the University of Kent in Canterbury, confirms that "compared to men, women hold less [income] back, both absolutely and relatively, for their personal use." (Crittenden 2001: 121-22, 125)

Though money might not be able to buy happiness, in the right hands it has enormous power to accomplish social good, and that, apparently, is where happiness thrives.

Since it is clear that human nature is not inherently selfish, some biological arguments attempt to establish an intractable difference between men's "nature" and women's "nature" such that only women (and only because of biological imperatives beyond their control) can possibly conduct themselves in such a pro-social manner. Though they continue to be popular, we have given ourselves the permission not to engage with biological, deterministic arguments or any arguments that claim women and men are "essentially" different. Currently, at least, these arguments are a less popular but still extant perspective from which to explain behavioral differences among races, ethnicities, and nationalities. Many distinguished scholars (Chodorow 1978; Fausto-Sterling 2000; Lorber 1995; Kimmel 2004;

Risler 2007; Bardo 1999; Caprioli, Hudson *et al.* 2007) have already admira-
bly refuted a range of claims that use essentialism or biological determin-
ism as well as explained the mutability and social–historical context of
constructs such as gender, race, ethnicity, disability, and sexual orientation. We join them in maintaining that selves are not biologically determined, but that cultural, social, economic, and ideological structures
provide the context for mutualistic, pro-social, cooperative behavior and
the development of relational selfhood (see discussion in Part 1 beginning
on page 109). In this view, anyone is theoretically capable of developing
relational selfhood.

Pro-social caring for others is so closely associated with the social construct of femininity that despite its correlation with increased happiness,
economic stability and the decline of poverty, caring work is often perceived as weak and inferior – unworthy of men because it erodes masculine strength and independence. In their book *On Kindness,* Adam Phillips
and Barbara Taylor explain:

> Yet ironically, one of the key outcomes of the egoism–kindness
> quarrel was to feminize kindness, divesting it from humanity as
> a whole while leaving a residue of womanly kindness, notably
> maternal solicitude. In recent times kindness has been largely
> a feminine prerogative, with men consigned to lonely egoism.
> (Phillips and Taylor 2009: 16)

Riane Eisler calls the dichotomy between men as superior leaders, and
women as inferior servants, the "dominator configuration" (Eisler 2007:
95). Under this configuration, all that is associated with femininity, females
and women (including care-giving work, contributions to social good, and
pro-social behavior) are perceived suspiciously and, as the surgeon said of
the organ donor, "abnormal and perverse." Eisler writes:

> The first component of the dominator configuration is a struc-
> ture of rigid top–down rankings maintained through physical,
> psychological and economic control . . . the second core com-
> ponent is a high level of abuse and violence from child and
> wife beating to chronic warfare . . . in the dominator system
> we find the institutionalization and idealization of abuse and
> violence. This is needed to maintain rigid rankings of domina-
> tion – man over women, man over man, race over race, religion
> over religion and nation over nation. It provides a mental map
> that children learn for equating *all* differences . . . Along with
> the ranking of male over female comes the ranking of quali-
> ties and behaviors classified as "hard" or masculine over those

classified as "soft" or feminine. "Heroic" violence and "manly" conquest, as in funding for weapons and wars, are valued more than caring, non-violence, and care giving.

Cultures . . . that orient closely to [the dominator system] teach that it's honorable and moral to kill people of neighboring nations or tribes, stone women to death, enslave "inferior" people and beat children to impose one's will. War is "holy" . . . and . . . these four components . . . shape all social and economic institutions of the dominator system. (Risler 2007: 96-97 [emphasis in the original])

According to Eisler, dominator economies rest on a stark contrast between "men's" work (which might also be done by women oriented to socially identified masculine characteristics) and "women's" work (which might also be carried out by men who identify with feminine qualities). There are also gradations of superior and inferior work based on such things as race, socioeconomic class, nationality, and religion. In male-dominated societies, the life-supporting, pro-social work that women contribute is devalued, both economically and in terms of social prestige. As discussed earlier, because domination and exploitation are so commonly associated with businesses that operate in capitalistic economies, the minority women in this study work hard to differentiate themselves from conventional business owners, but at the same time, they also have to convince others that they are hard-nosed enough to participate successfully in the capitalist marketplace.

Both Margaret Henningsen and Kathy Deserly commented that they work with "tough" women "who don't like to be crossed," and Judi Henderson-Townsend is careful not to characterize herself as an environmentalist. Rita Chang laments the expectation that women, especially those who are teachers, should "give everything away" and are socially stigmatized if they work for economic benefit. Unfortunately, the mentality that "good" women should not work for economic benefit diminishes the amount of money women control and therefore their ability to use their income to contribute to social good. Eisler points out that it is not capitalism *per se*, but domination that is significant, and domination can inform any economic, social, or religious system. **Based on the narratives presented here, businesses in a capitalist economy need not be configured on domination, but instead can be the conduit for personal, moral, and political development within a context of commitment to social good.**

Eisler is among many to make a connection between conventional capitalism and violent domination. In *The Shock Doctrine: The Rise of Disaster Capitalism,* Naomi Klein (2007) argues that capitalism, putatively a natural consequence of self-interested human nature, is instead imposed on societies that have suffered artificial crises and orchestrated disasters. According to Klein, the architect of "disaster capitalism" is Milton Friedman, the "Chicago School" economist who, as previously mentioned, believed "the business of business is to make a profit, not to engage in socially beneficial acts" (Reich 2007: 173). Klein explains:

> Friedman first learned how to exploit a large-scale shock or crisis in the mid-seventies, when he acted as adviser to the Chilean dictator, General Augusto Pinochet. Not only were the Chileans in a state of shock following Pinochet's violent coup, but the country was also traumatized by severe hyperinflation. Friedman advised Pinochet to impose a rapid-fire transformation of the economy – tax cuts, free trade, privatized services, cuts to social spending and deregulation . . . It was the most extreme capitalist makeover ever attempted anywhere, and it became known as a "Chicago School" revolution . . . Friedman predicted that the speed, suddenness and scope of the economic shifts would provoke psychological reactions in the public that "facilitate the adjustment." He coined a phrase for this painful tactic: economic "shock treatment." . . . Pinochet also facilitated the adjustment with his own shock treatments; these were performed in the regime's many torture cells, inflicted on the writhing bodies of those deemed most likely to stand in the way of the capitalist transformation. Many in Latin America saw a direct connection between the economic shocks that impoverished millions and the epidemic of torture that punished hundreds of thousands of people who believed in a different kind of society. (Klein 2007: 8)

The U.S. has imposed similar capitalistic economies in various nations, most recently Iraq. "Operation Iraqi Freedom" was begun on the assumption that the Iraqi government possessed weapons of mass destruction and was harboring Al-Qaeda operatives. Both accusations were proved false in short order but the invasion continued, with the new goal of installing a democratic government and spreading democracy in the region. Various estimates of Iraqi civilian deaths range between 85,000 and 1,000,000. The war began with so-called "shock and awe" waves which bombed populated areas, and continued with extensive use of torture of those identified by the U.S. military as "enemy combatants." Critics point out that, as of 2009, current costs to American taxpayers exceed US$3 trillion, but multinational corporations such as Halliburton, Bechtel, Custer Battles, Exxon-Mobil and Chevron have profited handsomely from the war. Companies such as CACI and Titan, private firms contracted by the U.S. government for "intelligence" work, have provided "interrogators" to such sites as Abu Ghraib prison where torture has been extensively documented in photos disseminated through the popular press.

In his research on the first war between the U.S. and Iraq, Stephen J. Ducat contends that support for the war had a gendered component: "men were more likely to endorse statements that linked military victory with one's own self-esteem . . . and . . . the hawks . . . were more concerned than the doves with not being feminine" (Ducat 2004: 180). Ducat links general aggression and support of aggression, including war, to the fear of being corrupted by feminizing forces, a fear he refers to "femiphobia," which he defines as an "inner-directed expression of misogyny, an unconscious hatred for and dread of a part of the self experienced as feminine" (Ducat 2004: 47). He writes:

> In the broadest sense, this involves the devaluation of all things associated with women – their work, their artistic or literary creations, their philosophical contributions, their athletic achievements and their scientific accomplishments. Much of the devaluation of women is directed more specifically at their childbearing and nurturing capabilities . . . The feminizing danger may seem to come from multiple sources – gay or transgender men and women, a maternally construed "big government," advocates of national health insurance, environmentalists seeking to increase regulatory constraints of corporate activities, or peace activists. (Ducat 2004: 43, 47)

Both peace and war are concepts, orientations, and sets of behaviors associated with gender: peace and cooperation are feminized, while war and conflict are associated with masculinity. In their article "Putting Women in their Place," Caprioli, Hudson *et al.* found that in addition to increased political and economic stability, "women's equality [with men] is a harbinger of peace" (Caprioli, Hudson *et al.* 2007: 17). Arguing that gender equality and nonviolence are linked through social norms of tolerance rather than based on women being "naturally" or biologically more peaceful, they found that *high social status for women and low levels of violence against women correlate more closely with intranational and international peace than the factors of national economic stability, religious culture, or democratic government.* They report:

> Domestic norms of violence inherent in structural inequality transfer to the international arena just as domestic norms of peaceful conflict resolution do . . . In sum, the promotion of

> gender equality goes far beyond the issue of social justice. It is
> a necessary condition for international peace. (Caprioli, Hud-
> son *et al.* 2007: 15)

But Danny Gordon already knows that. Featured in Nick Paumgarten's article "The Girl Counter," Gordon was hired to count the number of people
who use the restrooms at Bryant Park, and he makes a distinction between
women and men (Paumgarten 2007). Located in the heart of Manhattan and
touted as an urban oasis, Bryant Park is run by Dan Biederman, President
of the Bryant Park Corporation and a protégé of urban sociologist, the late
William Hollingsworth Whyte. Whyte observed that the "most-used places
also tend to have a higher than average proportion of women . . . Women
are more discriminating . . . more sensitive to annoyances. If a plaza has a
markedly lower than average proportion of women, something is wrong"
(Whyte 1980: 18). Accordingly, the presence of women "indicates civic
health" (Paumgarten 2007). Biederman's advice is: "Go to any public space
in the world. If it's skewing overwhelmingly male, get out as soon as possible" (Paumgarten 2007).

That understanding is at the basis of new initiatives targeting women,
such as the one in South Korea known as "Happy Women, Happy Seoul."
In an effort to draw women into the city, convenient parking places have
been set aside for them and are designated with the traditional women's
icon: a stick figure wearing a skirt. The initiative also includes a plan to
make sidewalks more "high-heel-friendly," a job-search program for unemployed women, more public female restrooms, better lighting in public
spaces, safe parks for women, a women's taxi service, and more public
day care (Zaragovia 2009). Efforts are also under way in India to make
women more comfortable. Responding to the high level of harassment
Indian women routinely face on public transport, a persistent obstacle for
women commuting to work, the government has "decided to remove the
men altogether" (Yardley 2009). Pilot cities for women-only trains include
New Delhi, Mumbai, Chennai, and Calcutta. Though women occupy some
of the most powerful political posts in India and the Indian constitution
guarantees gender equality, the increased numbers of women in the workplace has been met with increased violence against women (Yardley 2009).
Interviewed on her experience, Kiran Khas, a teacher, relates her experience on the women-only trains "as if she is describing a miracle" (Yardley 2009). Khas says, "Here on this train, you can board anywhere and sit
freely" (Yardley 2009).

If the absence of women means that something is wrong, then something
is wrong in the upper echelons of the business world. In Whyte's parlance

and in Biederman's understanding, a public space is an outdoor area: for example, Bryant Park in Manhattan. The concept of public space, however, can be expanded to include physical workplaces as well as the concepts that dominate business and entrepreneurship discourse, pedagogy, practices, and goals. As a public place in this larger sense, business has skewed overwhelming male, and because current social definitions of masculinity include aggression and dominance, perhaps it is not surprising that the business world has been showing signs of civic decay, even abuse and crime.

Entrepreneurship research, literature, training, and textbooks have maintained a largely male-dominated, White, educated, perspective that gives primacy to material wealth and profit-driven enterprises (Ogbor 2000). Perhaps because they do not fit the assumptions about entrepreneurs as "one-dimensional human beings, who are dedicated to one mission in their business lives – to maximize profit" (Yunus 2006), women and minorities are frequently left out of the discourse, images, and data gathering. Yunus contends that "By defining 'entrepreneur' in a broader way we can change the character of capitalism radically, and solve many of the unresolved social and economic problems within the scope of the free market" (Yunus 2006). This suggests a new central theorem for business: the reconsideration of relationships, of the interconnectivity between and among individuals, communities, and environmental health. Such a restructuring of values would inevitably lead to the prioritization of pro-social enterprises.

Opportunities for 'caring economics': business as a complex problem

In *Getting to Maybe: How the World is Changed*, Westley, Zimmerman *et al.* contend that all innovations start with new ways of thinking (Westley, Zimmerman *et al.* 2006: 6). First, there must be a belief that intractable problems can be solved. Then:

> there must be an individual or group of individuals poised and ready to act – but these do not have to be perfect people. The trick is to see the relationship among all these elements . . . To understand social innovations we must see the world in all its complexity. (Westley, Zimmerman *et al.* 2006: 7)

Some methods of seeing the world arise from using metaphors that focus only on selective parts of complex systems – from machines: "like clockwork," or "a well-oiled machine"; from farming: humans are "resources" and businesses are "harvested"; from economics: "human capital"; or even from body parts: "hired hands," "put your heads together" and "gut instinct." They write that the reduction of complex systems to individual parts makes it easy to neglect "the living aspect of our world and our work" and recognize that life is "unpredictable, emergent, evolving and adaptable" (Westley, Zimmerman *et al.* 2006: 7). Paraphrased below, Westley, Zimmerman *et al.* suggest an eloquent yet powerful rubric to differentiate among three types of problems: simple, complicated, and complex:

> **Simple problems** – like building a chair – can be addressed using patterns and behaviors established by routine craft or commonly held knowledge; while **complicated problems** – like building a plane – require a high level of technical sophistication and precision, and tight coordination through rigid protocols. Success in a complicated problem will result from sticking to these rigid protocols and strict application of pre-established rules and roles. Laxness or negligence likely leads to catastrophic results in addressing a complicated problem. By contrast, a **complex problem** – like raising a child – requires sensitivity to the uniqueness of the situation at hand, and recognition that approaches used to address simple or complicated problems may not work or may be counter-productive in such a context. Complexity involves thinking about the problem in a different way, both in terms of being aware of and sensitive to the connections that need to be made as well as in terms of the knowledge needed to address it. (Raufflet and Mills 2009: 2-3 [emphasis in the original])

Adhering to directions for simple problems assures easy, replicable success. Complicated problems can be solved if protocols are followed and there is a high likelihood of replication. However, complex tasks such as "raising one child provides experiences but is no guarantee of success with the next" (Westley, Zimmerman *et al.* 2006: 7). Unlike a simple chair that can be built with instructions specifying where each part fits, and a complicated plane that can be assembled with a blueprint, in complex problems, the parts cannot be separated from the whole because the "essence exists in the relationship between different people, different experiences, different moments in time" and the outcome therefore remains uncertain (Westley, Zimmerman *et al.* 2006: 7).

Business has traditionally been approached as a complicated problem, one with identifiable parts that have a set relationship to each other – there are markets, margins, products, financial statements, and sales predictions. The presumption was that based on blueprints of cost analyses, profit and loss, supply and demand, we could predictably determine whether a business would be competitive with other businesses. A profitable business was the equivalent of a successful business, and a very profitable business was a very successful one.

However, treating the development of successful businesses as a complicated problem underestimates the complexity of the social, political, cultural, economic, and environmental systems that are touched by business practices, and neglects to acknowledge that these systems are all inextricably related. Building a caring business in a social context is not a complicated problem; it is a complex one. The sum of the parts is not equal to the whole. The relationships and connections among the parts define success or failure. The minority women interviewed here demonstrate there is no need to adhere to the rigid protocol of prioritizing profit; they do not need to deny their emotional attachments to family and community – they can celebrate them. They do not have to decide between social values and ethical behavior on the one hand, and instrumental, amoral behavior on the other. Those rules laid out as imperatives for a business to stay afloat are characteristic of complicated systems, but not of complex ones. The minority women interviewed here treat their entrepreneurial processes as a set of ongoing, emergent relationships that fulfill a wide range of needs and objectives. They demonstrate an understanding of entrepreneurship that transcends its conventional representation in research, pedagogy, and literature; they see entrepreneurship, and show it to us, in all its complexity.

Challenges to adopting caring economics and creating socially conscious businesses

Eisler writes:

> It becomes evident that we can't continue to exploit and pollute our natural environment. It also becomes evident that to live more fulfilling and less stressful lives, we must adequately value caring and caregiving not only in the market but in all economic sectors, from the household to nature ... (Eisler 2007: 20)

The current definition of business, the one most often taught in colleges and universities to aspiring entrepreneurs and business people, is the primary pursuit of "economic goals (profit) in order to remain competitive in the context of market forces and survive over the long term" (Neck, Brush *et al.* 2009: 14). This definition does not distinguish car manufacturers from drug dealers, restaurateurs from human traffickers, or bankers from munitions smugglers. Using the same logic and principles of the most egregious examples of exploitation and avarice, our mainstream definition of business is absent social merit. We need fundamental changes that transform our social, political, economic, and domestic systems. These changes must be sweeping shifts away from domination, exploitation, and instrumental rationality, and toward the valuation of economic equity, mutuality, social good, and environmental conservation. Mere modifications of the established systems will not be sufficient to turn the tide of overwhelming economic inequality, severe ecological damage, and dwindling natural resources.

As Gladwell reminds us, dramatic change originates from outside of the establishment, from those who are new to the game. Against the backdrop of many quantitative studies suggesting similar behavior, the minority women entrepreneurs featured here imbue their business decisions with a complex set of moral and economic imperatives, contextualized within and motivated by social considerations that serve to consciously create and develop relational selfhood. They demonstrate that it is possible to maintain an economically healthy business without having to choose between a profit-driven and a values-driven venture. Their businesses are both. Business educators and economists might continue to claim this balance is impossible; they might refuse to acknowledge its existence, but that refusal is based on loyalty to instrumental rationality and profit-maximization as the acceptable motivations for business enterprises. In other words, the refusal to recognize socially conscious ventures as viable, lucrative, and sustainable is based on the rejection of humanistic social values and the populations associated with those values.

Similarly, we possess the solutions to remedy educational, social, and economic inequality – we have had those solutions for decades. They are not mysterious and unknown, however much the problems are portrayed as inevitable and insoluble. We see these solutions in the work of Mohammad Yunus, Claude Steele, Jane Margolis, Uri Treisman, Riane Eisler, and many others. To implement these solutions systematically would mean major shifts in power, prestige, resources, and material wealth. Although there is public outrage at exploitive business practices – especially during economic crises – and similar outcry about the large number of impoverished populations struggling to survive, there is also overwhelming resistance to the very changes that would relieve these problems. Research that outlines solutions to these problems is often lost, discredited, or ignored.

The layers of embedded inequality that characterize capitalism, bureau-cratic government, private education, and cultural and religious systems of oppression can seem too dense, too daunting, too overwhelming ever to be rectified. Addressing this sense of discouragement, Robert Jensen writes:

> No system, no matter how overwhelming and oppressive, is beyond challenge. Borrowing a metaphor from Naomi Sche-man, we can think of . . . concrete in the city. It covers almost everything. It is heavy and seemingly unmovable, and it paves the world. But the daily wear and tear produces cracks, and in those cracks, plants grow, weeds, grass, sometimes a flower. Living things have no business growing up out of concrete, but they do. They resist the totality of the concrete. No system of power can obliterate all resistance. All systems yield space in which things can grow. (Jensen 1988: 108)

Recognizing the frequency and complexity of social and economic change, one thing has remained with overwhelming durability: there have always been populations of people who have dependably delivered pro-social behavior and developed relational selfhood. It is this large, established, enduring population which possesses the mentality and sensibility to guide the future of business away from the debacle of exploitive, destruc-tive ends and towards socially conscious, humanistic goals. The first step is to grant socially conscious entrepreneurs the visibility and credit they deserve. As Pauline Lewis says:

> I've never understood "the protect yourself by not sharing, not giving, or [by] being territorial and not lending a hand to folks" . . . It's just never been a part of who I am, and I think that people who have a tendency to think that way – this is not the time for them.

References

Ali, A.H. (2007) *Infidel* (New York: Free Press).

Allen, E., N. Langowitz, and M. Minniti (2006) *Global Entrepreneurship Monitor: National Entrepreneurship Assessment, United States of America, 2005 Executive Report* (Babson Park, MA: Babson College).

Allen, P.G. (2007) "Where I Come from is Like This," in L. Richardson, V. Taylor, and N. Whittier (eds.), *Feminist Frontiers* (New York: McGraw-Hill, 7th edn).

Alvesson, M., and Y.D. Billing (1997) *Understanding Gender and Organizations* (Thousand Oaks, CA: Sage).

Appiah, K.A. (2006) *Cosmopolitanism* (New York: W.W. Norton).

Asthana, A. (2007) "Names really do make a difference: Research shows that girls with 'feminine' names steer clear of 'masculine' maths and science," *The Guardian*; www.guardian.co.uk/science/2007/apr/29/theobserversuknewspages.uknews, accessed May 1, 2009.

Baker, L.D. (1996) "Ida B. Wells-Barnett and Her Passion for Justice"; www.duke.edu/~ldbaker/classes/AAIH/caaih/ibwells/ibwbkgrd.html, accessed October 19, 2007.

Baker, T., H. Aldrich, and N. Liou (1997) "Invisible Entrepreneurs: The Neglect of Women Business Owners by Mass Media and Scholarly Journals in the U.S.A.," *Entrepreneurship and Regional Development* 9: 221-38.

Bakken, L.L. (2005) "Who are Physician–Scientists' Role Models? Gender Makes a Difference," *Academic Medicine* 80.5: 502-506.

Banks, M. (2006) "Moral Economy and Cultural Work," *Sociology* 40.3: 455-72.

Bardo, S. (1999) *The Male Body* (New York: Farrar, Straus & Giroux).

Baxter, J. (1994) "Is Husband's Class Enough? Class Location and Class Identity in the United States, Sweden, Norway and Australia," *American Sociological Review* 59: 220-25.

Becker, H.S. (1970) *Sociological Work: Method and Substance* (Chicago: Aldine).

Beldecos, A., S. Bailey, S. Gilbert, K. Hicks, L. Kenschaft, N. Niemczyk, R. Rosenberg, S. Schaertel, and A. Wedel (1988) "The Importance of a Feminist Critique for Contemporary Cell Biology," *Hypatia* 3.1: 61-76.

Bennett, D. (2009) "Happiness: A Buyer's Guide – money can improve your life but not always in the ways you think," *The Boston Globe*, August 23, 2009; www.boston.com/bostonglobe/ideas/articles/2009/08/23/happiness_a_buyers_guide, accessed August 23, 2009.

Berger, J., B.P. Cohen, and M. Zelditch, Jr (1966) "Status Characteristics and Expectation States," in J. Berger, M. Zelditch, Jr, and B. Anderson (eds.), *Sociological Theories in Progress* (New York: Houghton Mifflin): 29-46.

——, H. Fisek, R. Norman, and M. Zelditch, Jr (1966) "Status Characteristics and Social Interaction," *American Sociological Review* 37: 241-55.

——, H. Fisek, R. Norman, and M. Zelditch, Jr (1977) *Status Characteristics and Social Interaction* (New York: Elsevier).

Biernacki, R. (1995) *The Fabrication of Labor* (Berkeley, CA: University of California Press).

Bonacich, E., and J. Modell (1980) *The Economic Basis of Ethnic Solidarity: Small Businesses in the Japanese American Community* (Berkeley, CA: University of California Press).

Bottomly, H.K. (2007) "Words to the Community," *Wellesley* 92.1 (Fall 2007): 29.

Bourdieu, P. (1977) *Outline of Theory and Practice* (Cambridge, UK: Cambridge University Press).

Breyer, S. (1999) "Justice Harry A. Blackmun: Principle and Compassion," *Columbia Law Review* 99.6 (October 1999): x, 1393-96.

Broverman, I.K., S.R. Vogel, D.M. Broverman, F.E. Clarkson, and F.S. Rosenkrantz (1972) "Sex-Role Stereotypes: A Current Appraisal," *Journal of Social Issues* 28: 59-78.

Brush, C. (1997) "Women-Owned Businesses: Obstacles and Opportunities," *Journal of Developmental Entrepreneurship* 2.1 (Spring/Summer 1997): 1-24.

Butler, J.S. (1991) *Entrepreneurship and Self-help among Black Americans: A Reconsideration of Race and Economics* (New York: State University of New York Press).

—— (2005) "Regional Wealth Creation and the 21st Century: Women and 'Minorities' in the Tradition of Economic Strangers" (unpublished manuscript; IC²/Herb Kelleher Center, University of Texas at Austin).

Caprioli, M., V. Hudson, R. McDermott, C. Emmett, and B. Ballif-Spanvill (2007) "Putting Women in Their Place," *Baker Center Journal of Applied Public Policy* 1.1: 12-22.

Casper, W.J., D. Weltma, and E. Kwesiga (2007) "Beyond Family Friendly: The Construct and Measurement of Singles-Friendly Work Culture," *Journal of Vocational Behavior* 70.3: 478-501.

Cassidy, J. (2009) "Rational Irrationality," *The New Yorker*, October 5, 2009: 30-35.

Charmaz, K. (2001) "Grounded Theory," in R.M. Emerson (ed.), *Contemporary Field Research: A Collection of Readings* (Prospect Heights, IL: Waveland Press, 2nd edn).

Chodorow, N. (1978) *The Reproduction of Mothering: Psychoanalysis and the Sociology of Gender* (Berkeley and Los Angeles, CA: University of California Press).

—— (2001) "Family Structure and the Feminine Personality," in L. Richardson, V. Taylor, and N. Whittier (eds.), *Feminist Frontiers* (New York: McGraw-Hill, 5th edn).

Clark, K.B., and M.K. Clark (1939) "The Development of Consciousness of Self and Racial Identification in Negro Pre-school Children," *Journal of Social Psychology S.P.S.S.I. Bulletin* 10: 591-99.

Coffey, B., and P.A. McLaughlin (2009) "Do Masculine Names Help Female Lawyers Become Judges? Evidence from South Carolina," *American Law and Economic Review* 11.1: 112-24.

Collier, P.J., and D.L. Morgan (2007) "Role Mastery as Cultural Capital," paper presented at the *102nd Annual American Sociological Association Meeting*, New York, August 2007.

Collins, P.H. (1991) "Controlling Images of Black Women's Oppression," in J.J. Macionis and N.V. Benokraitis (eds.), *Seeing Ourselves: Classic, Contemporary, and Cross-cultural Readings in Sociology* (Upper Saddle River, NJ: Pearson Prentice Hall, 7th edn [2007]).

Collins, R. (1992) *Sociological Insight* (New York: Oxford University Press).

Collins, S., and J. Hoopes (1995) "Anthony Giddens and Charles Sanders Peirce: History, Theory and a Way Out of the Linguistic Cul-de-sac," *Journal of the History of Ideas* 56.4: 625-65.

Cooley, C.H. (1902) *Human Nature and the Social Order* (New York: Schocken Books [1964]).

Coughlin, J.H. (2002) *The Rise of Women Entrepreneurs* (Westport, CT: Quorum Books).

Crittenden, A. (2001) *The Price of Motherhood* (New York: Metropolitan Books).

CWBR (Center for Women's Business Research) (2009) "The Economic Impact of Women-Owned Businesses in the United States" (McLean, VA: CWBR; www.womensbusinessresearchcenter. org/Data/research/economicimpactstud/econimpactreport-final.pdf, accessed October 30, 2010).

Davies, P.G., S.J. Spencer, and C.M. Steele (2005) "Clearing the Air: Identity Safety Moderates the Effects of Stereotype Threat on Women's Leadership Aspirations," *Journal of Personality and Social Psychology* 88.2: 276-87.

Davis, N., and R. Robinson (1988) "Class Identification of Men and Women in the 1970s and 1980s," *American Sociological Review* 53: 103-12.

Day, P. (2009) "BBC Interview" (National Public Radio, April 10, 2009; www.bbc.co.uk/worldservice/business/2009/04/090403_peter_day_comment_mar_31.shtml, accessed November 18, 2010).

Dedham, B. (1988) "The Color of Money," *The Atlanta Journal Constitution* (Atlanta, GA: The Cox Enterprises Group, May 1–4, 1988; powerreporting.com/color/color_of_money. pdf, accessed November 3, 2010).

Ducat, S.J. (2004) *The Wimp Factor: Gender Gaps, Holy Wars and the Politics of Anxious Masculinity* (Boston, MA: Beacon Press).

Dunn, E.W., L.B. Aknin, and M.I. Norton (2008) "Spending Money on Others Promotes Happiness," *Science* 319.5870: 1687-88; DOI: 10.1126/science.1150952.

Durkheim, E. (1897) *Suicide: A Study in Sociology* (London: Penguin Books [2006]).

Duval-Couëtil, N. (2007) personal conversation with Mary Godwyn, October 12, 2007.

Eagly, A.H., and M.J. Johannesen-Schmidt (2001) "The Leadership Styles of Women and Men," *Journal of Social Issues* 57.4: 781-97.

Eby, L.T., W.J. Casper, A. Lockwood, C. Bordeaux, and A. Brinley (2005) "Work and Family Research in IO/OB: Content Analysis and Review of Literature (1980–2002)," *Journal of Vocational Behavior* 66.1: 124-97.

The Economist (2009) "A Special Report on Entrepreneurship. An idea whose time has come: Entrepreneurialism has become cool," *The Economist,* March 12, 2009; www. economist.com/node/13216053?story_id=13216053, accessed May 1, 2009.

Eisler, R. (2007) *The Real Wealth of Nations* (Williston, VT: Berrett-Koehler Publishers).

Elliott, J.R., and R. Smith (2004) "Race, Gender, and Workplace Power," *American Sociological Review* 69.3: 365-86.

Ely, R., and I. Padavic (2007) "A Feminist Analysis on Organizational Research on Sex Differences," *Academy of Management Review* 32.4, 1121-43.

Emerson, R.M. (1983) *Contemporary Field Research: Perspectives and Formulations* (Prospective Heights, IL: Waveland Press).

Espiritu, Y.L. (1997) "Ideological Racism and Cultural Resistance: Constructing Our Own Images," in L. Richardson, V. Taylor, and N. Whittier (eds.), *Feminist Frontiers* (New York: McGraw-Hill, 5th edn [2001]).

Fausto-Sterling, A. (2000) *Sexing the Body: Gender Politics and the Construction of Sexuality* (New York: Basic Books).

Fleischmann, F. (2006) "Entrepreneurship as Emancipation: The History of an Idea" (lecture, Free University of Berlin, July 12, 2006).

Fourcade, M., and K. Healy (2007) "Moral Views of Market Society," *Annual Review of Sociology* 33: 285-311.

Fox, J. (2009) "The way we'll work," *Time* 173.20: 41.

Frank, R. (2009) "The Wealth Report: Rich Women Give More to Charity than Men," *Wall Street Journal*, July 13, 2009; www.middlebergcommunications.com/documents/WSJBlogsJuly1309.pdf, accessed August 2, 2009.

Franklin, V.P. (1995) *Living Our Stories, Telling Our Truths: Autobiography and the Making of African American Intellectual Tradition* (Oxford, UK: Oxford University Press).

Fraser, I. (2007) "Microfinance comes of age," *Scottish Banker Magazine*; www.ianfraser.org/microfinance-comes-of-age, accessed November 6, 2010.

Friedan, B. (1963) *The Feminine Mystique* (New York: W.W. Norton & Co.).

Friedman, T.L. (2005) *The World is Flat: A Brief History of the Twenty-first Century* (New York: Farrar, Straus & Giroux, 1st edn).

Fronczek, P. (2005) "Income, Earnings and Poverty from the 2004 American Community Survey," *American Community Survey Reports*; www.census.gov/prod/2005pubs/acs-01.pdf, accessed October 13, 2007.

Galinsky, A.D., J.C. Magee, M.E. Inesi, and D.H. Gruenfeld (2006) "Power and Perspectives not Taken," *Psychological Science* 17.12: 1068-74.

Gilbert, A. (2002) "Computer Science's Gender Gap"; www.news.com/2102-1082_3-833090.html?tag=st.util.print, accessed 16 October 2007.

Gilligan, C. (1982) *In a Different Voice* (Cambridge, MA: Harvard University Press).

Gladwell, M. (2005) *Blink* (New York: Little, Brown & Co.).

—— (2008) *Outliers* (New York: Little, Brown & Co.).

—— (2009) "How David beats Goliath," *The New Yorker*, May 11, 2009: 48.

Godwyn, M. (2009a) "Hugh Connerty and Hooters: What is Successful Entrepreneurship?" in E. Raufflet and A.J. Mills (eds.), *The Dark Side: Critical Cases on the Downside of Business* (Sheffield, UK: Greenleaf Publishing).

—— (2009b) "Can the Liberal Arts and Entrepreneurship Work Together?" *Academe: The Bulletin of the American Association of University Professors* 95.1: 36-38; www.aaup.org/AAUP/pubsres/academe/2009/JF/Feat/godw.htm, accessed September 3, 2010.

—— (2009c) " 'This Place Makes Me Proud to be a Woman': Theoretical Explanations for Success in Entrepreneurship Education for Low-Income Women," *Research in Social Stratification and Mobility* 27.1: 50-64; DOI:10.1016/j.rssm.2008.10.003.

Goffman, E. (1963) *Stigma: Notes on the Management of Spoiled Identity* (New York: Simon & Schuster).

Gonzales, P.M., H. Blanton, and K. Williams (2002) "The Effect of Stereotype Threat and Double-Minority Status on the Test Performance of Latino Women," *Personality and Social Psychology Bulletin* 28.5: 659-70.

Grandin, T., and C. Johnson (2009) *Animals Make Us Human: Creating the Best Life for Animals* (New York: Mariner Books).

Green, W.S. (2005) "Entrepreneurship, Education, and Freedom: Reflections on the Kauffman Campuses Initiative," *Kauffman Occasional Paper Series*: 1-7.

Greene, P.G., and C.G. Brush (2004) "Women Entrepreneurs: An Explanatory Framework of Capital Types," in J.S. Butler and G. Kozmetsky (eds.), *Immigrant and Minority Entrepreneurship: The Continuous Rebirth of American Communities* (Westport, CN: Praeger).

—— and M. Johnson (1995) "Social Learning Middleman Minority Theory: Explanations for Self-employed Women," *National Journal of Sociology* 9.1: 60-83.

Hacker, H.M. (1951) "Women as a Minority Group," *Social Forces* 30: 60-69.

Hamper, B. (1986) *Rivethead* (New York: Time Warner Books).

Heilman, M.E., C.J. Block, R. Martell, and M. Simon (1989) "Has Anything Changed? Current Characterizations of Men, Women, and Managers," *Journal of Applied Psychology* 74.6: 935-42.

Hochschild, A. (1983) *The Managed Heart: Commercialization of Human Feeling* (Berkeley, CA: University of California Press).

—— (1989) *The Second Shift* (New York: Avon Books).

Hoddinott, J., and L. Haddad (1993) "Understanding How Resources are Allocated within Households," paper presented at the *Canadian Economics Association Meeting*, Ottawa, Canada.

Holland, K. (2009) "Is it time to retrain B-schools?" *New York Times*, March 9, 2009; www.nytimes.com/2009/03/15/business/15school.html, accessed June 6, 2009.

Hubbard, R. (1988) "Science, Facts and Feminism," in N. Tuana (ed.), *Feminism and Science* (Bloomington, IN: Indiana University Press): 119-31.

—— (1990) *The Politics of Women's Biology* (Piscataway, NJ: Rutgers University Press).

—— (1995) *Profitable Promises: Essays on Women, Science and Health* (Monroe, ME: Common Courage Press).

Hull, G., P.B. Scott, and B. Smith (eds.) (1982) *All the Women are White, All the Blacks are Men, But Some of us are Brave: Black Women's Studies* (New York: Feminist Press).

Jensen, R. (1998) "Patriarchal Sex," in S.P. Schacht and D.W. Ewing (eds.), *Feminism and Men* (New York: New York University Press).

Johnson, J.W. (1912) *The Autobiography of an Ex-Colored Man* (New York: Dover Publications [1995]).

Johnson, M.A. (2004) "New Approaches to Understanding the Gendered Economy: Self-employed Women, Microcredit and the Nonprofit Sector," in J.S. Butler and G. Kozmetsky (eds.), *Immigrant and Minority Entrepreneurship: The Continuous Rebirth of American Communities* (Westport, CN: Praeger).

Khurana, R. (2007) *From Higher Aims to Hired Hands: The Social Transformation of American Business Schools and the Unfulfilled Promise of Management as a Profession* (Princeton, NJ: Princeton University Press).

Kimmel, M. (2004) *The Gendered Society* (New York: Oxford University Press, 2nd edn).

Klein, N. (2007) *The Shock Doctrine: The Rise of Disaster Capitalism* (New York: Henry Holt & Co.).

Kolbert, E. (2009) "Leading Causes," *The New Yorker*, October 5, 2009: 23-24.

Kristof, N.D., and S. WuDunn (2009) *Half the Sky: Turning Oppression into Opportunity* (New York: Alfred A. Knopf).

Kuratko, D.F., and R.M. Hoggetts (2007) *Entrepreneurship: Theory, Process, Practice* (Mason, OH: Thomson South-Western, 7th edn).

Kusstatscher, V. (2006) "Cultivating Positive Emotions in Mergers and Acquisitions," in C.L. Cooper and S. Finkelstein (eds.), *Mergers and Acquisitions* (Amsterdam: Emerald Group Publishing).

Langowitz, N., and C. Morgan (2003) "The Myths and Realities of Women Entrepreneurs," in J.E. Butler (ed.), *New Perspectives on Women Entrepreneurs* (Greenwich, CT: Information Age Publishing).

——, N. Sharpe, and M. Godwyn (2006) "Women's Business Centers in the United States: Effective Entrepreneurship Training and Policy Implementation," *Journal of Small Business and Entrepreneurship*, May 2006: 167-81.

Lareau, A., and E. Weininger (2003) "Cultural Capital in Educational Networks: A Critical Assessment," *Theory and Society* 32: 567-606.

Lee, M., and E.G. Rogoff (1998) "Do Women Entrepreneurs Require Special Training? An Empirical Comparison of Men and Women Entrepreneurs in the United States," *Journal of Small Business and Entrepreneurship* 14.1: 4-30.

Lehmann, J. (1994) *Durkheim and Women* (Lincoln, NE: University of Nebraska Press).

Levin, W. (1994) *Sociological Ideas* (Belmont, CA: Wadsworth Publishing Co., 4th edn).

Levy, A. (2005) *Female Chauvinist Pigs: Women and the Rise of Raunch Culture* (New York: Free Press).

Lewis, P. (2008) *oovoo Design 2008 Fall/Winter Catalog.*

Lorber, J. (1995) *Paradoxes of Gender* (New Haven, CT: Yale University Press).

Lorde, A. (1984) *Sister Outsider: Essays and Speeches* (Trumanburg, NY: The Crossing Press).

—— (2001) "The Master's Tools will Never Dismantle the Master's House," in L. Richardson, V. Taylor, and N. Whittier (eds.), *Feminist Frontiers* (New York: McGraw-Hill Humanities): 22-23.

Lui, M., B. Robles, B. Leondar-Wright, R. Brewer, and R. Adamson (2006) *The Color of Wealth: The Story behind the U.S. Racial Wealth Divide* (New York: The New Press).

Lye, J. (1997) "Ideology: A Brief Guide"; www.brocku.ca/english/jlye/ideology.html, accessed October 11, 2007.

MacFarquhar, L. (2009) "The Kindest Cut: What sort of person gives a kidney to a stranger?" *The New Yorker*, July 27, 2009: 38-51.

MacKay, D.G. (1983) "Prescriptive Grammar and the Pronoun Problem," in B. Thorne, C. Kramarae, and N. Henley (eds.), *Language, Gender and Society* (Rowley, MA: Newbury House): 38-53.

MacLeod, J. (1995) *Ain't no Making It: Aspirations and Attainment in a Low-Income Neighborhood* (Boulder, CO: Westview Press).

Margolis, J., and A. Fisher (2001) *Unlocking the Clubhouse: Women in Computing* (Cambridge, MA: MIT Press).

Martell, R.F., and A.L. DeSmet (2001) "A Diagnostic-Ratio Approach to Measuring Beliefs about the Leadership Abilities of Male and Female Managers," *Journal of Applied Psychology* 86: 1223-31.

Martin, E. (1991) "The Egg and the Sperm: How Science Has Constructed a Romance Based on Stereotypical Male–Female Roles," *Signs: Journal of Women in Culture and Society* 16.3: 485-501.

Marx, K. (1844) *Estranged Labor, Economic and Philosophic Manuscripts of 1844* (Amherst, NY: Prometheus Books [1988]).

—— (1887) *Capital* (Volume I; London: Penguin Books [1990]).

—— and F. Engels (1848) *The Communist Manifesto* (New York: International Publishers [1982]).

MBDA (Minority Business Development Agency) (2008) "Minority women-owned businesses grow nationwide: Female minority entrepreneurial efforts increase more than other business owners regardless of race and gender," *U.S. Department of Commerce News*, October 14, 2008; www.allbusiness.com/company-activities-management/company-structures-ownership/11649176-1.html, accessed November 6, 2010.

McGee, S. (2007) "Scientists, Wellesley High School students star in teacher-inspired DVD series," *Wellesley Townsman,* October 4, 2007: 15.

McGill, A.L. (1993) "Selection of a Causal Background: Role of Expectation versus Feature Mutability," *Journal of Personality and Social Psychology* 64.5: 701-707.

McIntosh, P. (2007) "White Privilege and Male Privilege," in V. Taylor, N. Whittier, and L.J. Rupp (eds.), *Feminist Frontiers* (New York: McGraw-Hill, 7th edn).

McKinnon, J. (2003) *The Black Population in the United States: March 2002* (U.S. Census Bureau, Current Population Reports Series P20-541, Washington, DC; www.census.gov/prod/2003pubs/p20-541.pdf, accessed October 13, 2007).

Mead, G.H. (1934) *Mind, Self and Society* (ed. C.W. Morris; Chicago: University of Chicago Press).

Milkman, E. (1988) *Gender at Work: The Dynamics of Job Segregation during WWII* (Urbana, IL: University of Illinois Press).

Miller, D. (2001) *The Dialectics of Shopping* (Chicago: University of Chicago Press).

Miller, D.T., B. Taylor, and M.L. Buck (1991) "Gender Gaps: Who Needs to Be Explained?" *Journal of Personality and Social Psychology* 61.1: 5-12.

Miller, T. (2005) *Making Sense of Motherhood* (Cambridge, UK: Cambridge University Press).

Minniti, M., and W. Bygrave (2003) *Global Entrepreneurship Monitor: National Entrepreneurship Assessment, United States of America, 2002 Executive Report* (Babson Park, MA: Babson College; sites.kauffman.org/pdf/gem_2003_us_report.pdf, accessed November 17, 2010).

——, P. Arenius, and N. Langowitz (2005) *Global Entrepreneurship Monitor 2004 Report on Women and Entrepreneurship* (Babson Park, MA: Center for Women's Leadership; London: London Business School).

Moltz, D. (2010) "Freshman Abandon Business," *Inside Higher Ed*; www.insidehighered.com/news/2010/01/21/freshmen, accessed February 10, 2010.

Moore, C.J. (2004) *In Other Words: A Language Lover's Guide to the Most Intriguing Words around the World* (New York: Walker & Co.).

Morris, M., D.R. Kuratlo, and M. Schindehutt (2001) "Towards Integration: Understanding Entrepreneurship through Frameworks," *Entrepreneurship and Innovation*, February 2001: 35-49.

Morris, W. (ed.) (1976) *The American Heritage Dictionary of the English Language: New College Edition* (Boston, MA: Houghton-Mifflin Co.).

Munch, R. (1994) *Sociological Theory from the 1850s to the 1920s* (Chicago: Nelson-Hall).

Murray, S. (2000) "Getting Paid in Smiles: The Gendering of Childcare Work," *Symbolic Interaction* 23.2: 135-60.

Neck, H., C. Brush, and E. Allen (2009) "The Landscape of Social Entrepreneurship," *Business Horizons* 52: 13-19; DOI: 10.1016/j.bushor.2008.09.002.

Nemeth, C.J. (1986) "Differential Contributions of Majority and Minority Influence," *Psychological Review* 93.1: 23-32.

Net Impact (2009) *MBA Perspectives*; www.netimpact.org/associations/4342/files/Undergraduate_Perspectives_2010_final.pdf, accessed November 17, 2010.

Nkomo, S. (1992) "The Emperor has no Clothes: Rewriting 'Race in Organizations,'" *Academy of Management Review* 17.3 (July 1992): 487-513.

Norberg-Hodge, H. (1991) *Ancient Futures: Learning from Ladakh* (San Francisco: Sierra Club Books).

NSBA (National Small Business Association) "Fact Sheet"; www.nsba.biz/vote/70_MAV_Factsheet.pdf, accessed June 3, 2009.

Ogbor, J.O. (2000) "Mythicizing and Reification in Entrepreneurial Discourse: Ideology-Critique of Entrepreneurial Studies," *Journal of Management Studies* 37.5: 605-35.

Olshansky, S.J., D.J. Passaro, R.C. Hershow, J. Layden, B.A. Carnes, J. Brody, L. Hayflick, R.N. Butler, D.B. Allison, and D.S. Ludwig (2005) "A Potential Decline in Life Expectancy in the United States in the 21st Century," *New England Journal of Medicine* 352.11: 1138-45.

Ozbilgin, M.T., A. Beauregard, and M.P. Bell (2009) "A Critical Review of Theory and Methods in Work-Life Literature" (unpublished; presented at *Gender and Management Practice, Academy of Management Annual Meeting 2009*, Chicago).

Padavic, I. (1991) "The Re-creation of Gender in the Male Workplace," *Symbolic Interaction* 14.3: 279-94.

Paumgarten, N. (2007) "Girl-counter," *The New Yorker*, September 3, 2007; www.newyorker.com/talk/2007/09/03/070903ta_talk_paumgarten, accessed November 6, 2010.

Phillips, A., and B. Taylor (2009) *On Kindness* (New York: Farrar, Straus & Giroux).

Porter, N., and F. Geis (1981) "Women and Nonverbal Leadership Cues: When Seeing is not Believing," in C. Mayo and N.M. Henley (eds.), *Gender and Non-verbal Behavior* (New York: Springer-Verlag).

Preston, C. (2008) "Most small companies make charitable donations, survey finds," *The Chronicle of Philanthropy*, November 20, 2008; philanthropy.com/news/prospecting/6349/most-small-companies-make-charitable-donations-survey-finds, accessed August 4, 2009.

Pugh, M.D., and R. Wahrman (1983) "Neutralizing Sexism in Mixed-Sex Groups: Do Women have to be Better than Men?" *American Journal of Sociology* 88.4: 746-62.

Ransome, J. (2008) "Tax Insights: Analysis of Gift Tax Returns by Gender," September 12, 2008; www.grantthornton.com/staticfiles/GTCom/files/services/Tax%20services/Tax%20Flashes%20and%20Legislative%20Updates/Tax%20Insights_Analysis%20of%20gift%20tax%20returns.pdf, accessed August 2, 2009.

Raufflet, E., and A.J. Mills (eds.) (2009) *The Dark Side: Critical Cases on the Downside of Business* (Sheffield, UK: Greenleaf Publishing).

Reich, R.B. (2007) *SuperCapitalism* (New York: Knopf).

Reskin, B. (1997) "Bringing the Men Back in: Sex Differentiation and the Value of Women's Work," in L. Richardson, V. Taylor, and N. Whittier (eds.), *Feminist Frontiers* (New York: McGraw-Hill, 4th edn).

Richardson, L. (2007) "Gender Stereotyping in the English Language," in L. Richardson, V. Taylor, and N. Whittier (eds.), *Feminist Frontiers* (New York: McGraw-Hill, 7th edn).

Ridgeway, C.L. (2001) "Gender, Status, and Leadership," *Journal of Social Issues* 57.4: 637-55.

Roediger, D.R. (1994) *Towards the Abolition of Whiteness* (London: Verso).

Rudman, L.A., and P.S. Glick (2001) "Prescriptive Gender Stereotypes and Backlash toward Agentic Women," *Journal of Social Issues* 57: 743-62.

Schumpeter, J. (1934) *Capitalism, Socialism, and Democracy* (New York: Harper & Row).

Scott, J.W. (1992) "Experience," in J. Butler and J.W. Scott (eds.), *Feminists Theorize the Political* (New York: Routledge): 22-40.

Scott, M.B., and S.M. Lyman (1970) "Accounts," in G.P. Stone and H.A. Farberman (eds.), *Social Psychology through Symbolic Interaction* (New York: John Wiley).

Shane, S., and S. Venkataraman (2000) "The Promise of Entrepreneurship as a Field of Research," *The Academy of Management Review* 25.1: 217-26.

Shipman, C., and K. Kay (2009) "Women will rule business," *Time* 173.20: 47.

Shirky, C. (2010) "A Rant about Women"; www.shirky.com/weblog/2010/01/a-rant-about-women, accessed November 1, 2010.

Smith, A. (1776) *The Wealth of Nations* (New York: Bantam Classics [2003]).

Spinoza, C., F. Flores, and H.L. Dreyfus (1997) *Disclosing New Worlds: Entrepreneurship, Democratic Action, and the Cultivation of Solidarity* (Cambridge, MA: MIT Press).

Stebbings, P. (2007) "How a girl's name can determine what her career will be," *Daily Mail*, October 12, 2007; www.dailymail.co.uk/pages/live/articles/news/news.html?in_article_id=451542&in_page_id=1770, accessed May 3, 2007.

Steele, C. (1997) "A Threat in the Air: How Stereotypes Shape the Intellectual Identities and Performance of Women and African-Americans," *American Psychologist* 52: 613-29.

—— (2003) "Stereotype Threat and African American Student Achievement," in T. Perry, C. Steele, and A. Hilliard III (eds.), *Young, Gifted and Black* (Boston, MA: Beacon Press).

Stewart, M. (2006) "The Management Myth," *The Atlantic*; www.theatlantic.com/doc/200606/stewart-business, accessed August 3, 2009.

Stoddard, D. (2007) "Legacy Bank" (unpublished case study funded by Center for Women's Business Research).

Tharoor, I. (2006) "Paving the way out of poverty," *Time*, October 13, 2006; www.time.com/time/world/article/0,8599,1546100,00.html, accessed March 8, 2010.

Thomas-Hunt, M.C., and K.W. Phillips (2004) "When What You Know Is Not Enough: Expertise and Gender Dynamics in Task Groups," *Personality and Social Psychology Bulletin* 30.12: 1585-98.

Timmons, J.A., and S. Spinelli (2007) *New Venture Creation* (Boston, MA: McGraw-Hill).

Tolman, D.L. (2007) "Doing Desire: Adolescent Girls' Struggles for/with Sexuality," in L. Richardson, V. Taylor, and N. Whittier (eds.), *Feminist Frontiers* (New York: McGraw-Hill, 7th edn).

Treisman, U. (1992) "Studying Students Studying Calculus: A Look at the Lives of Minority Mathematics Students in College," *The College Mathematics Journal* 3.5: 362-72.

Tuana, N. (1988) "The Weaker Seed: Sex Bias in Reproductive Theory," *Hypatia* 3.1: 35-59.

Turkle, S. (2007) "The Secret Power of Things," *New Scientist*, June 9, 2007: 50-52.

U.S. Census (2005) "ACS Demographic and Housing Estimates," factfinder.census.gov/servlet/ADPTable?_bm=y&-geo_id=01000US&-qr_name=ACS_2007_3YR_G00_DP3YR5&-ds_name=&-_lang=en&-redoLog=false, accessed June 6, 2009.

—— (2006) "Facts for Features. Special Edition. April 9–15," March 27, 2006; www.census.gov/newsroom/releases/pdf/cb06-ffse03.pdf, accessed November 17, 2010.

Valian, V. (1998) *Why so Slow? The Advancement of Women* (Boston, MA: MIT Press).

Weber, M. (1904) *The Protestant Ethic and the Spirit of Capitalism* (New York: Charles Scribner's Sons [1958]).

Wells, I.B. (1997) *Southern Horrors and Other Writings: The Anti-lynching Campaign of Ida B. Wells, 1892–1900* (Boston, MA: Bedford St. Martin's).

Westley, F., B. Zimmerman, and M.Q. Patton (2006) *Getting to Maybe* (Toronto: Vintage Canada).

Westphal, J.D., and I. Stern (2007) "Flattery will Get you Everywhere (Especially if you are a Male Caucasian): How Integrating Boardroom Behavior, and Demographic Minority Status, Affect Additional Broad Appointments in U.S. Companies," *Academy of Management Journal* 50.2: 267-88.

Whyte, W. (1980) *The Social Life of Small Urban Spaces* (Ann Arbor, MI: Edward Brothers).

Willis, P. (1977) *Learning to Labour* (New York: Columbia University Press).

Winter, R.O., and B.A. Birnberg (2003) "Tuesdays with Morrie versus Stephen Hawking: Living or Dying with ALS," *Family Medicine* 35.9: 629-31.

Wirth, L. (1945) "The Problem with Minority Groups," in R. Linton (ed.), *The Science of Man in the World Crisis* (New York: Columbia University Press): 347-72.

Wise, T. (2005) *White Like Me: Reflections on Race from a Privileged Son* (Brooklyn, NY: Soft Skull Press).

Yardley, J. (2009) "Indian Women Find New Peace in Rail Commute," *New York Times*, September 16, 2009: A1.

Yunus, M. (2006) "Nobel Lecture," December 10, 2006; nobelprize.org/nobel_prizes/peace/laureates/2006/yunus-lecture-en.html, accessed January 9, 2010.

—— (2007a) *Creating a World without Poverty: Social Business and the Future of Capitalism* (New York: Public Affairs).

—— (2007b) "Foreword," in Grameen Bank, Annual Report; www.grameen-info.org/index.php?option=com_content&task=view&id=548&Itemid=590, accessed March 8, 2010.

—— (2008) "Nobel Laureate Dr. Muhammad Yunus: Women Borrowers," YouTube video; www.youtube.com/watch?v=NjI-nsHp0I0, accessed June 6, 2009.

Zaragovia, V. (2009) "Will high-heel-friendly streets keep Seoul's women happy?" *Time*, August 5, 2009; www.time.com/time/world/article/0,8599,1914471,00.html, accessed September 23, 2009.

Zelizer, V.A. (1989) "The Social Meaning of Money: 'Special Monies,' " *American Journal of Sociology* 95.2: 342-77.

Appendix
Themes in women's entrepreneurship as a basis for qualitative interview analysis

- Please note whether the theme was mentioned; if mentioned, the number of times and the intensity of the theme for the entrepreneur (how much does she seem to *care* about it?)

- Please write down specific phrases (quotations from the interviewee) to justify your response

- Please ensure you write down and detail any other themes the interviewee mentions that do not appear here

- Thank you very much for being part of this research!

Reasons for starting her business

1. **Turned to entrepreneurship because of low-paying dead-end jobs or glass ceiling? (Johnson 2004: 154).**

Mentioned?   ___Y / ___N

If Y, approximate number of times?

____ Occasionally (once or twice)
____ Moderately (three to five times)
____ Frequently (more than five)

Intensity (level entrepreneur cares about issue)

____ Not very important
____ Moderately important
____ Very important

How do you know? (please provide specific quotations from entrepreneur)

2. Lack of respect in workplace?

Mentioned?   ___Y / ___N

If Y, approximate number of times?

____ Occasionally (once or twice)
____ Moderately (three to five times)
____ Frequently (more than five)

Intensity (level entrepreneur cares about issue)

____ Not very important
____ Moderately important
____ Very important

How do you know? (please provide specific quotations from entrepreneur)

3. Lack of role models or affinity group in workplace (feeling of being an outsider)?

Mentioned?   ___Y / ___N

If Y, approximate number of times?

____ Occasionally (once or twice)
____ Moderately (three to five times)
____ Frequently (more than five)

Intensity (level entrepreneur cares about issue)

____ Not very important
____ Moderately important
____ Very important

How do you know? (please provide specific quotations from entrepreneur)

4. As an attempt to balance work and family? (Brush 1997:11)

Mentioned?   ___Y / ___N

If Y, approximate number of times?

____ Occasionally (once or twice)
____ Moderately (three to five times)
____ Frequently (more than five)

Intensity (level entrepreneur cares about issue)

____ Not very important
____ Moderately important
____ Very important

How do you know? (please provide specific quotations from entrepreneur)

5. Emphasis on employee development? (Brush 1997: 18)

Mentioned?   ___Y / ___N

If Y, approximate number of times?

____ Occasionally (once or twice)
____ Moderately (three to five times)
____ Frequently (more than five)

Intensity (level entrepreneur cares about issue)

____ Not very important
____ Moderately important
____ Very important

How do you know? (please provide specific quotations from entrepreneur)

6. Personal vision of what workplace should be like (also extends to product service, customer relations) (Johnson 2004: 155).

Mentioned? ___Y / ___N

If Y, approximate number of times?

____ Occasionally (once or twice)
____ Moderately (three to five times)
____ Frequently (more than five)

Intensity (level entrepreneur cares about issue)

____ Not very important
____ Moderately important
____ Very important

How do you know? (please provide specific quotations from entrepreneur)

7. Thought she could do a better job of running a business than her supervisor did?

Mentioned? ___Y / ___N

If Y, approximate number of times?

____ Occasionally (once or twice)
____ Moderately (three to five times)
____ Frequently (more than five)

Intensity (level entrepreneur cares about issue)

____ Not very important
____ Moderately important
____ Very important

How do you know? (please provide specific quotations from entrepreneur)

8. Bored or unfulfilled in workplace?

Mentioned? ___Y / ___N

If Y, approximate number of times?

____ Occasionally (once or twice)

____ Moderately (three to five times)
____ Frequently (more than five)

Intensity (level entrepreneur cares about issue)

____ Not very important
____ Moderately important
____ Very important

How do you know? (please provide specific quotations from entrepreneur)

9. Wanted more autonomy and more control over her professional life?

Mentioned? ___Y / ___N

If Y, approximate number of times?

____ Occasionally (once or twice)
____ Moderately (three to five times)
____ Frequently (more than five)

Intensity (level entrepreneur cares about issue)

____ Not very important
____ Moderately important
____ Very important

How do you know? (please provide specific quotations from entrepreneur)

Challenges of being an entrepreneur

10. Trouble with financing? (Johnson 2004: 156)

Mentioned? ___Y / ___N

If Y, approximate number of times?

____ Occasionally (once or twice)
____ Moderately (three to five times)
____ Frequently (more than five)

Intensity (level entrepreneur cares about issue)

____ Not very important
____ Moderately important
____ Very important

How do you know? (please provide specific quotations from entrepreneur)

11. Trouble being taken seriously as business owner/entrepreneur? (Brush 1997: 9)

Mentioned? ___Y / ___N

If Y, approximate number of times?

____ Occasionally (once or twice)
____ Moderately (three to five times)

____ Frequently (more than five)

Intensity (level entrepreneur cares about issue)

____ Not very important
____ Moderately important
____ Very important

How do you know? (please provide specific quotations from entrepreneur)

12.   Trouble with growth and acquiring expansion capital? (Brush 1997: 12; Greene and Brush 2004)

Mentioned?   ___Y / ___N

If Y, approximate number of times?

____ Occasionally (once or twice)
____ Moderately (three to five times)
____ Frequently (more than five)

Intensity (level entrepreneur cares about issue)

____ Not very important
____ Moderately important
____ Very important

How do you know? (please provide specific quotations from entrepreneur)

13.   Childcare and domestic responsibilities? (Brush 1997: 11-12)

Mentioned?   ___Y / ___N

If Y, approximate number of times?

____ Occasionally (once or twice)
____ Moderately (three to five times)
____ Frequently (more than five)

Intensity (level entrepreneur cares about issue)

____ Not very important
____ Moderately important
____ Very important

How do you know? (please provide specific quotations from entrepreneur)

14.   Lack of entrepreneurial education and training? (Brush 1997: 14)

Mentioned?   ___Y / ___N

If Y, approximate number of times?

____ Occasionally (once or twice)
____ Moderately (three to five times)
____ Frequently (more than five)

Intensity (level entrepreneur cares about issue)

____ Not very important
____ Moderately important
____ Very important

How do you know? (please provide specific quotations from entrepreneur)

15. Lack of confidence? (Langowitz, Sharpe *et al.* 2006)

Mentioned?   __Y / __N

If Y, approximate number of times?

____ Occasionally (once or twice)
____ Moderately (three to five times)
____ Frequently (more than five)

Intensity (level entrepreneur cares about issue)

____ Not very important
____ Moderately important
____ Very important

How do you know? (please provide specific quotations from entrepreneur)

16. Lack of community and/or family support? (Langowitz, Sharpe *et al.* 2006)

Mentioned?   __Y / __N

If Y, approximate number of times?

____ Occasionally (once or twice)
____ Moderately (three to five times)
____ Frequently (more than five)

Intensity (level entrepreneur cares about issue)

____ Not very important
____ Moderately important
____ Very important

How do you know? (please provide specific quotations from entrepreneur)

17. Lack of colleagues/loneliness? (Langowitz, Sharpe *et al.* 2006)

Mentioned?   __Y / __N

If Y, approximate number of times?

____ Occasionally (once or twice)
____ Moderately (three to five times)
____ Frequently (more than five)

Intensity (level entrepreneur cares about issue)

____ Not very important
____ Moderately important
____ Very important

How do you know? (please provide specific quotations from entrepreneur)

18. Lack of role models or mentors? (Butler 2005)

Mentioned? ___Y / ___N

If Y, approximate number of times?

____ Occasionally (once or twice)
____ Moderately (three to five times)
____ Frequently (more than five)

Intensity (level entrepreneur cares about issue)

____ Not very important
____ Moderately important
____ Very important

How do you know? (please provide specific quotations from entrepreneur)

19. Lack of people like her?

Mentioned? ___Y / ___N

If Y, approximate number of times?

____ Occasionally (once or twice)
____ Moderately (three to five times)
____ Frequently (more than five)

Intensity (level entrepreneur cares about issue)

____ Not very important
____ Moderately important
____ Very important

How do you know? (please provide specific quotations from entrepreneur)

20. To escape racism, sexism, or other discrimination in workplace setting?

Mentioned? ___Y / ___N

If Y, approximate number of times?

____ Occasionally (once or twice)
____ Moderately (three to five times)
____ Frequently (more than five)

Intensity (level entrepreneur cares about issue)

____ Not very important
____ Moderately important
____ Very important

How do you know? (please provide specific quotations from entrepreneur)

Opportunities

21. Learn/develop new technology? (Brush 1997: 16-18)

Mentioned?   ___Y / ___N

If Y, approximate number of times?

____ Occasionally (once or twice)
____ Moderately (three to five times)
____ Frequently (more than five)

Intensity (level entrepreneur cares about issue)

____ Not very important
____ Moderately important
____ Very important

How do you know? (please provide specific quotations from entrepreneur)

22. Increase acceptance of new management/leadership styles? (Brush 1997: 16-18)

Mentioned?   ___Y / ___N

If Y, approximate number of times?

____ Occasionally (once or twice)
____ Moderately (three to five times)
____ Frequently (more than five)

Intensity (level entrepreneur cares about issue)

____ Not very important
____ Moderately important
____ Very important

How do you know? (please provide specific quotations from entrepreneur)

23. Increased acceptance of women and/or of minorities in management/leadership positions? (Brush 1997: 16-18)

Mentioned?   ___Y / ___N

If Y, approximate number of times?

____ Occasionally (once or twice)
____ Moderately (three to five times)
____ Frequently (more than five)

Intensity (level entrepreneur cares about issue)

____ Not very important
____ Moderately important
____ Very important

How do you know? (please provide specific quotations from entrepreneur)

24. Ability to help employees? (Brush 1997: 16-18)

Mentioned? ___Y / ___N

If Y, approximate number of times?

____ Occasionally (once or twice)
____ Moderately (three to five times)
____ Frequently (more than five)

Intensity (level entrepreneur cares about issue)

____ Not very important
____ Moderately important
____ Very important

How do you know? (please provide specific quotations from entrepreneur)

25. Ability to express personal vision in business enterprise and to contribute to wider change (such as workplace policies, new products, and/or social change generally)? (Johnson 2004; Fleischmann 2006)

Mentioned? ___Y / ___N

If Y, approximate number of times?

____ Occasionally (once or twice)
____ Moderately (three to five times)
____ Frequently (more than five)

Intensity (level entrepreneur cares about issue)

____ Not very important
____ Moderately important
____ Very important

How do you know? (please provide specific quotations from entrepreneur)

26. Financial independence?

Mentioned? ___Y / ___N

If Y, approximate number of times?

____ Occasionally (once or twice)
____ Moderately (three to five times)
____ Frequently (more than five)

Intensity (level entrepreneur cares about issue)

____ Not very important
____ Moderately important
____ Very important

How do you know? (please provide specific quotations from entrepreneur)

27. Ability to help others like herself? (Butler 2005)

Mentioned?   ___Y / ___N

If Y, approximate number of times?

____ Occasionally (once or twice)
____ Moderately (three to five times)
____ Frequently (more than five)

Intensity (level entrepreneur cares about issue)

____ Not very important
____ Moderately important
____ Very important

How do you know? (please provide specific quotations from entrepreneur)

28. Ability to be with others like herself (such as other women, minorities, family members)? (Butler 2005)

Mentioned?   ___Y / ___N

If Y, approximate number of times?

____ Occasionally (once or twice)
____ Moderately (three to five times)
____ Frequently (more than five)

Intensity (level entrepreneur cares about issue)

____ Not very important
____ Moderately important
____ Very important

How do you know? (please provide specific quotations from entrepreneur)

Index

About the authors

Mary Godwyn is an Assistant Professor in the History and Society Division at Babson College. She holds a BA in Philosophy from Wellesley College and a PhD in Sociology from Brandeis University. She has lectured at Harvard University and taught at Brandeis University and Lasell College, where she was also the Director of the Donahue Institute for Public Values. Dr. Godwyn focuses on social theory as it applies to issues of inequality in formal and informal organizations. She studies entrepreneurship as a vehicle for the economic and political advancement of marginalized populations, especially women and minorities. She has published in journals such as *Research in Social Stratification and Mobility*, *Symbolic Interaction*, and the *Journal of Small Business and Entrepreneurship*. Dr. Godwyn also consults to colleges and universities about how to integrate entrepreneurship into liberal arts programmes. In 2008, her business ethics case,

"Hugh Connerty and Hooters: What is Successful Entrepreneurship?", won the Dark Side Case Competition sponsored by the Critical Management Studies Division of the Academy of Management. Dr. Godwyn's research has been funded by the Coleman Foundation, the Ewing Marion Kauffman Foundation, the Harold S. Geneen Charitable Trust, and the Babson College Board of Research Fund.

Donna Stoddard is Associate Professor of Information Technology Management (ITM) and teaches undergraduate, graduate, and executive education courses related to management information systems and business strategy. Before joining the Babson faculty, Dr. Stoddard was on the faculty at Harvard Business School where she taught in the MBA and executive education programs. She is a graduate of Creighton University, University of North Carolina at Chapel Hill, and Harvard Business School where she received her BS, MBA, and DBA, respectively.

Dr. Stoddard is currently exploring how small and large companies leverage enterprise systems to improve communication and collaboration. In addition, she has conducted research related to digital government, electronic commerce, managing the IT infrastructure, IT business innovation, the State of Minority Business Enterprises in Massachusetts, and women of color entrepreneurs. Dr. Stoddard has written a number of cases and articles on re-engineering and the impact of information technology on the structure and strategy of the firm. Dr. Stoddard's articles have been published in such journals as *Harvard Business Review, California Management Review, MIS Quarterly*, and *Journal of MIS*.

Before entering the doctoral programme at the Harvard Business School, Dr. Stoddard spent several years in various marketing positions at IBM where she worked with large financial services and manufacturing companies and she was on the audit staff at Peat Marwick Mitchell. Dr. Stoddard has served as a keynote speaker at management and senior executive conferences sponsored by KPMG Peat Marwick, Ernst & Young, The Travelers, MIT, Boston University, State Street Boston Corporation, Johnson & Johnson, and Siemens Rolm Communications.

Photos by Tim Morse, Morse Photography/M&M Films